The Illustrated Handbook of FURNITURE RESTORATION

The Illustrated Handbook of
FURNITURE
RESTORATION

George Buchanan

1817

HARPER & ROW, PUBLISHERS, New York

Cambridge, Philadelphia, San Francisco, London
Mexico City, São Paulo, Singapore, Sydney

To Elizabeth

THE ILLUSTRATED HANDBOOK OF FURNITURE RESTORATION.

Copyright © 1985 by George Buchanan.

FIRST U.S. EDITION

ISBN: 0-06-015558-2

LIBRARY OF CONGRESS CATALOGING-IN-PUBLICATION DATA

Buchanan, George.
  The illustrated handbook of furniture restoration.

  Bibliography: p
  Includes index.
  1. Furniture—Repairing. 2. Furniture finishing.
1. Title.
TT199.B83 1986   749'.1'0288   85-45540
ISBN 0–06–015558–2

86 87 88 89 90 10 9 8 7 6 5 4 3 2 1

Contents

Acknowledgements

I am extremely grateful to all those who have helped me in the preparation of this book.

In particular, I wish to thank Mrs Janet Gibbs of Cotswold Caners, Cirencester, for teaching me the techniques of split cane weaving and correcting that part of my manuscript.

My thanks also to Ben White, Peter Buchanan and David Playne for the photographs, to John Yate, antique restorer of Coln St Aldwyns, who gave me some useful hints and allowed us to photograph his workshop, and to Jacquie Govier, for her advice and criticisms of my drawings. Also to Elizabeth Buchanan, Ian Fiddes Gooding, David Sloan and Simon Tuite for their advice and encouragement in this project.

Simon Creese-Parsons and Paul Caffell of Tetbury Antiques, Don Parsons of the Tetbury Secondhand Furniture Company, and Mick Wright of the Antique Centre, Gloucester, very kindly allowed us to photograph some of their furniture.

I am grateful to Peter Harding for the jacket photograph and the photograph of the wood samples.

1 The Workshop

A well organised workshop will be a pleasant place to work in. Although size is an advantage, the workshop need not be large. A room the size of a garage is quite sufficient for one person working on his own. There must be room for a bench, a piece of furniture (in pieces) and room to walk unimpeded around the workpiece. Unless the room is very large, it is best not to store furniture or any wood (apart from wood in use and some offcuts) in the workshop, otherwise the working space becomes compromised by the need for storage.

Good lighting is the key to first-class repair work. If repairs are invisible or acceptable in brightly illuminated conditions, they will be perfectly satisfactory in the indirect light of a home. Light from windows should be supplemented by neon strip lights, and these should be left on whenever finishing work is in progress. A light from a window will throw strong shadows, and it is easy to overlook areas that need attention if they are hidden in shadow or sparkle with low-level reflected sunlight.

Without a gentle background warmth, glues and polishes will not dry. All kinds of heaters are available, but a stove that can burn shavings and the wood off-cuts is very convenient. Small workshops can be adequately heated with a bottled gas, or an electric convector heater. Take great care to place heaters well away from polishes and solvents. Inflammable substances should be outside the working area, and out of danger of accidental ignition.

ORGANISATION OF THE WORKSHOP

The shape of the workshop, and the need to use the space efficiently, determines its organisation. Plan the arrangements from the outset. The lay-out of the workshop must allow room for manhandling large pieces of furniture without accident or injury and, if possible, for the installation of extra machines that may be bought and will need to be situated where they can be used to best advantage.

The location of the doorway will often determine the internal arrangements in a small workshop. It is important that large pieces of furniture can be carried in and out without difficulty. The doorway should therefore be kept clear and lead directly to the workspace inside. In a small workshop it can help to use the doorway to increase the length of wood stock that can be fed through a circular saw or planer. These machines, rather than the workbench, have a prior claim to a

place near the door, and are best sited in line with the opening, compatible with an unobstructed entry.

The bench

The bench should be close to the workspace. As the vice is normally installed at one end of the bench, it is necessary to keep the vice end away from any walls or cupboards that might interfere with the working of long pieces of timber held in the vice.

Electrical fittings

These can be installed once the positioning of the bench and the machines has been decided.

All power supplied should be encased in metal conduit and the sockets should be metal-cased workshop fittings. Have a power outlet at each end of the bench, and others as close as possible to the machines. A double power point close to the work-space is necessary and it should be placed so that cables to the work area do not cross the workshop floor where people are likely to be walking. The main fuse box and earth trip will be located at the discretion of the electrician, but an emergency power cut-out should be installed where it is easily visible and close to the door.

Lighting

Install a single high-wattage light bulb, or a double fluorescent fitting on the wall above the workbench. A single fluorescent bulb emits a flickering light which is disconcerting when reflected from the edge of a chisel etc. Doubling the tubes eliminates this effect, but a normal light bulb is cheaper and simpler.

Fluorescent lights should be installed slightly to one side of the work area, and close to the machine tools. Double fittings again should be used, as the stroboscopic effect can be reflected in a rotating circular saw blade or planer cutter.

Neon lights give a strong diffused bluish light. This has the advantage of subduing the red, brown and yellow tints in a piece of furniture. The restorer can be sure that if a refinished piece glows with a rich brown hue in the workshop's artificial light, it will be even more attractive in daylight, or under less glaring household conditions. It is useful to be able to supplement the strip lighting with a car inspection lamp. This is particularly handy for looking inside or under furniture.

Storage

The stove, workbench and machines are the only permanent fixtures that need to stand on the floor of the workshop. Any additional items are going to use valuable floorspace and make the floor more difficult to keep clean and tidy.

Wherever possible, shelving and hanging cupboards should be used

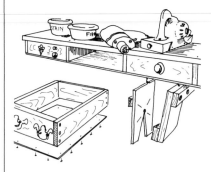

to store the stains and glues, nails and screws that the restorer uses.

Large quantities of inflammable supplies such as methylated spirits, turpentine, etc., should be stored in a steel cupboard away from the stove. A second-hand filing cabinet makes a very good storage cupboard.

Where the workshop has a pitched roof, it might be possible to use the roof space for extra storage, provided that the necessary alterations do not result in a depressingly low ceiling. Roof spaces can become very warm in summertime, so inflammable liquids and waxes should not be stored there. A roof space is ideal for the bulk storage of clean spare rags, and supplies of wire wool, powder stain, etc.

Waste disposal

The restorer generates great quantities of waste, and some difficult decisions must be made concerning its disposal. Sawdust and shavings can be burnt (if the stove will accept them), or should be

bagged and dumped. Do not allow shavings and sawdust to accumulate on the floor of the workshop. A deep pile of cedar and pine shavings looks attractive and smells delightful, but it is dusty and a fire hazard, and if any small item is dropped, it is as good as lost. Sweep regularly, after every operation in the restoration process. Never allow the mess to accumulate. Bag the waste – old rags, used wire wool, etc., – and take it outside.

Wood store

If small pieces of wood are stored for future use, they will accumulate so rapidly that it will be impossible to locate pieces when they are needed. Make no distinction between old wood and new. Discard all pieces that are less than 24 in. (600 mm) long, and 2 × 3 in. (50 × 80 mm) wide.

There are two exceptions: if the wood is particularly rare – rosewood or ebony for instance – keep it safe, and store it where it can be found. Secondly, if a birthday or Christmas is drawing near, and you like making presents, keep the nicest pieces for that.

This is a necessary rule. If you don't know what you have in your woodpile, you may as well not have it.

The restorer must adopt some method of storing wood which enables him to find what he needs easily without moving great quantities of lumber.

The system must start with some strict rules of admittance to the wood store. There should be a minimum wood size limitation (mentioned earlier). Large pieces that are seriously split, or that, on handling, seem riddled with nails or worm, should be discarded. No attempt should be made to sort timber according to its type – this may lead to useful pieces of timber being overlooked because of faulty identification.

Wood should be sorted according to length, and stored on end. It will remain drier, and be easier to search through, than wood stacked horizontally. A simple series of partitions is usually adequate to separate the sizes. They need not be substantial as the floor of the woodstore will take most of the weight.

Veneers should be stored in a dry, cool atmosphere, to prevent them from becoming too brittle and cracking when handled. Lay them on a flat board, and wrap them in newspaper. Place a board and weights on them to keep them flat.

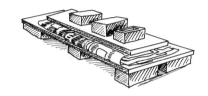

TOOL STORAGE

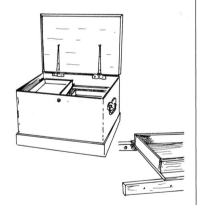

Tools that are used rarely can be stored in a chest tucked in beneath the workbench. An old pine box or blanket box is ideal. A tray fitted inside enables small tools to be separated from the larger tools in the base.

The tools that are always in use must be placed close at hand and easily visible. A board fixed to the bench and supported against the wall can be arranged to make a very convenient display.

Electric hand tools

Drills, jigsaws, routers, etc. should be kept separate from the hand tools to avoid the danger of the cables being nicked or tangled. Keep them on a shelf near the bench. Router bits and saw blades should be stored with them. Tools which are used regularly will not rust. A wipe with an oily rag will keep bright tools that are seldom used.

Tools

Most household tool kits will include at least some tools that will do, but it is likely that others will have to be bought. When choosing tools, always buy the best. As old tools wear out, replace them with tools of better quality.

Buy your tools second-hand or from a tool store that has a wide choice of tools and knowledgeable assistants. Choose tools that carry a quality brand name; do not buy edge tools with disposable blades. Hold the tool and feel the edge of the casting for roughness and signs of careless finishing. Screw threads must turn easily, wooden handles should be comfortable, smooth and well finished. The tool, whether it is a plane, a chisel or a new saw, should feel nicely balanced and pleasant to hold. The following basic hand tools will be needed.

Saws: rip and crosscut handsaws, dovetail saw, coping saw, fretsaw, hacksaw

Planes: jointer plane, smoothing plane, block plane, rebate plane, combination plane

Scrapers: cabinet scraper

Drills: 1/4 in. (6.4 mm), 3/8 in. (9.5 mm), 1/2 in. (12.7 mm) brad point drills; others as needed

Plug cutters: 3/8 in. (9.5 mm)

Chisels: 1/4 in. (6.4 mm), 3/8 in. (9.5 mm), 5/8 in. (16 mm) bevel or paring chisels, 1 1/4 in. (32 mm) firmer chisel, 1/4 in. (6.4 mm), 3/8 in. (9.5 mm) mortice chisels

Gouges: as needed

Rules: 6 ft (2 m) rule (flexible)

Squares: 1 set square, 1 mitre square

Dividers: 1 pair, lockable

Bevel: 1 sliding bevel

Gauges: 1 marking gauge, 1 mortice gauge

Hammers: 1 tack hammer, 1 medium-weight hammer

Punches: centre punch, nail punch

Screwdrivers: 1 for general use

Pliers: 1 pair

Nail cutters: 1 pair

Pincers: 1 pair

Files: assorted files, as needed

Snips: 1 pair

Clamps: the more the better

Cramps: the more the better

Bolsters: 1 bricklayer's bolster, 1 floorboard lifter

USED TOOLS

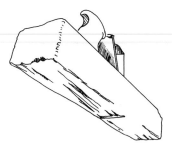

Old tools can be found for sale in bric-à-brac shops and antique markets. They are very often high quality and serviceable tools. When considering buying edge tools (chisels, gouges and planes) look carefully at the condition of the blade. Chips in the cutting edge can be ground out and do not matter, but if the blade is pitted with rust it will be useless.

Beechwood block planes can represent good value, if the blade is in a good state. The steel is usually very good, thicker than modern plane blades, and will not overheat in use.

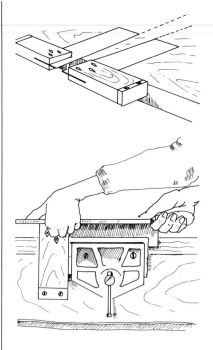

The problem with these planes is that the sole of the plane wears into grooves or becomes twisted. This can be corrected by removing the blade and planing the sole flat. This unfortunately increases the width of the slot, which in turn reduces the plane's ability to make fine cuts. If a well balanced plane has these problems it may be worth cutting the sole back and glueing a new one in place, and chiselling out a new slot for the blade.

Second-hand marking gauges are easy to come by and are inexpensive. New ones are probably cheaper than the brass inlaid versions to be found in antique shops.

Chisels, screwdrivers, punches and bradawls are all easily available second-hand and often well worth buying. Fretsaws and hacksaws can be bought second-hand, but avoid buying used handsaw and tenon saws. Start with a new saw, and look after it well.

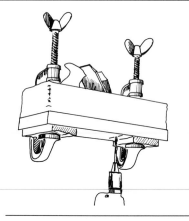

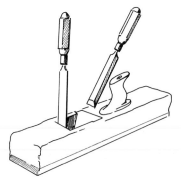

Second-hand set squares need to be checked for accuracy as shown in the drawings. The blade can be corrected by careful filing, but take care to avoid introducing a curve into it. Used ebony or rosewood brass-bound set squares and bevels are very attractive, and far nicer to handle than the modern plastic-handled alternatives.

Do not keep a duplicate set of saws or edge tools for rough use. Have one set of tools and treat them with respect.

HOME-MADE TOOLS

The restorer can supplement his commercially-made tools with some home-made ones. The following tools and jigs are simple to make, will simplify the woodworking operations and will speed the restoration process.

These tools need to be designed with care. Make them before they are needed, and familiarise yourself with their use.

The following section describes those that should be ready for use in the workshop.

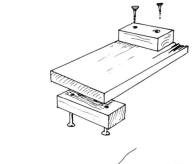

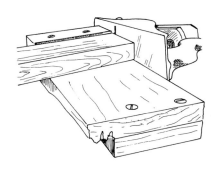

Bench hook. Make this from hardwood. Keep one end block short for sawing, bring the other flush for use as a small shooting board. Make sure that the end boards are at right angles to the sides of the bench hook

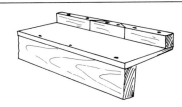

Mitre block. This small bench hook is used when cutting mitres in beadings, etc. The 45° slots which guide the saw blade enable mitres to be cut with a minimum of marking

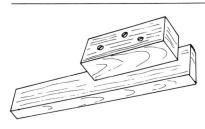

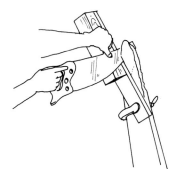

Saw guide. Nail or screw the two pieces together. Trim them square. Periodically check the faces for accuracy and, if necessary, true them up

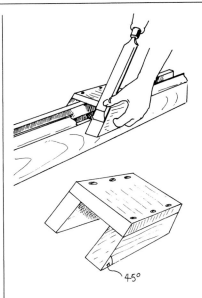

Small mitre box. Make this accurately; hold the two guides together with a strong hardwood board. The front edge of the board as well as the front edges of the guides should be bevelled to 45°

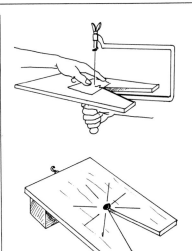

Fret sawing V. Make this from ⅜ in. (8 mm) plywood. Nail a hardwood block beneath the board so that it can be held in the vice

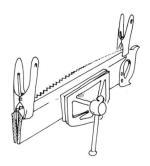

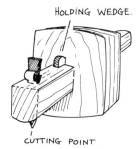

Two pairs of cheeks are needed: one for holding handsaws, the other for dovetail and tenon saws. Shape the face so that maximum clamping pressure is applied just below the line of the teeth. Use as illustrated

Cutting gauge. This tool should be made with care; the fence must slide smoothly over the stock, and is fixed with a wedge or screw. Make this a comfortable tool to hold. The blade can be ground from an old jigsaw or hacksaw blade

The screw moulder, scratch stock, chair scraper and toothed plane are extremely useful. Use good quality hardwood for these, and shape and smooth them carefully. They are tools that require some effort to operate, and so should be comfortable to hold.

Screw moulder. This simple tool should be made from hardwood. Fashion it to fit comfortably in the hand

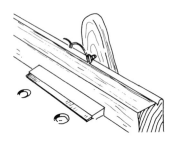

Scratch stock. Make this large and easy to hold. The cutter can be ground from a used machine hacksaw blade or filed from any flat stock

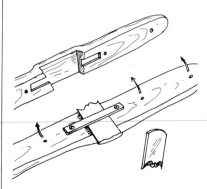

Chair scraper. Make the scraper comfortable to hold. Rest the blade against the rear half of the body of the scraper, and restrain it with a bar and two

bolts. Make up a pair of fences that can slip between the handles, held in place by tightening the handle bolts

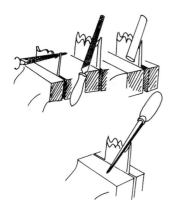

File the blade of the chair scraper to the correct profile, taking into account that the blade will not be held vertically in the tool. Hone to a sharp edge and turn a hook with a burnishing tool

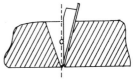

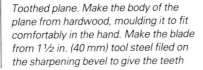

Toothed plane. Make the body of the plane from hardwood, moulding it to fit comfortably in the hand. Make the blade from 1½ in. (40 mm) tool steel filed on the sharpening bevel to give the teeth

The following items and blades for the previously described tools will require the use of a metalwork vice. In a small workshop it is not always practical to have a permanently installed metalwork vice set on a separate bench. A simple alternative is to bolt the metalwork vice onto a strong plywood board and clamp this to the workbench. After use, the vice and board can be removed and stored, and the bench swept clean of metal offcuts and filings. The following metal tools and accessories can be made as the need for them arises.

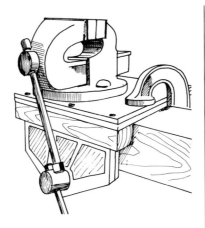

Nail puller. Make this from ⅛ in. (3 mm) flat stock. File a bevel in the top of the nail slot, and a shallower bevel on the underside to enable the tool to grip the nail without marring the surface of the wood. Bend the tool so that when it is rocked the nail is lifted clear

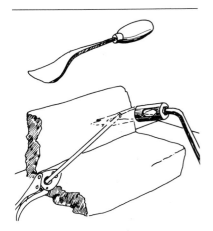

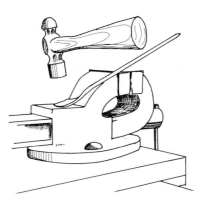

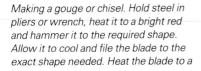

Making a gouge or chisel. Hold steel in pliers or wrench, heat it to a bright red and hammer it to the required shape. Allow it to cool and file the blade to the exact shape needed. Heat the blade to a

cherry red, and temper it by plunging it in cold oil. Heat the tang and drive the previously bored handle over the hot metal. Grind, hone and strop to a fine edge

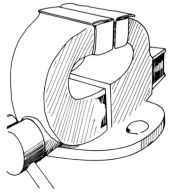

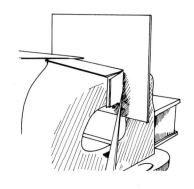

Punches. Make a selection of these from wire nails. Curved ones are handy for removing pegs in awkward corners

Vice jaw liners. Cut these from thin sheet steel or brass. Mark and cut them as illustrated and beat them into shape on the vice

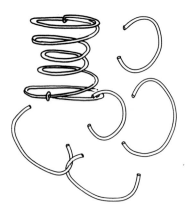

Spring clamps. Cut these from used upholstery springs.

Nail extractor. File teeth around the top of some small diameter steel pipe. Do not harden or set the teeth. The tool should fit in the chuck of an electric drill and is used to bore round immovable nails and screws

Tools that are made in the workshop should be well finished, and easy to use. Rough edges should be rounded, handles smooth. The following tools are an exception to this rule. These are the faking tools and here roughness and coarseness can be an advantage. In ageing new wood, irregular marks must be applied to the wood surface in a rapid yet convincing manner. For this business, instruments of vandalism which reflect their purpose are needed.

Tools for ageing new wood (clockwise from top left): broken brick, rusty chain, wheel chain, iron castors mounted in an arbor, wire brush, stick with hobnails and nails

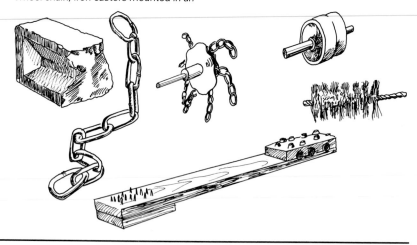

BENCH AND TRESTLE PLANS

The following design for a workbench is functional, quick to build and very strong. Use seasoned rough sawn wood (larch is good, as it is both heavy and cheap) purchased straight from a sawmill. The top can be planed level and smooth when it is finished. The joints are simple and held by coach bolts and nails. The top is nailed to the legs, and the nail heads are recessed and plugged in ½ in. (13 mm) dowel.

A cutting list that allows easy reference when selecting the timber in a woodyard should be made.

As well as a workbench, a pair of trestles will be needed. These should be of equal height, strong, and long enough to cope with fairly large pieces of furniture. The nails at the top of the legs should be hammered well in. The legs need to be able to move slightly – this allows the loaded trestle to settle firmly on a slightly uneven floor.

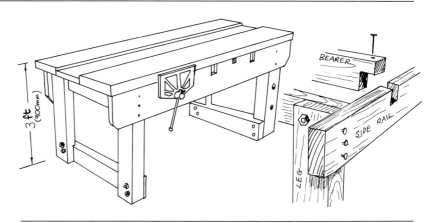

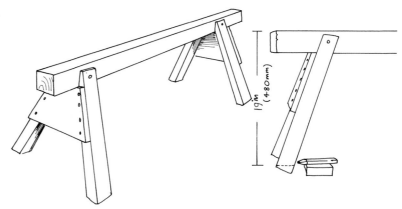

2 Wood and its Identification

Freshly felled logs contain a large proportion of water, most of which is lost in the drying process before the wood can be used for indoor joinery and cabinet making. Newly cut oak, for example, will lose over a third of its weight during seasoning, and many woods lose an even greater proportion.

If the loss of moisture is too rapid, a log will end-check (split from the ends where the moisture loss is most rapid) and large parts of the trunk may be rendered unserviceable. To slow down the loss of moisture, many good quality hardwood logs are left felled on the forest floor, where they can dry slowly in the damp and shady conditions. It is also to inhibit the loss of moisutre which may cause cracking or twisting, that woodcarvers and turners who work on large pieces of wood will wrap the piece in polythene or slightly dampened hessian before leaving the workshop at the end of the day.

SAWING

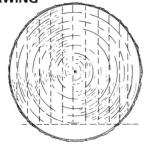

Most sawmills convert their logs into boards by using a large bandsaw, fed by a rolling table on which the log is rested, supported by wedges. Unless a specific request is made to the sawyer, the log will be plain sawn. This is the easiest and quickest way of converting the log and it also produces the most boards from a single trunk. Many of the boards sawn in this way, however, will be prone to warping and excessive shrinkage.

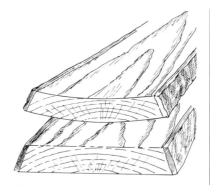

Shrinkage. Quarter-sawn boards do not cup as they dry. Shrinkage is normally limited to a slight tapering across the section of the board

Better quality logs will be cut on the quarter. This entails far more handling of the log, more adjustment to the bandsaw fence and, for the most part, fewer wide boards. The advantages, however, are that the boards will be more stable, will shrink less, and may show on their sides the strikingly beautiful medullary rays, known as figure.

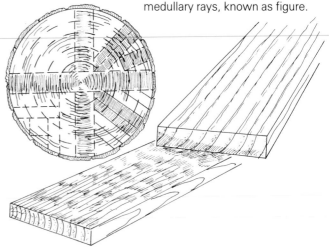

SPLITTING TIMBER FOR TURNING

Where dowels, pegs or long, thin turnings are needed, it is best to split the stock rather than saw it to size. This enables the wood to break at its weakest point, eliminating cross grain weaknesses, and reducing the likelihood that the finished turning will distort with age and stress.

This is only a practical proposition for lengths up to about 24 in. (600 mm), although of course logs far bigger than that are riven, and then reduced to size with the adze and side axe.

All that is required for splitting a log, cut to length by chainsaw, is a selection of hardwood wedges and a sledge hammer. Leave logs needed for turning on their side in the shade. When a length of stick is needed, roll one of the logs into the workshop and inspect the ends for radial cracks. Select a promising crack, insert a wedge in it and strike it with a sledge hammer. Do not continue striking wildly at the wedge, hoping for the log to cleave cleanly in two. After a couple of blows, stop and inspect the sides and ends for signs of a running crack. If one is noticed, drive a wedge into the crack close to the first wedge. Use as many wedges as you need to open the crack. Once the required pieces have been obtained the log should be returned out of doors and left in the shade and damp. Most logs, except

elm, can be riven in this way, but those with crooks, large burrs or signs where branches have been pruned away, will not split cleanly.

SEASONING

The success of the seasoning process is dependent upon the wood drying slowly and evenly. It is because of this that the wood is best sawn in the winter. The typically cold and damp days prevent the fresh sawn wood from drying too quickly.

Apart from the sense of urgency that should inspire summer work, the procedure for stacking, and the care of the wood pile remain the same.

STACKING

Preparation for stacking fresh sawn wood

Before cutting the log into boards, prepare a place for the wood pile to stand. The ideal conditions are a shaded, level outdoor area, protected from the wind.

A very imprecise general rule is that a board cut to 1 in. (25 mm) thickness will need one year to air dry. With this in mind, site the stack where it will be out of the way and if possible out of sight. Also, before cutting, have a general notion of the order in which the wood will be needed from the stack.

Building the wood stack

Prepare a level base. Vegetation should be cut and the area covered with plastic fertiliser bags or old roofing felt, to act as a moisture barrier.

The stack should be raised from the ground on piles of bricks or concrete blocks. These should be built in pairs, the width of the stack, and spaced at about 24 in. (600 mm) intervals. Lay some 2 in. (50 mm) square sticks across them and sight down the stack. Eliminate any twist or unevenness in the cross members by packing beneath them with shims of slate or formica.

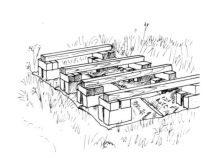

An alternative and equally satisfactory way to build the foundation is to rest the entire pile on a pair of very substantial beams, lifted clear of the ground by a pile of blocks at each end. The availability of bricks as against beams will probably determine which method is adopted.

Stacking the pile

Once the wood has been sawn and delivered to the site of the stack, it should be graded in a number of ways.

The very best boards should be selected and put to one side to be placed in the middle of the pile.

Bowed boards should be paired and put to one side.

Select some straight, poor quality

boards for the first layer; lay these across the bearers. Over each cross member place a small 1 in. (25 mm) square stick. These must be perfectly aligned over the supports, and the subsequent rows of sticks perfectly aligned as well, otherwise stresses will develop in the woodpile, and the boards will warp and twist when they are removed.

Build the pile, adding sticks at each layer of wood, supporting short ends and overhangs inside the pile with extra sticks.

Lay bowed boards face to face, bowing out, so that the weight of the pile presses them flat. Place the best boards at the middle, and any pieces that are already cupping should be placed cup downwards to allow any rainwater that enters the stack to run off.

Finish the pile with a final layer of poor quality boards, and then some sheets of corrugated plastic, iron, plywood, or offcuts scraps from the woodyard, to cover the stack and make it watertight.

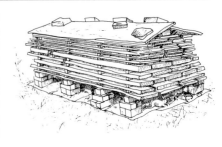

Immediate treatment for the ends

Once the pile has been built, the exposed ends of the planks should be coated with a thick oil-based paint. (Any household weatherproof paint will do.) This will help prevent the boards from end-checking as they dry. Once this has been done, the pile can be left, and the air flow through the stack will dry the wood. If the wood is cut in the summer, it is a good precaution to cover the pile with old tarpaulins or sacks to slow down the current of warm dry air between the boards; remove these in the autumn.

USE OF WOODS
Preparation for use

Air-dried timber will lose moisture until it reaches an equilibrium with the outside air, after which it will dry out no more. This is not usually sufficiently dry for use in cabinet making; for this, the wood should be removed from the pile, taken indoors, and piled well away from any radiators, where it should remain warm, dry and undisturbed for a couple of months.

Before using the wood, scrub it well with a wire brush, and dust it to remove grit and dust that may damage woodworking tools.

Abnormal woods

In many cases there will be very little choice when it comes to selecting a suitable piece of wood for a restoration project. The grain patterns, the frequency of knots, etc., will all help determine the selection. There are however, tell-tale signs to scan for when selecting stock, that if detected should warn of problems ahead in working or finishing a piece of wood. This does not mean that wood which displays suspect features should be discarded, but it should certainly be treated with caution and perhaps used for back or bottom repairs, glue blocks, or temporary holding jigs.

Knots

Knots occur where a twig or branch begins its growth from the centre of the tree trunk. If the branch is lopped off, or if it dies naturally as the crown of the tree spreads and starves it of light, the stub will be enveloped in the growing trunk of the tree. Knots of this kind occur in most trunks, particularly at the centre of the tree, where a lot of false starts are recorded in the presence of small black knots. Most knots are accepted as a matter of course in woodwork, but large ones will cause trouble, and so will those that are surrounded by a layer of bark. (This appears as a black ring around the knot.)

Knots present end grain wood, across the width of a flat sawn board, and will tend to shrink more than the surrounding wood. Cracks may form across the face of the knot and the knot may even drop out. The wood surrounding a knot will tend to have a confused and (generally) denser grain pattern. These patterns can be very attractive, but areas of such turbulent grain sometimes warp and bulge into unusual and unpredictable shapes long after the furniture is finished.

The position of knots should be considered when planning joints. Knots should be avoided at joints, unless they are small and are not associated with major distortions in the grain. Similarly, where large section timber is to be used, the outside grain patterns should be scrutinised for unexplained irregularities, as these may indicate the presence of a buried knot just where a joint is to be cut, or some delicate carving planned.

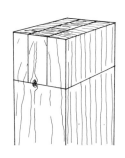

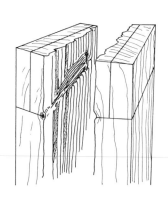

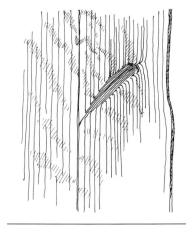

Quarter-sawn boards tend to show knots as spike shapes, extending in some cases across the face of the board. Where this is the case, due thought should be given to the general weakening effect this will have on the strength of the board.

Conditions in many timber yards make a careful selection of timber rather difficult. Once one is familiar with the grain patterns of a straight grained log, it is easier to spot one that may cause trouble.

Cracks and shakes: both sides should be free from cracks; end-checking is acceptable, provided an allowance is made for it when the wood is measured for paying.

Furry surface: timber that has been planed or sawn, and retains a feathery fibrous surface, may just need dusting off. If not, the furryness indicates that the wood is poor grade reaction timber, deformed during growth by excessive stress on the tree. This may be very difficult to finish cleanly, will stain badly, and

shrink longitudinally far more than a normal plank.

Crooked logs: rough sawn boards that have twisted or bent out of straight are only useful for very short work. Bending indicates inner tensions in the plank that will continue to plague the restorer after the plank has been planed and sawn.

These inner tensions will also be revealed when the piece is fed into a circular saw. If the sawn piece springs away from the stock, or springs back and presses against the blade, it will be unsound and unreliable.

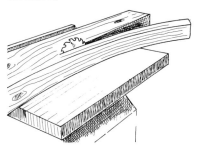

Cracks across the grain

Be on the lookout for fracture lines across the width of the plank. Brash failure occurs in hardwood logs, caused by the impact of the falling tree when it crashes to the ground. A dark line across the board and down its sides reveals the presence of such a fracture. The wood above and below these lines is usually quite sound.

IDENTIFYING TIMBER

Various criteria should be applied in identifying timber. Unfinished woods of the same species can look very different, due to such factors as soil mineral content, manner of growth, and health of the tree.

Where different woods can be found in furniture

Turnings	Beech, birch, box, mahogany
Chair legs	Beech, ash, birch
Painted furniture	Beech, birch
Bent wood	Beech, birch, ash, yew, willow
Chair seats	Elm, maple
Table tops – dairy	Sycamore
Table tops – country	Oak, elm, pear, cherry, chestnut, walnut, ash
Table tops – quality	Mahogany, oak
Backing to wood veneers	Oak, pine
Drawer sides	Chestnut, oak, mahogany, pine
Backs to frame furniture	Poplar, alder, chestnut, birch
Modern machined	Beech, birch, sycamore, ash

Identification guide

(*see identification chart between pp. 96 and 97*)

The woods described in this guide are grouped according to their natural, unstained colour, and are listed in order of weight (kilo/cubic metre at 15% moisture content).

White woods
Hemlock   A straight, well-defined grain, non-resinous, with occasional brown or grey streaks along the grain. *Furniture use:* general use in modern furniture.

Poplar   White, sometimes with a yellowish tinge, soft, even texture, and fibrous. Splits easily. Used for making matches and matchboxes.

Furniture use: plywood, shelving and backs to country furniture.

Willow   White, fine-textured, soft wood. Steam-bends well. Most common use is for the blade of cricket bats; other uses are steam-bent chair backs, clogs, turnings.

Sycamore   Hard, fine and even textured wood. Iridescent quality when cut on the quarter. Used in backs of violins, table tops – especially dairy furniture. Known as harewood when stained grey.

Whitewood (yellow poplar)
Usually white, but the heartwood is often pale brown and streaked with black, green and red. Fine, even texture, and straight grain. *Uses:* panels, linings, carcassing, chairs.

Beech   Pale, occasionally pink. Straight grain, with dense, even texture. Characteristic brown flecks in the grain and heavy weight make this easily recognised. Used in turned, bent and machined work; often the wood beneath a grained finish.

Ash   White heartwood. Some hedgerow trees may be a rich brown colour. Marked grain patterns, growth rings clearly evident in end grain. Steam-bends well, and is extremely tough and resilient. Cuts like cheddar cheese, and has a ripe musty smell when worked. *Uses:* country furniture, especially chairs, and turnings.

Plane   Pale brown, fine even texture, straight grain. Flecks are more obvious than in beech. *Uses:* as a veneer.

Rock maple   Pale in colour, normally straight-grained, hard, fine and even texture. Sometimes grain produces a bird's-eye effect. *Use:* veneers for quality furniture.

Birch   'Poor man's walnut'. Almost white. Grain varies from straight to the wavy figure of flame birch. Fine texture, close grain. *Uses:* turnings, bent wood furniture, and to imitate more expensive woods.

Ramin   Almost white, straight grain

and even texture, with a tendency to splinter. *Uses:* general furniture making, and can be stained to match more decorative woods, for mouldings, etc.

Oak   Pale in colour, varying from yellow brown to pinkish white. Sap wood generally darker. Straight grain, coarse texture. Very strong and durable. Can be turned, steam-bent, and brought to a high finish. Acrid odour when being worked; high tannic acid content corrodes ferrous fastenings imbedded in it. *Uses:* much old furniture was made from oak, better quality modern furniture, also figured oak veneers used to decorate particle and block board furniture.

Holly   White, or greyish white. Straight grain, even texture. *Uses:* inlay; when stained black it is used as a substitute for ebony.

Yellow woods
Cedar   Varies in colour from pale yellow to pale brown. Straight grain, fine and even texture. *Uses:* furniture, framework in particular.

Parana pine   Pale yellow to pale brown. Sometimes streaked with red. A knot-free, straight-grained wood, with a fine even texture. *Uses:* cabinet framing, drawer sides, mouldings.

Box   Yellow, heavy, fine-grained and very dense. *Uses:* fine carving, decorative inlays.

Satinwood   Cream to yellow; fine, even texture, iridescent grain. *Uses:* inlay and marquetry.

Brown and light-brown woods
Redwood (Scots pine)   Reddish-brown heartwood. Knotty. Varies in texture. Used in pine furniture.

Mahogany   Medium to deep red-brown. Cuban mahogany is darker, heavier (and rare), South American mainland mahogany is paler, lighter, with an open-grained, rather plain appearance. *Uses:* high class furniture, used in the solid or as a veneer.

Redgum Pale sapwood (hazel pine), reddish brown heartwood (satin walnut). Irregular and interlocked grain. Fine even texture. *Uses:* furniture of all sorts.

English elm Pale brown, irregular grain, coarse texture. Sour smell when worked. *Uses:* chair seats on simple country furniture, and table tops.

Sweet chestnut Pale brown, like oak in appearance. *Uses:* country furniture.

Douglas fir Pale to medium red-brown; straight grain. *Uses:* carcassing for pine furniture, plywood.

Alder Pale, but darkens on exposure to light. Fine texture, no distinctive figure. *Uses:* widely used in the U.S.A. for furniture making.

Sometimes found in country furniture.

Cherry Pale brown with tinges of green. Darkens and reddens on exposure. Generally has straight grain and fine textured. Has a glittery, irridescent quality which makes the wood glow when it is finished. *Uses:* good quality furniture of all kinds.

Teak Golden brown to dark brown. Coarse, open grain, slightly greasy. Fashionable in modern furniture, often as a veneer.

Afrormosia Golden brown, with fine, interlocked grain. Sometimes used as a cheap alternative to teak, but can be distinguished by its finer grain texture.

Yew Orange-brown, darkens after exposure. Irregular grain. Fine even texture. *Uses:* hoops of Windsor

chairs, high quality furniture. Veneer.

Walnut Grey brown, straight grain, medium fine texture. A very pleasant wood to work, easy to carve, and takes a high polish. Can be bleached and stained yellow orange, or brown/red. Typical use is for gunstocks, but is used in all kinds of high-quality furniture.

Rosewood Highly figured black, orange, and sometimes purple streaked wood. Heavy and brittle, also rather oily. *Uses:* as veneer on fine furniture.

Ebony Black, although colour and tone vary greatly. Fine even texture. *Uses:* inlay, stringing, turned handles. Often imitated by holly or sycamore (both white woods) stained black.

WOOD AND ITS IDENTIFICATION

3 Preparing for Work

GUIDE TO STYLE AND DATE OF FURNITURE

This is never an entirely straight-forward and simple matter. Many apparently old pieces are recent copies of period designs. Genuine country furniture is quite often newer than its style suggests. There has always been a delay between the designing of furniture for fashionable houses and the adoption of the new designs and construction techniques by provincial craftsmen. This, coupled with the conservative taste of many households, has resulted in a great deal of furniture being made in a style long-since superseded by new designs from fashionable workshops.

Style alone is a very poor criterion by which to judge the age of a piece, but it remains a very useful reference point. Subsequent detective work can establish whether the technical details of a piece of furniture are consistent with its style and apparent age.

Some of these broken pieces of furniture are well worth repairing

Pre-1700 mule chest, bureau, bible box, joint stool, dresser base, Cromwellian chair, restoration chair. Details of typical drawer construction techniques, and mouldings. Note grain direction in drawer bottoms, crude dovetails and applied mouldings. Handmade metal fittings, mouldings scribed, chamfered or cut with a mason's mitre. Oak and, later, walnut used for making furniture

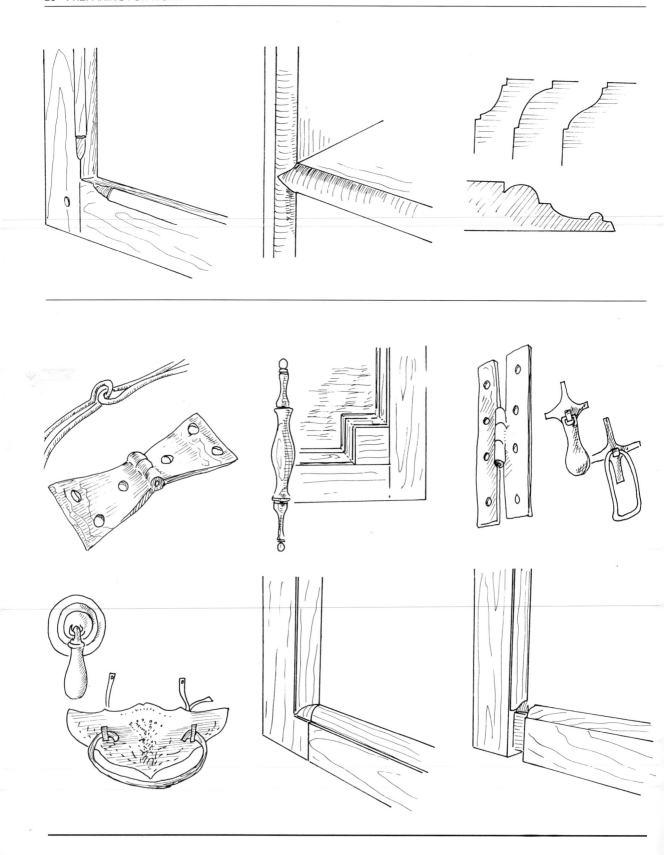

1700-1750 kneehole desk, lowboy, gateleg table, chest of drawers on a stand, corner cupboard, dining chair, toilet mirror, wing arm chair. Typical handles and feet of the period. Drawer dovetails are finer. Lip moulding, recessed behind mahogany crossbanding, is typical of drawer front decoration. Walnut, fruitwood, oak and, towards mid-century, the increasing use of mahogany, firstly in the solid (using heavy Cuban mahogany), later as a veneer laid over pine or oak

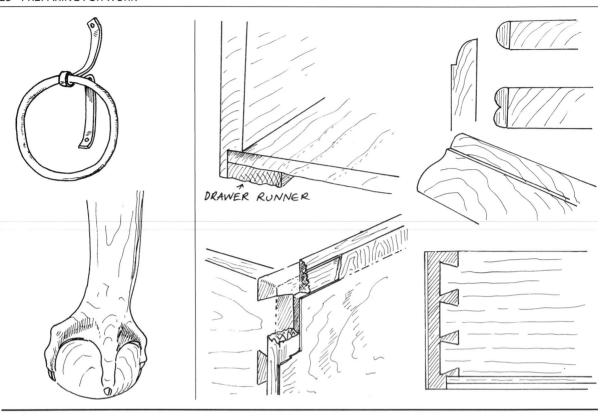

DRAWER RUNNER

1750-1800. Chest on chest, Hepplewhite-style dining chair, Sheraton-style arm chair, birdcage table, Chippendale-style dining chair, tea table, bureau, Windsor chair, linen press, bow-fronted corner cupboard, ladder back and spindle back chairs on a chest of drawers, Pembroke table with a tea caddy on top. Refined drawer construction — grain of the bottom boards parallel with the front of the drawer. Cock beading decoration. Typical handles and feet

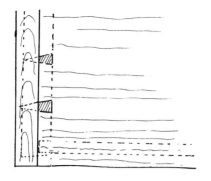

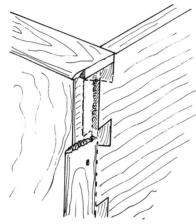

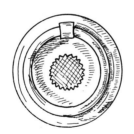

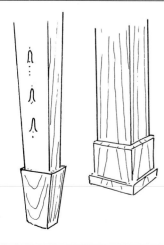
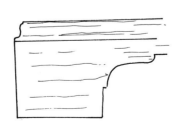
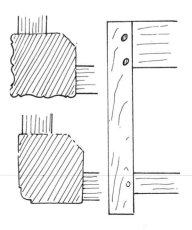

Regency – 1800-1830. Farmhouse table with H stretchers, Windsor and spindle back chairs on top. Canterbury, arm chair, breakfast table with reeded legs, sarcophagus-shaped tea caddy, sabre leg dining chair, cricket table, bookcase, hanging shelves, bookcase with drawers beneath, small stretcher table, dresser. Some typical handles, fittings and decoration of the Regency period. Simulated bamboo and rope twist are very common motifs

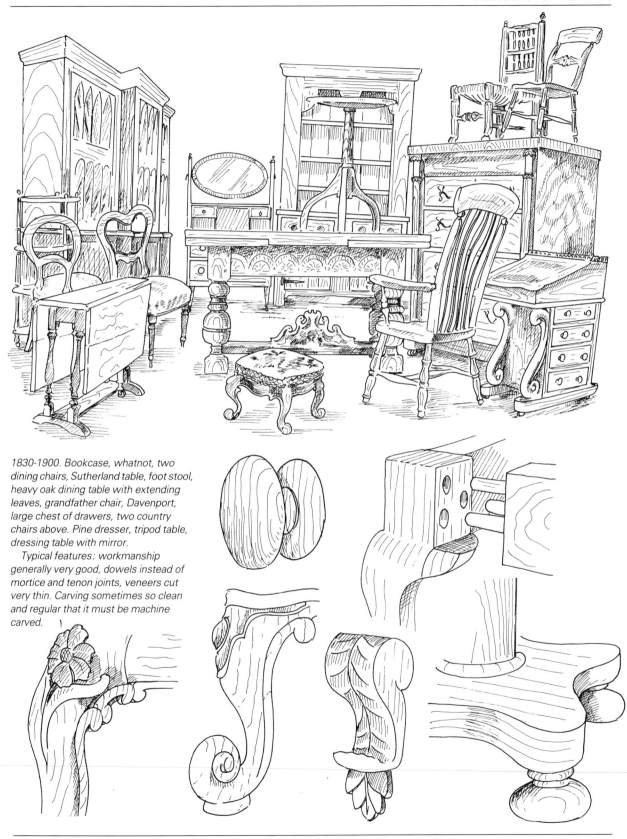

1830-1900. Bookcase, whatnot, two dining chairs, Sutherland table, foot stool, heavy oak dining table with extending leaves, grandfather chair, Davenport, large chest of drawers, two country chairs above. Pine dresser, tripod table, dressing table with mirror.

Typical features: workmanship generally very good, dowels instead of mortice and tenon joints, veneers cut very thin. Carving sometimes so clean and regular that it must be machine carved.

1900-present. Windsor chair, beech
bentwood chair, inlaid Edwardian corner
chair, hall stand, sideboard, chest of
drawers, dressing table, fitted wall
shelving, ladder back chair and extending
dining table. Sideboard and oak wardrobe
with simple decorative carving. Bookcase
and solid wood contemporary chair.

Typical features: use of man made
resin-bonded boards, paper-thin veneers,
plastic finished to simulate wood. Thin
stamped metal fittings, machined
dovetails, sparkling, brilliant finish.
Serious structural failures with little sign
of wear

Estimating the age and origins of antique furniture

1. *Quick assessment*

(a) The proportions of old furniture are slightly more generous than later copies. Chairs, for instance, are broader and deeper, with more sweep to the back legs. The timber used will be thicker in section than that used in reproductions.

(b) The wood of old unpainted furniture will glow and show a depth of colour not evident in new wood. Surfaces will be blemished, edges chipped and veneer and parts of moulding missing.

(c) Look for sharp edges, perfectly flat surfaces, and immaculate jointing. These are often the hallmark of machine manufacture. Handmade furniture has a charm that is partly the result of the imperfections in the wood and workmanship, and in the movement of the timber due to stress and years of loving abuse.

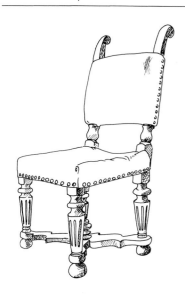

The degree of dilapidation should never be taken as evidence of great age. A rapid assessment of the proportions, condition, and style of a piece of furniture should be a prelude to a thorough investigation into the details of construction, fastenings etc.

Chippendale-style dining chair. Look for wide and bold proportions, with good rake to the back legs. The back should be worn smooth, and there should be signs of wear and bruising on the rail legs and stretchers. Previous repairs may be evident

Quick assessment. This is a copy of a Chippendale-style dining chair. Smaller section wood, less sweep to the back, few signs of wear. Narrow and shorter seat

Lowboy. Plywood back, machine dovetails, identical and perfect machine-turned legs indicate this is a new piece of furniture

Chest of drawers. Look inside for signs of hand crafting – sawing, planing, etc. Check drawer dovetails, quality and machining of back boards. Inspect the handles to see if they are original or replacements. The type of nails and screws will give a good indication of the piece's age

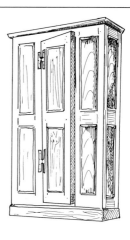

Pine cupboard. Look for original hand-forged hinges. Does it have solid or plywood panels? Is there evidence of wear or rot? Check the back to see if it was once a built-in piece of furniture that has been rescued and rebuilt

Clean flat surfaces, sharp corners, few signs of wear, use of plywood, machine dovetailing and grooving all point to recent manufacture

2. *Details*

Brasswork. Handles and escutcheons will be worn and in places damaged. Their screws and nuts should be brass, and appear undisturbed. Woodwork near brass fittings tends to discolour – dirt and polish accumulate beneath and around the handle. Incorrect or new handles do not prove a piece of furniture is a fake. Original handles can reinforce an opinion that the piece is genuinely old.

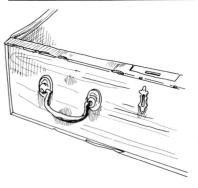

HAND CRAFTED

MACHINE MADE

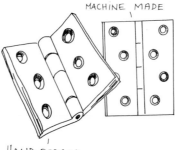

MACHINE MADE

HAND FORGED

Screws, nails and fittings. The fittings and fastenings on furniture that pre-dates the 1850s should all show marks of hand crafting. Screw head slots are often very narrow, and off-centre; screw threads are hand filed, and do not taper to a point. Nail heads are often forged (not extruded and stamped as modern ones are) and will show the blacksmith's marks on the head. Old hinges are generally heavier than modern ones, and are made from solid plates of metal. Old metal hinges often evince signs of deterioration into thin,

irregular shims. This delamination results from the initial beating it underwent during the hand forging, and usually indicates age. Where iron fastenings are embedded in wood a discoloration in the adjacent timber will result. This is particularly obvious in woods with a high tannic acid content, such as oak; the wood in contact with the metal turns black. If a screw has a black stain around it, it is likely to be very difficult to remove it. If it can be turned easily, it would suggest that the black stain is probably a deception.

Pegged joins. These should be smooth and undisturbed. There should not be any sign of hammering around a join. If filler has been used (revealed by flat, featureless areas in the timber, or unsightly swellings near a peg) it may suggest recent repair work.

Carvings will become worn. Fine detail is often worn away on the high spots. Backgrounds on a carved panel should be smoothed with a chisel, rather than punched flat. Chisel marks should still be visible. Carved mouldings should be irregular, and show hand-tool marks.

Veneers. These will be cracked and probably lifted and broken in areas. The movement of solid wood panels (the groundwork) beneath the veneers may have resulted in ragged tension cracks in the veneer, which do not correspond with the grain pattern of the veneer.

Drawers. Should be dovetailed. If they are nailed, the sides, back, and

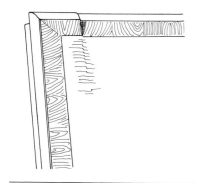

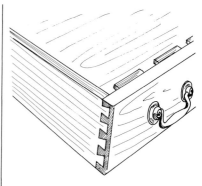

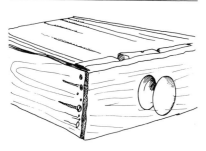

A drawer exhibiting many signs of age: loose and cracked dovetails, worn sides, shrinkage at the bottom covered by a strip of cloth. Note direction of grain of drawer bottom – this might indicate that it was made before the modern practice of running grain across the drawer became established. About 1760?

A new drawer. Equal-sized machine dovetails, few signs of wear or shrinkage

front should match perfectly, and the nails should be old and undisturbed. Cracking around the joints usually indicates that the drawer has been apart. The underside of the drawer should show signs of wear, which will correspond to marks on the drawer rail beneath.

Machine work. Hand-driven reciprocating machine saws have been in use for centuries, but they leave an irregular saw cut that differs

from a bandsaw cut in the frequency of marks caused by badly set teeth. A bandsaw tooth will leave its mark once with each circuit of the blade, while a badly set reciprocating saw leaves a mark at each stroke.

The circular saw came into general use in the middle of the nineteenth century. Circular saw marks should not appear on furniture made before that date.

Machine planers and jointers were

in use by the late eighteenth century and leave slight, regular-spaced ripples across the width of the board. A good furniture maker will plane these out, but sometimes the marks can be spotted on the surface or the underside of a plank.

Plywood was first used in furniture in the nineteenth century. Plywood furniture is light. Panels are very flat, and smooth on both sides. They are larger than solid wood panels, and surface cracks do not continue right through the panel.

Variations in quality

One of the most revealing discoveries that can be made when investigating the age of a piece of furniture is to find a discrepancy in the quality of workmanship between the parts of a single piece. This is to be expected if parts have been repaired; pieces of beading may be badly mitred or the tip of a foot poorly carved. However, if the front of a cupboard, for example, is neatly joined and pegged, and the back and sides are nailed together, the age and authenticity of a piece must be held in doubt.

Old furniture should be worn, but

only where one would expect wear to occur. Look closely for unusual and inexplicable signs of wear and repair. Patches of wood inlaid into drawer fronts probably hide the marks of previous handles rather than remedy accidental damage. One should not see – although occasionally one does – hobnailed boot marks across a table top. Hinge or lock marks where none are needed suggest replacement wood has been used, or that the item is made from used wood. Such marks are often found on the undersides of the flaps of drop leaf tables.

Signs of alteration

Signs of alteration to a piece of furniture should not escape detection. Careful alterations will often prolong the useful life of a piece of furniture with a consequent benefit to the people who possess it. Some typical alterations are illustrated here.

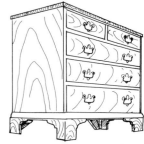

A cut-down chest of drawers is sometimes difficult to spot. Check the underside for evidence of recent work. Check behind brass handles for signs of previous wooden knobs. Victorian veneer is thinner than Georgian veneer – look for bubbles and areas of missing veneer to help to establish the age of the piece

This alteration has been undertaken to increase the leg room of a table. If the earpiece and under-rail of the table are cut from a single plank, it is likely to be a recent alteration. On old furniture, earpieces are made from separate pieces and glued in place to support a join. The electric jigsaw makes this alteration a quick and simple operation.

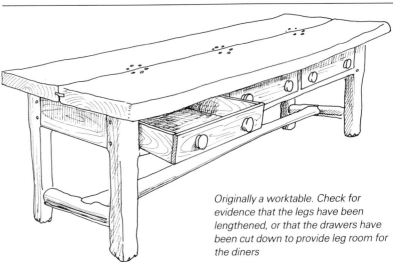

Originally a worktable. Check for evidence that the legs have been lengthened, or that the drawers have been cut down to provide leg room for the diners

Originally a mule chest. Front panels are cut to form doors and the top is nailed down. A useful piece of furniture that cannot pretend to be in its original state

Marriages. A marriage is created by uniting two originally separate pieces. Such a piece may have an attractive and convincingly original appearance. However, pieces originating from one workshop usually bear an imprint of the craftsmen who made them. To spot a marriage, it is best to look for discrepancies in construction techniques, quality of workmanship, fittings, markings, panelling, glue blocks, etc. Inconsequential differences in detail can give useful evidence of a piece's pedigree.

Most old pieces of furniture will have been repaired, sometimes very badly. If there seem to be many recent repairs, or if you sense that the piece is not all that it pretends to be, run your hand along the under-rails at the base and elsewhere.

Feel for rough or sharp edges. Dust and fluff that has been glued onto the underside of a piece feels coarse and gritty; evidence of this should indicate major restoration, alteration or entirely new work.

Most old pieces of furniture have had a chequered history. It is unusual to find a piece that is entirely original. All of the above clues need to be balanced against the apparent age of the piece itself in order to establish its approximate age. A genuinely old piece of furniture should have a presence that is timeless, and yet which reflects the ravages of time.

ASSESSMENT OF A RESTORATION PROJECT

Restorers are often asked to estimate the cost of repairing a piece of furniture. This is very difficult, particularly when dealing with old furniture, where more problems lurk beneath the surface than one would imagine possible. It is essential to give a good service, and to return the piece to the owner in excellent condition. All necessary work should be done but the owner, not the restorer, should pay for it.

Try to identify all of the jobs that require attention, and to discover whether they are caused or exacerbated by structural faults that will need correction.

1 Look for superficial damage. Rapidly explore and note down the areas of damage that need attention – missing beadings, stressed joints, lifting veneers, etc. Start by inspecting the front and the top, then the sides, back and underside. Drawers should be removed and checked, moving parts tested. Everything that needs attention should be listed in the notebook, a separate line for each job.

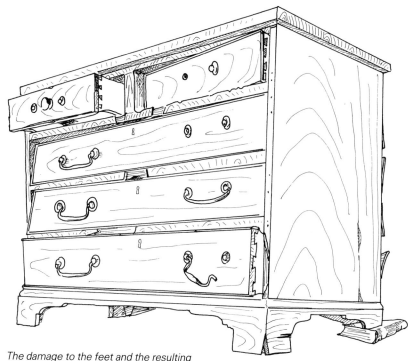

The damage to the feet and the resulting twist it gives to the carcass will certainly have added to the problems of this fine Georgian chest of drawers. Broken beading and missing (or replaced) handles indicate that the drawers do not run smoothly. Carcass joints, back boards, drawer runners and guides will all have to be repaired before attending to the more superficial problems

2 It is rare to encounter old furniture that has only suffered from accidental damage. Much external injury can be attributed to internal structural weaknesses, wear, or poor construction methods. The close inspection of the exterior of a piece should provide evidence of these internal problems. The following illustrations show the relationship between superficial damage and underlying cause. This is a fundamental connection to look for. A good restorer needs to correct the basic structural faults as well as the consequential damage.

Stressing of the framework and eventual failure of the joints may have been caused by the unequal lengths of the legs. This has been remedied by an inadequate repair. This Sheraton-style dining chair is not worth repairing unless it is part of a set, but it is worth storing in its present state until other similar chairs can be collected and repaired to form a harlequin set

Shrinkage across the wide boards of the table top has resulted in a wide crack running down the centre of the table. It will be impossible to pull the top boards together because the leaves, which are already canted out slightly, will be prevented by the table framework from hanging down. A fillet of new wood will have to be inserted in the top, and the rule joints attended to, before replacing the top

Sometimes a restoration job will entail the undoing of someone else's restoration work. Never underestimate the magnitude of such a task. Second-rate workmen who use modern glues and fastenings can present real headaches to a restorer. Be wary if there is any evidence of recent slipshod restoration work.

When all of these faults are noticed and listed in columns on your notepad, place an asterisk against the structural repairs. Do not specially underline any particular operations; some jobs may be a keystone of the restoration process, but they may not take any longer than some of the more superficial repairs noted above. In fact it is frequently the case that the fiddling jobs take the longest.

Order of repair

The order in which the job will be tackled should be fairly clear — structural faults must come first, superficial repairs after. Jobs of the same type (patching, tipping legs, etc.) should be done together: finishing is last.

How perfect should it be?

Once the general order of repair is established, a final and very important point needs to be decided: to what level of perfection should the piece be restored?

When a piece of furniture is in need of repair, one tends to look at the faults; the more obvious the damage, the easier it is to ignore other scratches and tiny breakages.

When the major work has been accomplished these minor blemishes become eyesores. It is essential, therefore, to decide and agree at the outset which repairs are necessary. This decision should be made with a vision of what a piece will be like when the work is complete.

Estimating the cost of repair

Although no two jobs are ever exactly the same, the processes involved will have been undertaken before. When estimating, think in terms of these processes — stripping, patching, tipping, etc. Always add some time as a contingency factor, and don't forget to include in the estimate the time for collecting, returning, and estimating the work.

Calculate an hourly rate to charge for the workshop services, and add extra costs – such as fittings and timber – to the estimate. A written estimate should specify what work will be undertaken and it should be quite plain that it is an estimate and not a guaranteed price. In the sometimes embarrassing event that the repair work is taking longer than calculated, it is best to meet your client and discuss the situation with him as soon as possible.

REPAIR GUIDELINES

There is a prejudice amongst some restorers who resist the introduction of modern techniques, believing that modern methods may compromise an authentic antique. I have no such scruples and the guidelines I use are listed below.

1 Furniture that has been restored needs to be safe, serviceable and completed with as little damage to the character of the piece as possible.

2 Original surfaces should be preserved where desirable.

3 Structural repairs should be, where possible, reversible.

4 Repairs to timber need not be reversible, but should be invisible.

5 Modern techniques and labour-saving devices should be welcomed and adopted where useful.

6 Repairs should enhance the quality of a piece. Repair work should never, in concept or execution, be inferior in quality to the piece itself.

4 Safety

Woodworking is a hazardous operation and, in some respects, the antique restorer is at even greater risk than the joiner or cabinet maker. The restorer will find that some of the conditions in which he must work are set for him by the particular breakages that he is asked to repair, and it requires very careful planning to make the best of some of these difficult situations.

ATTITUDE

Work deliberately and carefully. Never take risks. Always think well ahead, and plan for success. If necessary, be prepared to damage a piece further in order to simplify the total repair. Always keep the tools exceedingly sharp (so that cutting is smooth, controlled and predictable) and keep the hands behind the cutting edge.

Absorb yourself in the intricacies of the work, in the control and use of the tools, and not in preoccupations with speed, money, or radio programmes.

ACTIVITY

Walk in the workshop, never bustle about. Take as much work as possible to the work bench. Where this is impractical arrange temporary holding devices.

Do not allow shavings or other workshop debris to accumulate; clean up after each messy operation, or whenever cleaning is needed. Dispose of used rags and wire wool outside the workshop. Remove dirty working clothes before standing by an open fire; fumes from some products can ignite. Do not allow children to play in the workshop.

SAFETY EQUIPMENT

All guards, guides and safety devices should be in working order, and well adjusted.

Use pushing sticks to control the feeding of the stock into the saw. Use the pressure pad to feed work over the joiner/planer.

Wear protective goggles when routing, and a mask for all dust-creating operations. Gloves and an apron should be worn when stripping furniture.

PERSONAL

Do not smoke, or work near an open fire when stripping or finishing furniture. Keep the workshop well ventilated. Take all debris resulting from stripping outside the workshop.

FIRST AID

Keep a supply of sticking plaster, bandages and antiseptic ointment in a clearly marked first-aid box. Place the box where it can be seen and reached easily. Familiarise yourself in the use of the bandages, etc. and basic first-aid techniques. If working alone try to arrange means of attracting help in an emergency.

5 Tools

SHARPENING EDGE TOOLS

All woodworking edge tools need to be kept very sharp. It is a good habit to hone the tools that have been used during the day, just before closing the workshop in the evening. Always sharpen tools before they become dull and hard to use. Once an edge starts to break down it rapidly deteriorates, and the longer the delay before resharpening the greater will be the task when it is undertaken.

A sharp blade will cut cleanly and evenly. Minor variations in the grain of a piece of wood will not cause the tool to hesitate or stick. The balance of effort between pushing, guiding and restraining the tool will be easy to maintain.

Sharp edge tools make a faint singing sound as they slice through fibres of wood. A dull tool digs away, the efforts of the worker adding to the sound of chatter and splitting of the wood fibres. A simple test is to hold the edge of the blade to the light. A sharp blade will not reflect light from its cutting edge. A dull blade can quickly be identified, as the chipped or slightly blunted parts will glitter in the light.

Principles of sharpening

Except in the case of carving chisels, only one side of an edge tool should be ground and honed in the sharpening process. The correct method is to grind away any chips in the blade until an unbroken burr that extends across the width of the blade is created. This can be felt by stroking the thumb gently down the back of the blade. The burr should be removed by reversing the blade, and flatting the back against the oilstone.

Tools that are to be used in softwood have a more acute sharpening angle than tools used for hardwood. Softwood has a tendency to compress when being cut, and this effect is reduced by lowering the sharpening angle, in effect making the blade thinner. Hardwood, on the other hand, tends to rive or split when cut with a fine-angled tool. The stress that is built up ahead of the cutting edge must be relieved as the shavings are pared from the wood, and before they splinter ahead of the cutting tool. A high sharpening angle has the effect of acting as a chipbreaker.

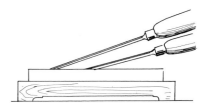

A 19° sharpening angle (top) is about right for working hardwood, and 12° (below) for softwood. Where both types of wood are being worked, sharpen to a compromise angle between these, and strop a steeper edge before cutting hardwood

Equipment

A grindstone (preferably power driven), a medium and smooth oilstone, and some stropping compound will be needed for sharpening flat-bladed edge tools. For sharpening gouges and carving chisels, small slipstones will be needed as well.

If the restorer has a lathe, he will be able to make a simple grinding wheel holder that is very effective and cheap. The grindstone can be spun between the lathe centres, with the lathe tool rest supporting

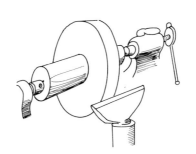

Grindstone holder. Turn part **A** first. Bore part **B** and then slip it onto **A**, and dowel it in place. Turn the ends and sides of **B**, tap out the dowel, slide on the grindstone, and bed it in P.V.A. glue.

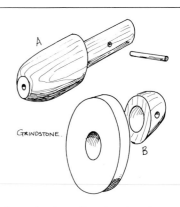

Press the sleeve **B** against the grindstone and dowel it in place

the blade. Arrange a perspex guard.

Oilstones are available at most hardware stores. Slipstones can be bought from a good tool store, or from manufacturers of woodcarving chisels. You can usually buy stropping compound from your local barber.

Safety

Wear safety glasses when using a power grindstone, and stand slightly to one side of the wheel. Grindstones should have a perspex window that can be lowered over the tool: use this as a supplement to safety glasses.

Sharpening method: stage 1

Run the grindstone at a moderate speed. The speed of rotation and the pressure on the tool determine the degree of heat build-up that occurs at the edge of the blade. Hold the blade firmly against the tool rest, and press it gently against the grinding wheel. Move the blade horizontally across the wheel. If the blade remains fairly cool continue to move it from side to side. Do not linger at the edge when changing direction, or the tip of the blade will overheat.

When the grindstone is in use,

take the opportunity to grind several tools at once. These can be sharpened in sequence. Tools awaiting their turn can be left in a tub of cold water to cool.

Once the tools have a regular and flat edge, and the sparks flying from the wheel flow over the tip of the tool onto your hand, leave the tools to cool. Switch off the grinder and wipe it clean.

If the lathe has been used to hold the grindstone, clean the lathe bed, head, and tailstock of abrasive particles.

Stage 2

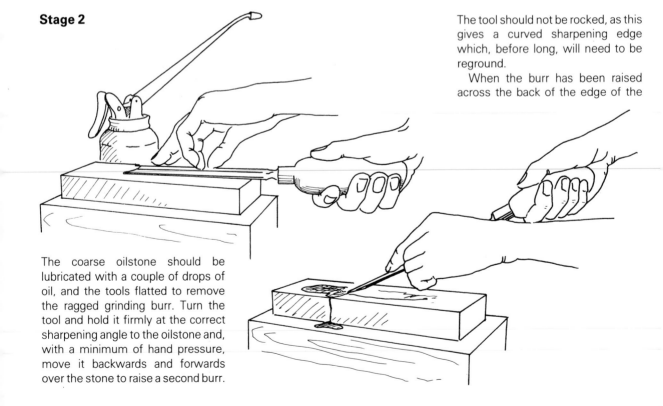

The coarse oilstone should be lubricated with a couple of drops of oil, and the tools flatted to remove the ragged grinding burr. Turn the tool and hold it firmly at the correct sharpening angle to the oilstone and, with a minimum of hand pressure, move it backwards and forwards over the stone to raise a second burr.

The tool should not be rocked, as this gives a curved sharpening edge which, before long, will need to be reground.

When the burr has been raised across the back of the edge of the tool, remove it again by flatting, and change to the smooth oilstone. Keep the same sharpening angle on this stone, and raise a third burr, which must then be removed as before. Very gentle hand pressure is needed at this stage or the edge of the tool will be distorted.

This process of honing and deburring is a delicate means of removing the unevenness in the tip of the blade, so as to leave a fine, keen cutting edge. Nicks and chips in the blade are revealed by lines left in the path of the blade as it is passed across the stone. Once the tool leaves an even smear of oil on the stone, with no scratch lines showing, remove the burr, and begin the third stage.

Stropping: stage 3

Rub some stropping compound onto a flat board. Hold the tool at the same sharpening angle as before, and draw it across the board. Do this five times, remembering to keep the tool at its sharpening angle. The path of the tool will be revealed by tiny trace lines in the paste. Turn the tool over, and flat the back against the board. This will remove the tiny burr that left the scratches. Repeat the operation with five more strokes across the board, and flat the back. When the tool no longer leaves small scratches across the compound it will be sharp. If it seems impossible to work out these marks, inspect the back of the tool for signs of rust pitting.

Tools that are sharp are a pleasure to use. Keep all of your edge tools sharp by regularly stropping them. Keep the strop clean of metal or other debris that may damage the carefully honed edge.

Sharpening gouges

The principal processes remain the same when sharpening gouges and shaped blades. Shaped slip stones are required, and outside bevels are achieved by giving the tool a rocking motion as it is moved across the flat oilstone.

Keep a special strop for sharpening carving tools. It should be of pine, about 1 in. (25 mm) thick. Every different cutting profile should have its own groove; it is handy if the stropping board is large enough to accommodate the needs of all of the carving tools. Work the tools across the pine. Smear the stropping compound into the grooves or channels cut by the tools.

Grind and hone carving tools to suit the needs of the work. It is often useful to grind a sharpening bevel on each side of a gouge, to give greater flexibility in the use of the tool, and to

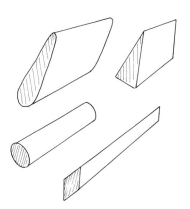

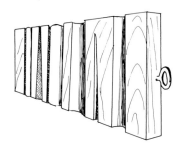

reduce the number of times tools are picked up and put down. Edges and sides to gouges can be ground away, but always ensure that the cutting edge, when seen from vertically above the tool, is straight, with sharp, well-defined, and square corners.

Sharpening scrapers

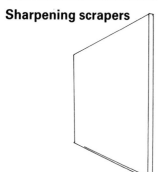

Cabinet scrapers

Cabinet scrapers are sharpened by raising a very fine hook at the edge of the scraper. This must be done very carefully, in the following manner.

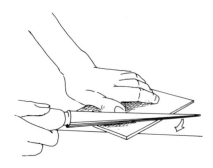

Stage 1. Use the back of a gouge, or a purpose-bought burnishing iron, to rub away the blunted or damaged hook.

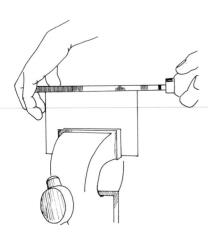

Stage 2. Place the scraper in the vice, with its edge about 1½ in. (4 cm) above and parallel to the jaws. Hold a flat, fine file at right angles to the blade, and make sufficient strokes to remove the traces of the previous edge. It is very important for the file to be held at right angles to the blade. If difficulty is experienced in doing this, a small block of wood held against one side, and moved with the file, will help to keep it level. As soon as a clean, square edge has been filed, remove the scraper from the vice and place it on a flat piece of scrap wood. When the smooth oilstone is placed on the bench next to this, the scraper should be able to touch the side of the stone.

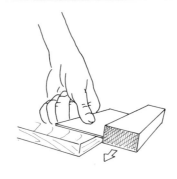

Stage 3. Rub the stone against the edge of the scraper until all file marks have been removed.

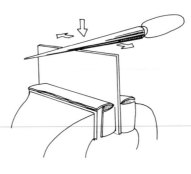

Stage 4. Replace the scraper in the vice. It will have a clean flat edge to it, and sharp corners. Take the burnishing tool, hold it at right angles to the blade, and make a few strokes down the blade. By this means the hook is started.

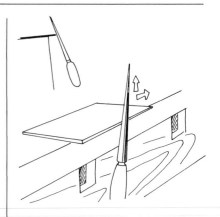

Stage 5. Remove the scraper and place it on the bench, overhanging the side by about ¼ in. (5 mm). Take a few slow and powerful strokes upwards and at an angle across its length. Very few strokes are needed. Take care not to overdo this part and turn the hook right back on itself. Repeat this last process on the second side, and the scraper should have two sharp, clean hooks – one on each side of its edge.

With steady use, the hook will gradually wear back. By gently working a pointed tool into the groove to open it out, then repeating the first and last operation, a useful edge will be restored to it.

Chair and moulding scrapers

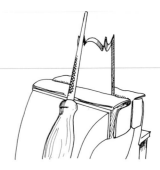

The procedure for sharpening these is more straightforward, although the end hook is the same. The moulding tool or chair scraping iron will be shaped to the required curvature or moulding with a file. A 60° sharpening angle should then be filed against the back edge of the blade. Hone this to a sharp cutting edge. This is then 'hooked' as for the cabinet scraper, except that the hook is not pressed over so far. Where the mouldings are small and delicate, it may be necessary to use the back of a V parting chisel for this.

Sharpening saws

Tools

You will need a selection of unused triangular files, a saw set, and some saw cheeks, with which to hold the saw. A pair of spring hand-clamps are also useful.

A sharp saw will cut in a clean straight line. Very little force should be required to make it cut the timber. When cutting dry wood, a sharp saw will make a high pitched chattering sound, and the sawdust will fly ahead of the blade on the cutting stroke.

A blunt saw is hard to control, and tends to bounce along in the cut. Keep all woodworking tools sharp and available for use.

Saw teeth

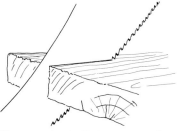

There are basically two types of saw teeth. The ripsaw tooth is sharpened at right angles to the blade; this type of tooth will remove wood with the grain, but makes a ragged cut when used to cut across the grain. The cross cut teeth are sharpened like small knives, and cut in both directions of the saw stroke; this type of tooth makes clean cuts across the grain, but is very slow in cutting with the grain.

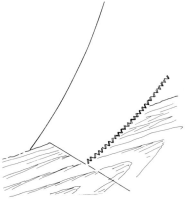

Saw teeth should be sharp and of equal height. The teeth must be bent slightly, in alternate directions, to allow the waste sawdust to be removed from the teeth and to prevent the saw jamming in the cut. This slight misaligning of the teeth is known as the set. The greater the set of the teeth, the wider will be the saw cut, and the greater the amount of wasted energy in sawing. When there is very little saw set, it is difficult to make minor adjustments to the direction of the cut, and energy can be wasted in correcting this. For a beginner, it is best to start with a fairly generous saw set, and reduce it as proficiency in the use of the saw is acquired.

The following instructions for sharpening apply to any saw. Less file pressure and fewer strokes are needed for small-toothed saws.

Rip saw sharpening

Hold the saw in the cheeks. Clamp the cheeks in place using the spring hand clamps. Hold the cheeks in the vice, and tighten.

Sight along the blade. If the teeth are of uneven length, they should be tipped. Hold a flat file at right angles to the blade, and file the edge of the saw until all of the teeth have been reduced to an equal height.

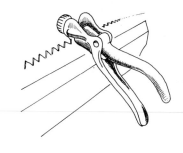

Bend the tip of the teeth using a setting tool. Count the number of the tooth points to the inch, and adjust the dial on the saw set to this number. Work the saw set up one side of the saw, pressing each alternate tooth. Repeat this on the opposite side to complete the setting.

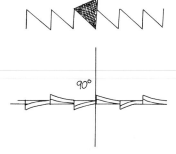

Take an unused triangular file. Hold it firmly at each end, at the angle shown in the drawing. Make three firm cutting strokes with the file and move to the next tooth. Each tooth should have an equal number of file strokes. Adjustments to the shape of the teeth can be made by increasing the sideways pressure when re-cutting the cutting edge or lowering the back of the tooth.

When the full length of the saw has been filed, inspect it for any tips that may still be blunt. Blunt teeth will reflect light from the point flattened during the tipping process. If there are several that need further attention file again, using only two strokes per tooth.

Test the saw by cutting into waste wood. The saw should cut smoothly, evenly and without jamming. Inspect the saw cut for signs of uneven setting. Small errors can be remedied by laying the saw flat on a board, and running an oilstone up the side of the teeth.

Major errors can be corrected by punching the teeth down with a small pointed piece of hardwood and a hammer. After remedial work of this kind, it is best to return the saw to the vice and file single, sharpening strokes to each tooth.

Cross cut saw sharpening

The same initial processes are repeated.

Tipping, setting

For sharpening cross cut teeth, tilt the file at a different angle, and make the strokes of the file about 60° to the blade. Alternate teeth are

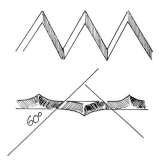

sharpened, and the saw should then be rotated, so that its other side is facing you. Sharpen the remaining teeth. It will be noticed that each file stroke simultaneously sharpens the front of one tooth and the back of the next.

For each side, start filing at the top of the saw and keep the same number of strokes per tooth. Only change the file at the end of a run of teeth. When starting on the second side of the blade, use a new side of the file. It is only through introducing these mechanical elements into the operation that it is possible to hand file teeth evenly and quickly.

For names of companies that specialise in selling and resharpening saws see the list of suppliers at the back of the book.

USING HAND WOODWORKING TOOLS

Woodworking tools must be handled deliberately and with care. The woodworker should try to control his temperament as well as his tools, and to concentrate on the task before him. Some jobs will not go well – these must be regarded as useful experiences. Lost time can never be made up by working frantically.

Marking knives

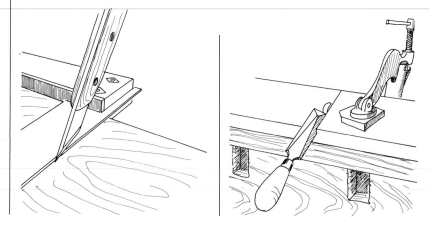

These must be pointed and sharp. All marks for cuts across the grain should be made with a knife. For a perfect saw cut, the waste side of the line can be relieved slightly using a paring chisel. The tenon saw can then begin its saw cut slightly below the surface of the timber.

When chiselling to a line the final cut can be made by starting the chisel in the knife cut, which will automatically align the chisel correctly.

When working with a set square or straight edge, the marking knife can be used to pinpoint a spot, and the

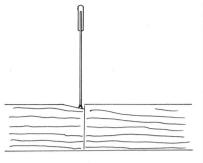

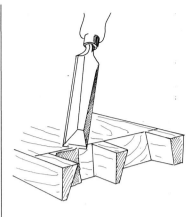

square or rule can be run against it.

Do not use a marking knife where the mark will be seen on the finished surface. Chamfers, bevels, etc. should be marked in pencil.

Gauges

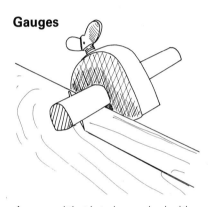

Any wood that is to be marked with a marking gauge should be firmly clamped. The fence of the marking gauge must be pressed tightly against the side of the timber, and the whole tool slightly tilted, so that the marking point trails. Move the gauge very slowly along the wood, or

irregularities in the grain will deflect the line.

Fine adjustments to the setting of the gauge can be made by tapping the end against the bench. This causes the fence to move slightly; a tap at the other end causes it to move in the reverse direction.

A cutting gauge is used in the same way as a marking gauge, but it has a blade rather than a point. It is a very useful tool, particularly for marking lines across end grain when, for instance, marking the shoulders and end laps of dovetails.

A mortice gauge has two marking points which mark the edge of the slot to be cut with a mortice chisel. The points of the gauge should be set to the mortice width before the fence is adjusted.

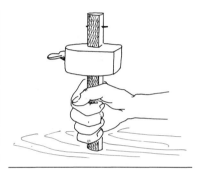

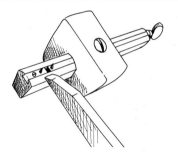

Set squares, bevels and dividers

These must be handled with great care, and if they are dropped, or suspected of being out of square, checked as described on p. 12. Use a set square to check the angle between adjacent faces of wood. When they have been checked and are found to be at right angles, it is customary to mark the wood in the following manner.

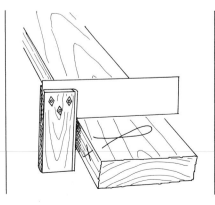

Sliding bevels are used for marking and checking angles other than 90°. If the blade rocks slightly when it is

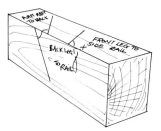

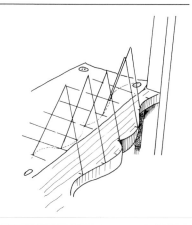

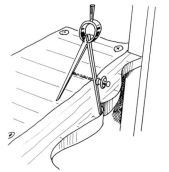

held flat against a piece of wood, it may be necessary to file down the head of the stock by the pivot. Where several different angles need to be marked out, a short piece of squared timber can be marked with the various angles and the bevel can be reset to these when required.

Dividers should be lockable. When dividers are used carefully they reduce the chance of an error resulting from inaccurate measurements. Dividers can also be used to transfer curves or wavy lines accurately and quickly.

Saws

Hand saws

These should be held in one hand. The other hand is used to guide the saw as it begins the saw cut, and to hold the waste wood as the cut is finished. For achieving a square saw cut, the cutting lines should be marked across the timber and down one side. Begin sawing at 45° to the surface of the wood, and saw both lines at once. For a long cut, the angle of the blade can be checked with a set square.

Thick pieces of wood should be marked with a cutting line on both sides, and sawn from both sides.

Saws used hurriedly, or forced into the wood, tend to wander off line. Only sufficient force to push and pull the saw is required. The weight of the arm and the cutting action of the teeth do the rest.

It is sometimes handy to be able to reverse a hand saw. Hold the saw vertically, with the cutting edge pointing away. Make small vertical strokes with the saw, lengthening the stroke as the technique becomes familiar. This is particularly convenient for cutting into large panels of plywood.

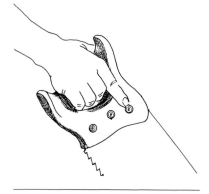

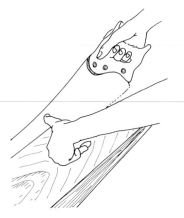

Tenon saw

Tenon saws are normally used in conjunction with a bench hook, but for sawing down the sides of a tenon the workpiece should be held in the

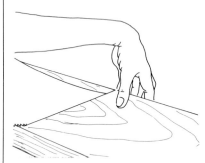

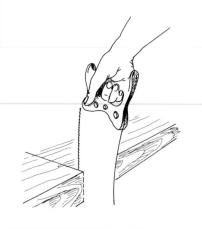

vice. All of the remarks for handsaws apply to the tenon saw. The technique of paring away at the waste side of the cutting line to ensure a perfect saw cut described earlier is particularly relevant to the handling of this tool.

It is tedious work cutting down the grain using a tenon saw, and I recommend the use of a ripsaw for cutting all but the most fragile of tenon sides.

Dovetail saw

This is smaller than the tenon saw, and often has a horizontal handle rather than a pistol-like grip. It is used for delicate work, and for cutting dovetails. This saw has very little set, and should be handled gently.

Coping saw

This is a frame saw. The sprung frame holds the replaceable blade in tension. At each end of the blade is a swivel, which permits the blade to be rotated relative to the frame. The sawblade should be inserted so that the saw cuts on the push stroke. Take great care that the blade is not twisted, or it will be impossible to control its direction.

Fretsaw

A cutting board with a V-shaped slot is essential when using a fretsaw. At the apex of the V is a small hole about ⅜ in. (7 mm) in diameter. It is a help

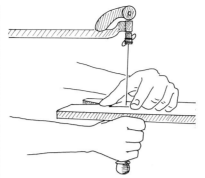

to draw lines radiating from this to enable you to locate the centre of the hole when it is obscured by the workpiece. The saw frame is tucked under the right arm and moved in a vertical direction. The very thin replaceable blades should cut on the down stroke. While the blade is moving up and down in the centre of the sawing hole, guide the workpiece to the blade with the free hand, twisting and turning it to follow the cutting line.

Very delicate patterns can be cut using a fretsaw once the gentle arm movement is mastered. Only a very small stroke of the arm is needed: the trick is to feed the work slowly and to reduce the rate of feed when approaching a sharp curve, or a right-angled bend. Always keep the saw moving.

If the pattern needs to be cut from the centre of a panel, use a bradawl to punch a hole in the wood, release one end of the blade, feed it through the hole, and refasten it. Tension the blade by using the lever or wing nut at the top of the frame. Place the workpiece over the V and cut out the required shape.

Mild steel or brass can be cut if the correct blade is selected. Detergent or oil, dropped onto the blade, will prevent the blade from overheating and breaking.

Bow saw

The bow saw has a thin steel blade, tensioned in a wooden frame. The blade has ripsaw teeth and very little set. The bow saw can be used for cutting curves or straight lines in wood. It can be held like a coping saw and, because it has a longer blade and bigger teeth, will cut more quickly. Where there is a lot of sawing to be done, the work can be clamped horizontally overhanging the workbench. Hold the saw vertically: the arms give a gentle feeding pressure to lead the saw into the wood, and the weight of the arms and saw supply the cutting force. When this tricky technique is mastered it provides a very efficient and relaxing means of cutting curved stock. Difficulties in guiding the saw through the wood are often caused by a twisted or over-set blade.

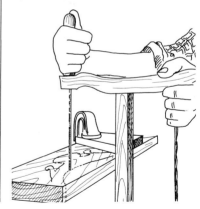

Planes

Planes should be looked after with great care, and rested on their sides when not in use. They should be stored with their sole propped against a small ledge sufficiently high to lift the blade clear of the shelf.

Plane blades tend to dull fairly rapidly. This is partly the inevitable

deterioration of the cutting edge in heavy use, but it is aggravated by the heat build-up in the blade. Planes move very fast across the timber, and if this movement continues in both directions (the cutting and the recovering stroke) for very long, the blade will overheat. Intervals between sharpening can be increased by lifting the plane clear of

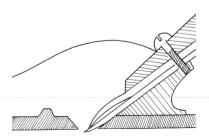

the stock on the return stroke.

Most plane blades have a chipbreaker tightly clamped to the front of the iron, a little above the cutting edge. This serves to locate the blade on the adjusting screw and may also break the shavings as they curl through the mouth of the plane. The chipbreaker should be screwed very tightly to the blade, as its other function is to pre-stress the blade to prevent if from vibrating as it slices through the wood. If a plane continues to suffer from chatter – a rippled finish achieved with a lot of effort – it may be worthwhile removing the blade and checking the blade support for unevenness or a build up of sawdust which may have resulted in an undesirable movement in the plane iron when in use.

Jointer plane

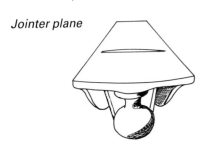

These are very long hand planes used for trueing the edge of a board. The blade should be sharpened with a slight curve, so that the area of maximum cut is at the centre of the blade, and the least cut at the sides.

Boards to be edge jointed or 'shot' should be held edge up in the vice.

The plane should be held in the manner illustrated, and walked along the edge. Once the blade is cutting, the left hand should apply downwards pressure at the front of the plane while the right hand pushes. A set square can be used to detect

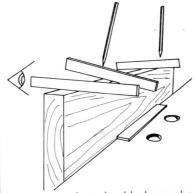

squareness, but should always be used to supplement winding sticks. After taking a few passes over the edge these straight- and parallel-sided sticks are balanced across the edge, and sighted. Any variation in angle can be detected by observing the slope of the sticks. Mark the high edges with a pencil, and using the fingers of the left hand ease the plane sideways as it is moved forwards. The high spots can be reduced by the centre of the plane iron, while the low areas are merely shaved by the edge of the blade.

This technique of achieving a varied depth of cut without inter-rupting the

continuity of the shaving is fundamental to the use of the jointer, and it can be used with any plane wherever perfectly square edges are required.

Smoothing plane

This is smaller and handier than a jointer, yet should have sufficient bulk to enable it to carry its momentum past patches of difficult grain. The blade is set at a compromise angle, suitable for hard and soft woods, but if a particularly fine finish is required on a hardwood surface an effective change in sharpening angle can be achieved by stropping the blade on the front face and flatting the sharpening angle. When smoothing boards or panels, downward pressure needs to be slight. For thin pieces of wood ensure that the bench or work surface is even and supports the timber, otherwise hollows will be scooped from the areas supported by high spots, while the low points allow the panel to bend out of reach of the cutting iron.

If the cutting iron is sharp, but the plane is difficult to push across the board, lubricate the sole with candle wax.

The shoulder or block plane

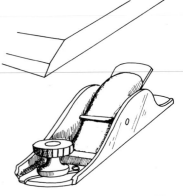

This is a small (about 6 in., 155 mm long) very versatile tool. The blade is set at an angle of between 12° and 20° to the sole, and in many tools the mouth of the plane is adjustable.

The sharpening bevel is ground on

the upper side of the blade, so the blade is supported right to the very cutting edge. This, and the low angle of the blade, prevent tool chatter. When the mouth opening is set to a minimum and very little blade is used, extremely fine cuts can be made on end-grain and difficult grained woods.

The plane should always be held with both hands, the left hand at the front applying downward pressure, the right guiding and pushing. When planing around the edge of a board, it is a sensible general rule to plane the end grain first (if necessary working from both sides to the centre) and then to follow by planing the sides.

Rebate plane

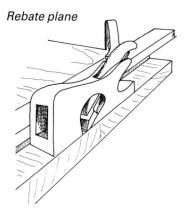

A rebate plane is used for working shoulders or 'rebates' in wood. Some planes incorporate a fence at one side. For those that do not, a batten of wood should be clamped or nailed to the workpiece, and the plane worked along it. If the rebate plane has a skewed blade, the leading edge of the blade should cut

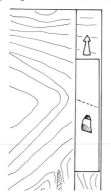

the inner side of the rebate. This skewing of the blade has the effect of pulling the plane into the rebate as it is cut. If the plane is used in the wrong direction it will tend to wander away from the guide.

Combination plane

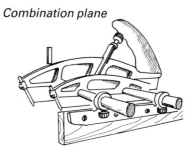

Combination planes can perform a number of tasks, including tongueing and grooving, and beading. They are often equipped with small knives at the leading edge of the sole that should be lowered when cutting grooves across the grain. These nick the grain fibres ahead of the cutting tool, and help prevent cross grain tearing. A combination plane can be used when roughing out stock prior to cutting a moulding. Always start roughing work at the edge of the moulding and work inwards. This gives the depth stop a level surface to slide on.

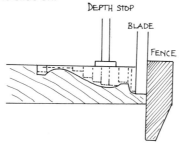

DEPTH STOP / BLADE / FENCE

Wooden planes

The second-hand wooden versions of the modern steel planes are often good value, and very pleasant to use. 'Used tools' on p. 12 outlines the qualities to look for when buying a second-hand wooden plane.

The blade in a wooden plane is held in place by a wooden wedge. Sometimes a chipbreaker is fitted to the front of the blade, and the wedge

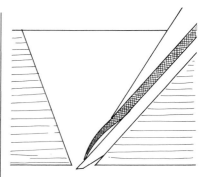

sits over this and presses the chipbreaker and blade against the tool support. In order to adjust the depth of cut, the blade and the chipbreaker should be put in place, with the blade just slightly above the level of the sole. The wedge is pushed in to hold the blade in this position, and given a few sharp taps with a light hammer. Invert the plane and sight down the sole. The blade should just be visible protruding through the mouth of the sole. If the blade is too far out, a couple of smart taps at the back of the plane will withdraw it. If the blade is down too far at one side, the iron should be hit sideways to correct it. To make the blade come out a little further, tap the nose or the end of the blade.

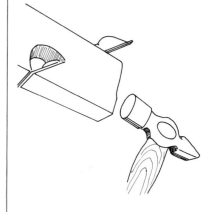

When sharpening moulding planes, great care must be taken to ensure that the line of the blade's edge follows the exact profile of the plane sole. Because moulding plane blades are so often badly out of shape when they are bought secondhand, I rarely bother to buy them. Rounds and hollows, however, are very useful and well worth buying.

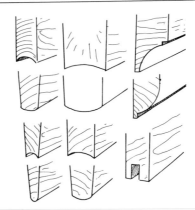

Spokeshaves

Spokeshaves are designed to be used with both hands. It is useful to have a round-soled, as well as the normal flat-soled, spokeshave. Second-hand wooden spokeshaves are light and efficient tools to use, but the mouth of the tool should be inspected for wear. If the slot ahead of the cutting iron is badly rounded or worn, the tool will be unpredictable in use.

Hold the wooden spokeshave with

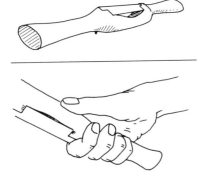

the first fingers of each hand, covering the side spur of the blade. This prevents the blade from pulling out. If, despite this, there is a tendency for the blade to free itself from the stock, remove it, and thrust a wood-shaving or small piece of paper into the hole to help wedge it in place.

The blade of a steel spokeshave is held by a clamp, and adjusted by two screw threads. These must be tight against the blade to prevent it from working back into the body of the spokeshave.

Cabinet scraper

This tool is held in both hands, with the thumbs pressed against the blade to give a slight bend to the steel. The movement of the blade should always start off the wood, and finish clear of the wood. Gentle passing strokes need to be made in the direction of the grain, and very fine, lace-thin shavings will be removed. Thin scrapers tend to overheat quickly and are unpleasant to use. A good quality scraper will be fairly heavy gauge steel, hard to bend, and will not chatter or swiftly lose its edge. Scrapers are ineffective on most softwoods. Problems in using a scraper are usually caused by poor sharpening.

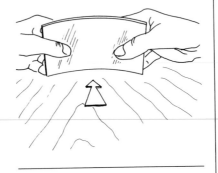

The chair scraper

The chair scraper is held in both hands, and either pulled towards the operator or pushed away from him. The initial passing cuts are made with the handles twisted forwards with the cutter trailing behind. As the moulding becomes deeper, the tool is twisted back, bringing the cutter

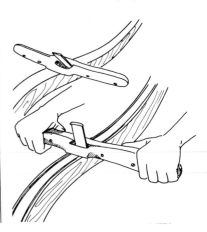

deeper into the moulding until, on the final strokes, the sole of the scraper rests on the moulding, helping to steady the cutter on its last smoothing strokes. Irregularities in the grain will cause the scraper to hesitate or chatter. Work these areas down before the moulding goes deeper. Rough parts can be eased down with a gouge or chisel. In order for a chair scraper to work effectively, it must be kept very sharp and the passing strokes should be light, but firm. A sharp cutter can be used to shape mouldings across end grain and against the grain. It is often very useful to arrange one or two fences on the tool, to help guide the scraper.

Scratch stocks

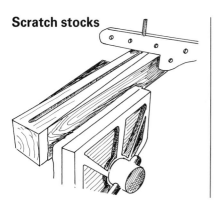

These are simple to make and easy to use. The blade is not sharpened to an edge or a hook, but is merely filed or ground to a right angle with the steel blade.

The tool is tilted so that the cutter trails behind the leading edge of the scratch stock, and the edge of the cutter scrapes the moulding. On the return stroke, it is tilted in the opposite direction. The tool will cut on both strokes and, provided the moulding is not very long, the cutting stroke on one side tends to clear the reverse side of the accumulated scrapings of the previous stroke. This a very useful tool, and very detailed mouldings can be made using it. It has the advantage over the scraper, that once the full depth of moulding has been cut, the tool continues to burnish the finished moulding. The scratch stock is not effective on most softwoods.

Scratch stock. The illustration shows a scratch stock working a moulding down the centre of a tapered leg. The leg is held in the vice by wedges, one of which acts as a guide to keep the moulding tool cutting down the centre line of the leg

Screw moulder

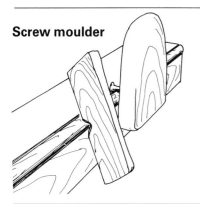

This simple tool makes a scraped line, parallel to the edge of a board. The profile of the line can be altered by using a round-headed screw rather than a countersunk head. Tighten the screw to bring the line closer to the edge of the board. If the screw is subsequently slackened, it may tend to wobble and spoil the moulding. A convincing antique beading can be achieved with this tool if the edge of the board is rubbed down with a piece of hardwood after the screw cutter has cut its line.

Chisels

Keep chisels and gouges in a tool roll. These can be bought from a good tool store. It is useful to have a large (1½ in., 38 mm) firmer chisel in the tool rack above the bench, and a (¾ in., 19 mm) paring chisel at hand on the bench. It is a good idea to keep mortice chisels separated from the others, as they are more cumbersome and difficult to store in a roll.

Mortice chisel
Mortice chisels are long and very heavily made. A good mortice chisel will have a leather washer between the handle and the blade to act as a shock absorber; it may also have a ferrule at the end of the handle to prevent it from splitting.

Bevel-edged and paring chisels

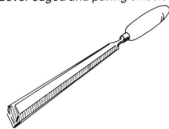

Paring chisels have a bevel-edged blade, and are longer than ordinary firmer or bevel-edged chisels. It is useful to have at least one such chisel, and other sizes can be shorter-bladed bevel-edged chisels. Workpieces must always be clamped or held firmly against a bench hook. The chisel must be perfectly sharp, and stropped regularly when in use. Hold the chisel handle in the right hand (this is the pushing hand) and guide and restrain the chisel with the left hand. Never use a chisel with one hand.

Lean into the work, using body weight, rather than strength, to slide the chisel through the wood fibres.

The left hand holds back the chisel and guides it, and the right hand acts as a ram pushed forward by the weight of the body. If the chisel slips and breaks out of the wood, over-balancing the worker, or if it slips and dives ahead of the cut, the wrong action is being used. Great force is not needed and should not be applied. Only small amounts of wood should be removed with each stroke of the chisel. If a large area of wood has to be pared away, for instance when a cross-halving joint is being cut, the area of waste wood can be weakened by making saw cuts down to the waste line. The saw cuts should be farther apart than the width of the chisel being used, and should not extend below the line of the joint.

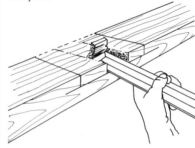

Chopping with a chisel

Any flat pine board will suffice as a chopping board. The bench should not be used without this, as its surface is often pitted with metal and other debris that may harm the chisel. The workpiece is placed over the board, the chisel is taken in the right hand and, with the left hand guiding it, is placed in position on the wood. The worker then leans right

over the chisel so that his right hand is by his right shoulder and, while still controlling the direction of the cut with his left hand, he moves his weight forward, applying it to the hand holding the chisel. A sharp chisel, held correctly, can make a clean and accurate slice across the grain. Strength is needed for this, but the force comes from the weight of the person wielding the tool; his strength is used to control the chisel and to transfer the driving weight to the handle of the chisel in a downwards direction.

For hammering and screwing, see section on glueing and fastening

A restorer is often proud of the array of ancient tools he has accumulated, which he may use occasionally where a primitive appearance needs to be given to a piece of new wood. The drawknife, adze and axe are all excellent and useful tools. All three should be sharpened on one face only, and kept razor sharp.

Drawknife

The drawknife is held with both hands, with the work gripped firmly in the vice. It is used for roughing down clean-grained stock, and leaves a smooth but angular finish. Chair rails that are to be rushed, and crude chamfering, are often shaped with a drawknife.

Adze

The adze is sharpened on the inner face of the curved blade. The tip of the blade should be adjusted so that it hangs correctly. Wedges driven into the head socket will correct the angle.

The adze is held with both hands; the left hand holds the end of the handle and acts as a pivot, while the

right arm lifts and guides the handle, following the action through as it swings down and across the timber. Handled with care, the adze can make regular and smooth cuts across the face of a board, in wide sweeping strokes. It is, however, a dangerous tool, and steel capped boots should be worn when using it to cut timber placed on the floor. Practise the use of the adze by sweeping the adze slowly over a flat board held on the floor. Once the action is mastered, long fine sweeping cuts can be made.

An adze should be hung so that a tape measure set at 2 ft (610 mm) suspended from the end of the handle, is flush with the head, and when swung sideways overhangs the tip of the blade by about ⅝ in. (15 mm). Wedge the blade into position and cut the handle flush with the outside curve of the adze head

Axe

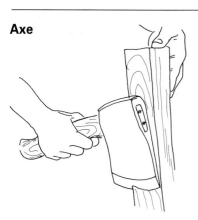

This is another roughing tool and is far more use to the restorer when it is sharpened on only one side of the blade. It can then be used fairly accurately to chop away bark and sapwood on wood to be used to replace the back framing of country furniture. This is a one handed tool; the other hand should support the workpiece at a point well away from the axe.

Clamps

When using clamps and furniture cramps always protect the workpiece by placing slips of wood to spread the load exerted by the clamping heads. Also, be sure to watch the bars of sash cramps, as they may bend slightly and rub against the face of a piece of furniture, leaving unsightly lines behind when they are removed.

When cramping framed or carcass pieces, always check the furniture for squareness in all possible directions. A diagonal stick is very useful for this. After a piece has been cramped up, and before it is dry, it is often a good idea to make one or two

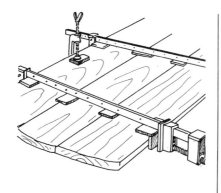

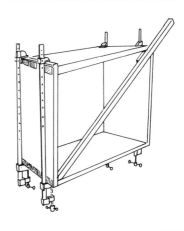

random spot sights just to check that the force exerted on the piece has not resulted in odd distortions elsewhere.

SETTING AND USING MACHINE WOODWORKING TOOLS

Machine tools must be adjusted with great care, and the operator should always use them with extreme caution. Wear safety spectacles when using circular saws, planers or routers, and a breathing mask if large quantities of stock are to be sawn.

Machine tools are often very noisy, and their noise and speed can mesmerise the operator. Light reflected from a blade or cutting head sometimes makes a strobo-scopic effect, which may distract the attention of the operator.

None of these factors alone makes machine tools too dangerous to use, but it is best to bear in mind that they can have a disorientating effect, and should not be used for long periods without a break.

Circular saws

Circular saws make straight, parallel cuts. Restorers should use tungsten-tipped saw blades because of the frequency with which nails and stones are found embedded in old wood.

The saw blade must be aligned parallel to the fence. A fence that converges with the blade will cause the blade to burn against the side of the wood as it is fed through, and may jam. If the saw and fence diverge, the stock will appear to pull away from the fence as it is pushed past the blade.

The alignment of the blade can be checked by placing a straight-edge against the blade (at a point where the set of the teeth does not interfere with the rule) and measuring from the straight-edge to the ends of the fence. Inspect the saw to discover how to adjust the fence alignment.

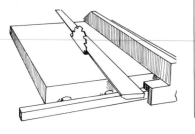

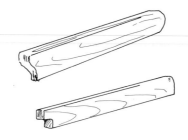

Using the saw
Stand to one side of the saw, and feed in the work slowly and steadily. If long stock is being sawn, erect supports on the feed and the outfeed side to support the stock. These will prevent the operator from having to exert his strength to control the wood as the saw nears the end of the cut. Push sticks should be close at hand and must be used to push and control the wood as it is fed into the blade.

When cutting stock that is thicker than the depth of the saw blade, the steel guide that sits in the kerf and holds the protective cap over the blade will have to be removed. The stock can then be inverted and fed through a second time. If the cuts don't meet, the saw cut will have to be finished with a handsaw or a bandsaw.

Sawing tenon cheeks
Provided that the saw is fitted with a rise and fall (which allows for an adjustable depth of cut), a tenon jig can be used to speed the process of sawing tenons. The jig holds the workpieces vertical while it is moved over the sawblade. Cut the inner side of the tenon first, then the face closest to the saw fence. This is because the face side of the stock, where it is pressed against the fence, will be weakened when the outer tenon is cut, and inaccuracies in cutting will result.

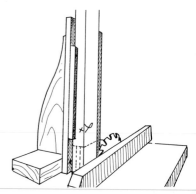

The circular saw is set to cut the length of the tenon. The fence is set to the marks of the mortice gauge so that the saw blade cuts on the waste side of the line

The bandsaw

All of the safety rules that apply to the circular saw also apply to the bandsaw. The hands should be kept clear of the blade and, where appropriate, push sticks should be used to control the stock. This is sometimes impossible when cutting curves, and great care is needed when handling wood close to the moving blade.

Setting up the bandsaw
Loosen the blade guides, and move them away from the bandsaw blade. Tension the blade to its normal operating tension, and push the top inner guide gently up to the blade.

Using a push stick with the circular saw. (The blade guard has been raised here for clarity.)

Screw the guide tight. Move the lower inner guide to the blade, and tighten that. These two guides should put no sideways pressure onto the blade, which should run straight and true.

Next, the top outer guide is moved to the blade, a slip of paper is held between the guide and the blade, and the guide is tightened. Remove the slip, and use it again on the lower guide. This should provide sufficient clearance to enable the blade to move easily, without wandering.

If a bandsaw blade persists in wandering while cutting straight stock, remove the fence, and try to cut the line without it. If the blade runs true, then the fence is out of alignment, and should be adjusted. If the blade is still difficult to control, and tends to have a bias to one side, remove it and send it away for resetting.

If the stock is pushed into the blade at a faster rate than can be easily cut, the blade will tend to wander off line.

Planer jointer

As with the other machine tools in this section, the jointer is designed to cope with a certain rate of feed. If this is exceeded a very poor finish, or damage to the motor or cutter, will result.

Position the jointer where there is good light and space to stand back from the tool. The woodworker must keep his hands well clear of the stock when it passes over the cutter, and should use push sticks where necessary. The pushing and pressure pad illustrated is easy to make and very useful. Small lengths

Planing pressure pad. Make this from pine. Arrange the dowels so that they can catch and guide the work being pressed across the planer

of timber are difficult and dangerous to plane; cut timber to length after planing.

Never pass the hands over the cutter. Hands should be withdrawn as the wood approaches the cutter, and deliberately raised and brought down well ahead of the cutter. This eliminates the possibility of slicing off a finger.

Setting up the cutter

Switch off the power supply. Different planers have their own systems for adjusting the knives. Whichever system is used, the knives must all be set at exactly equal distance from the centre of the spindle. This can be checked in the following way. Lower the outfeed table slightly. Take a piece of straight-sided hardwood, about 1 in.

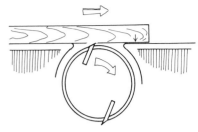

(25 mm) square, and rest it on the outfeed table, slightly overhanging the cutter. Rotate the cutter by hand, and the first knife that touches the wood will lift it slightly and drag it forward. If a rule is taped to the feed table the exact distance that the wood moved can be measured.

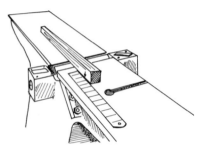

Continue to rotate the cutter slowly, and the next knife will also move the wood along. It should move the same distance. If it does not, the knives are badly adjusted. If the distance is less, the knife is too low, and vice versa. Make this check at both ends of the cutters and adjust the planer knives until they all have the same setting. This tedious job may take a long time, but it is time well spent. Once all of the blades are set to the same height, and tightened, the final setting is as follows.

Leave the stick resting on the outfeed table, slightly overhanging the cutter. Raise the outfeed table, until the stick just appears to rest on the blade. Rotate the cutter by hand and listen. The cutting knives should whisper as they pass the wood. They should not move the wood, nor should they miss it. The feed table can then be raised until it is just below the level of the outfeed table.

In order to make perfect joints, the

Showing the use of the push stick and pressure pad while using the power planer. (The operator is wearing safety spectacles.)

blades should be very sharp. Major regrinding will often be necessary and should be done by a specialist company. The blades can, however, be honed while in place by passing the edge of an oilstone along the back of the cutting edge. A slip stone is then rubbed along the front face of the cutting knives to remove the burr that results. Care should be taken not to curve the blade, nor to upset the height settings of the knives by grinding too heavily or frequently.

Using the jointer

When passing stock across the face of a jointer, the initial feed pressure should be applied to the front of the stock as it approaches the cutters. Once about 8 in. (200 mm) has passed the cutter and is resting flat on the outfeed table, transfer all downward pressure to the outfeed table. This will ensure a straight edge, provided that the tables are at the correct setting.

Router

Wear safety glasses, and keep hands well clear of the rotating cutter. Disconnect the router from the power supply when changing cutter bits.

The electric router is a versatile and useful tool. Tungsten carbide tipped tools are a necessity, except in the case of infrequently used moulding cutters. Apart from the normal functions of plunge routing, edge moulding, grooving, etc., the router can also be used for morticing.

Morticing box

This is a plywood box made with open ends and one side missing. The box should be held in the vice, with the open side uppermost. Clamp the wood to be morticed against the side of the box so that the face of the router can rest on the top side of the

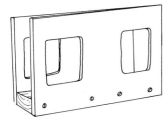

Morticing box. Make this from plywood. The top edges must be parallel and should be shaped if curved work is being routed

Morticing using a router and box

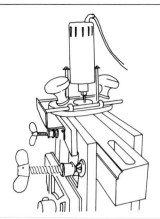

box, with the fence against the side of the box.

Adjust the fence of the router so that the cutter is directly above the mortice marks, tighten the fence locking screws, and plunge out the mortice. Move the router along the box after each downward stroke.

The morticing box is particularly useful where the stock is narrow and unable to support the face of the router, or where the wood to be morticed is shaped. If several identical pieces need morticing, then a depth stop for the workpiece to rest on, and end stops to limit the router's travel along the box, can be clamped or tacked in place.

Another useful jig used with a router is illustrated here. This should only be made if it seems likely that a number of turned legs will need to be tipped where the furniture frame-work is sound. Rather than dismantle the frame, this jig allows the turning to be performed on the furniture itself.

The router is mounted on the parallel bars, and the bottom clamp is tightened around the leg. The top pivot is tacked to the centre of the tip, and the router set in place on the bars. The router is then plunged to the required depth and slowly rotated around the leg. Any turned shapes can be cut in this way, although final finishing must be done by hand.

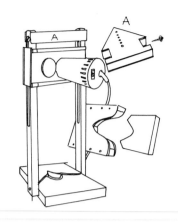

*Turning jig. This is a simple tool, which enables turning to be carried out on a leg without the furniture being dismantled. The top centre pivot board **A** has several holes which act as centres to permit the jig to cope with wide or square stock. As the wood is turned down, the centre is changed to bring the router back into the wood.*

6 Joints

EDGE JOINTS

Rubbed glue joints

These are commonly used edge-to-edge joints. Faces should be true and smooth. Assemble the edges to be joined on a pair of battens, and ensure that there is sufficient freedom of movement for the planks to be rubbed one against the other in a longitudinal direction.

Heat scotch glue and add a little water to it until the glue runs freely off the brush. Warm the edges to be joined against a radiator so that the glue doesn't chill when it is brushed on.

Take one plank, apply the glue quickly down its joining edge, and return it to the batten. Rub the edges

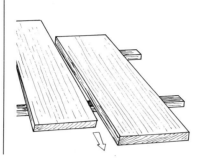

of the two planks together. Almost immediately a suction will be created and most of the glue will squeeze out. Align the ends and the surfaces of the boards, place battens above the lower ones, clamp and cramp the pieces together.

Where old rubbed joints have failed it will be necessary to reshoot

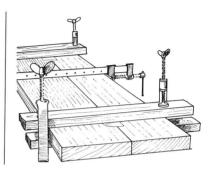

the edges. Take off as little as possible. If a jointer cannot be used, take slightly more from the centre part of the plank, leaving the ends a fraction high. When glueing check that the showing surfaces are level, as it is impossible to adjust them after the glue is dry without ruining the original finish.

Loose tongue joints

A strong edge joint can be made by inserting a tongue into grooves worked in both edges of the workpiece. The groove can be cut with a router or with a combination plane fitted with a grooving cutter. The advantage of using the router is that the groove can easily be stopped before the end of the plank so that the tongue will be invisible from the edges.

The same fence adjustment must be kept for both grooves, to ensure that the pieces remain level. Cut sufficient cross grain tongueing to fit the length required, place it in one groove and fit the other piece over it. The tongue should be a tight fit, and the boards should sit together without any rocking or gaps.

Use a slow drying glue. Quick-grab

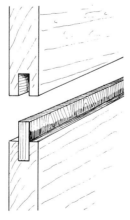

P.V.A. (polyvinyl acetate) and scotch glues will begin to set before the joint is completely together. Apply the glue to the groove, and tap the tongue in place. Add more glue to the edges if required. Run glue into the groove on the second piece, and clamp them together.

Tongue and groove joints

These are made in the same way, except that the tongue is incorporated into the edge of one board. It is cut with a special plane, or tongueing cutter set in a combination plane.

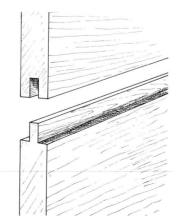

MORTICE AND TENON JOINTS

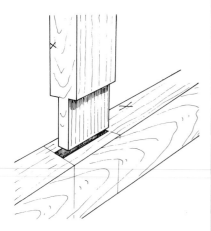

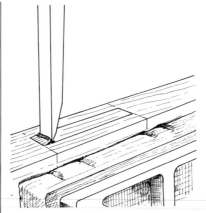

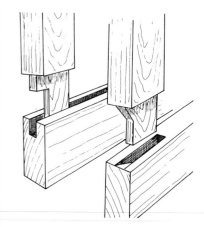

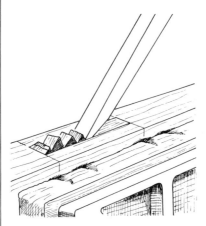

Strong joins, used for making concealed right-angled joins between pieces of timber.

Mark with a gauge in the manner illustrated. Use a mortice gauge, with two points (one adjustable) and a fence. The points should be set to the width of the chisel, which should be approximately one-third the thickness of the pieces to be joined.

Cut the mortice first. The workpiece should be held firmly on the bench or in the vice, and supported at the point where the mortice will be cut. If this is at the end of a piece, a clamp should be fastened to the sides to prevent the work from splitting. The mortice should be marked with a mortice gauge, the ends with a marking knife and set square. The chisel is held in the left hand, positioned very near the far end of the mortice, between the gauge marks, and at right angles to the grain. For the initial cuts, a single smart blow with a mallet is sufficient to loosen the wood in the mortice, and no rocking action is required. The tool is placed and hit at about ¼ in. (5 mm) intervals for the full length of the mortice, less about ¼ in. (5 mm) at each end; this is to protect the ends of the mortice from the bruising caused by levering out the waste chips. When the length of the mortice has been loosened, the chisel is returned to the far end of the

mortice, and the process is repeated, except that after each stroke of the mallet, the chisel should be rocked back sufficiently to remove a chip of wood from the mortice. In this way the mortice is cut out. Each layer of chips should be removed with the chisel before the next layer is begun. The ends are cut last. Take care not to bruise the ends of the mortice when making the final clear-out of the mortice. If the mortice passes right through the wood, the timber is turned around when the half-way point is reached, and the mortice is started again on the new side.

A mortice should be a tight fit with the tenon. If the mortice has wandered off its line as it has been cut deeper, it will need to be chiselled square later. This will weaken the joint. It is very important for the worker to stand back with his

mortice chisel at arm's length as he works, so that the cut of the chisel can be sighted as he works.

Any cuts to take a haunch (which is necessary only where the joint occurs at the end of a piece of wood) can be made at this stage.

Cut the tenon with a handsaw or a circular saw, using the tenon support described on p. 56.

The knife line marking the shoulders of the tenon should be cut with a paring chisel, and a tenon saw used to remove the waste. Mark the haunch with a marking gauge, and cut down and then across the tenon. clean the tenon and mortice, fit them together, and sight for accuracy.

Pegged mortice and tenon joints

Pegs can be used to draw mortice and tenon joints together and hold them tightly without the use of glue.

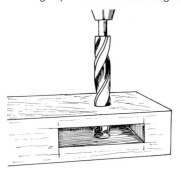

Select a drill of suitable size to take a peg, and bore through the mortice.

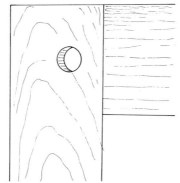

Insert the tenon into the mortice, and centre punch the tenon a little to the shoulder side of the hole. Remove the tenon, support it on some waste wood, and drill the hole marked with the centre punch. Replace the tenon,

and it will be seen that a slightly elliptical hole will pass through the entire joint. Cut a long tapered peg, leaving the last inch or so untapered, and hammer this into the hole with steady and unremitting blows.

As the peg is driven in, it will force the two parts of the join together. Drive the peg home and cut off the tapered part. It is useful to have a stock of pegs available for this kind of work; always make more than are needed, and store the rest for other jobs.

Foxed tenon and wedged tenon joints

These are made and cut in the normal way, but wedged to hold them tight. Always use strong, straight-grained wedges, and cut them accurately to size, so that the mortice is not damaged.

Foxed tenon

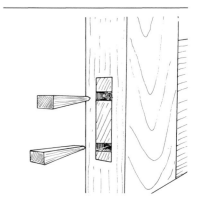

Wedged tenon

Mitred mortice and tenon joints

These joints are usually found around panelling where the supporting framework has an edge moulding.

Mark the joints in the normal way, except that the face side with the moulding should not be scribed, or marked with a marking knife. Instead, the shoulder lines are taken to each edge of the face side, and

then a mitre bevel is used to pencil in a line showing the line of the mitre on the moulding. This line is best carried across on to the flat of the face edge, as satisfactory cutting marks cannot be made across the moulding. A cutting gauge should then be set to the exact width of the moulding and run down beside the mortice.

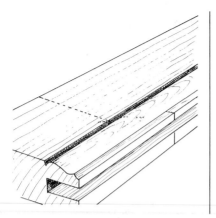

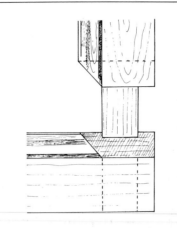

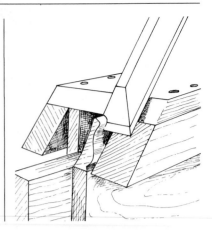

Remember that the face side of the tenon piece will be longer by the thickness of the moulding, so the mitre should extend ahead of the shoulder.

Both the mortice and the tenon are cut in the way described above. If the mortice is set in the groove to take a panel, the mortice and tenon will be shorter by the depth of the groove.

Once they are cut, the mitres are eased away in the way illustrated, and the joint pushed together.

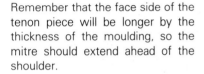

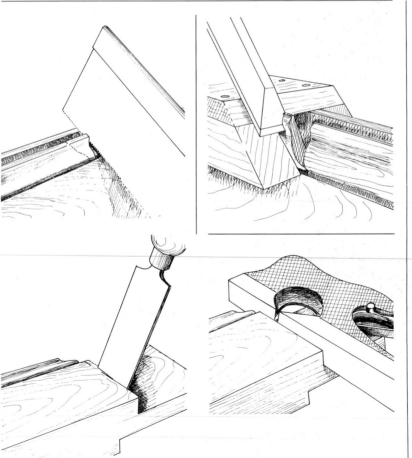

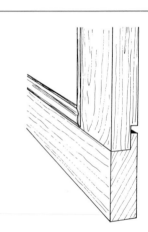

The rear shoulder of the tenon should be tight against the face of the mortice. If there is a gap, the front shoulder of the tenon (and the mitre if necessary) should be shaved back. If the inside shoulder rests against the morticed part before the face side is together, too much has been pared away.

A simple mitre cutting guide is useful for this work, and can be made up from spare wood to the design shown in the drawing.

Cleaning away decayed polish from a Regency sabre-leg
dining chair prior to staining and re-finishing

A very pretty walnut side table

A French oak dresser

A variation on the mortice and tenon joint is illustrated below. This joint is often used around a table top and is similar to the mortice and tenon joint, except that the shoulders are marked at 45° to the sides of the stock, rather than at right angles to it.

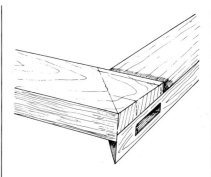

First cut the piece which is to have the mortice, making the 45° cut clean and square. Mark the mortice on the sides of the piece and across both edges. Chop out the mortice. Mark the shoulders of the tenon and cut the lower cheek of the tenon with a hand saw. Rest the tenon over the morticed end, check for squareness, and pencil in the line for the tenon.

Cut the tenon, allowing for a small haunch at each side, and then cut down and remove the second cheek. Clean the tenon and mark in and cut a groove at each end of the mortice to take the haunch. Fit the joint.

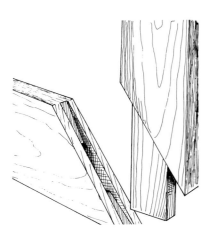

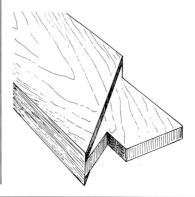

DOVETAIL JOINTS

Dovetailing has changed over the centuries, and replacement dovetails should always be in keeping with the contemporary style of the piece.

Through dovetails

The two boards to be joined should be of even and regular thickness and have their ends squared.

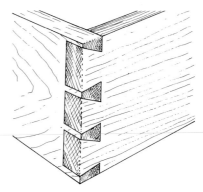

(a) Set a cutting gauge to the thickness of the pinned piece, allowing a small amount for overlap, and mark the shoulder for the dovetails. These can be measured with dividers and squared with a set square if preferred.

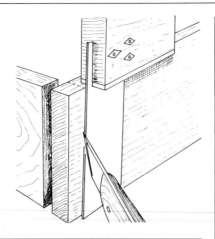

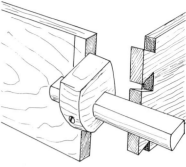

Cutting the pins

Reset the gauge to the thickness of the dovetailed board and mark the shoulders for the pins on the second board, using the gauge.

(b) Mark with pencil the position of the dovetails. This should be done by eye. Try to keep the tails of even-width and regularly spaced. Square across the end of the board at each mark.

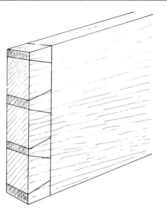

(e) Square round the board for the pins (as for the dovetails).

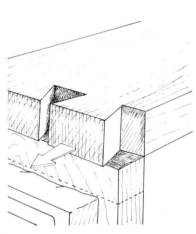

(c) Clamp the board in the vice. Take a dovetail or small tenon saw, hold it at an angle, and saw down one side of each dovetail right to the shoulder. Change the angle and saw down the other side of each dovetail.

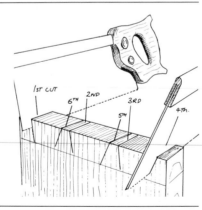

(f) Place the pin board, edge up, in the vice and place the dovetails over it. The shoulders of the dovetails should coincide exactly over the inside edge of the board.

(d) Remove the board from the vice and place it on a chopping board. Take a bevel-edged chisel and mallet and remove the waste between the tails. Turn the board over to finish the cut. Saw away the waste at the top and bottom edge of the board.

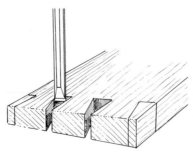

After the bigger cuts for the dovetail joint have been made with mallet and chisel, the finer cuts are made with the chisel only

To make perfectly tight dovetail joints

(g) Slip the dovetails further across the edge of the board that is to be marked with the pins. Because the pins taper, the further the dovetails are moved across the board, the greater will be the thickness of the pin. For hardwood this misalignment need only be very slight; for easily compressed softwood it can be more.

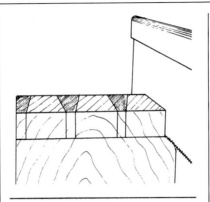

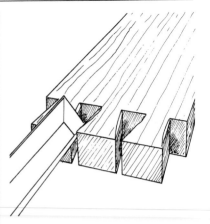

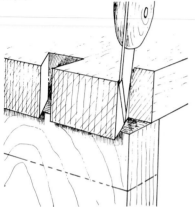

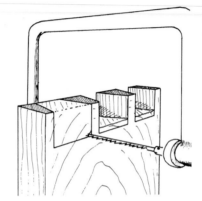

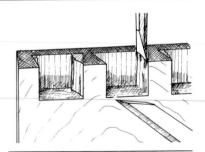

Place the dovetails over the pins. They should feel ready to slip together. If not, ease away at the pins until they do. Then slightly bevel the underface of each dovetail, and tap the joint together, spreading the shock of the hammer with a piece of softwood held against the back of the dovetails.

(h) Keeping the board over the pins, take a knife and mark the line and position of the pins (between the dovetails).

(i) Cut the pins with a dovetail saw, remembering to keep the saw vertical. Use a coping saw to remove the waste and finish with a bevel-edged chisel as for the dovetails.

Lapped dovetails

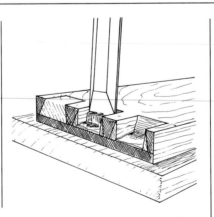

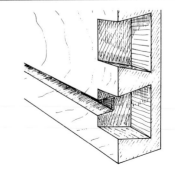

These are used in drawer fronts and are made in exactly the same way as the through dovetails, except that the waste between the pins must be chopped out using a chisel and mallet instead of a coping saw. Mark accurately, remembering to overlap the dovetails a little when marking the pins, and remember to include the drawer bottom groove as part of a dovetail rather than as a pin, or it will show in the ends of the drawer front.

Secret dovetails

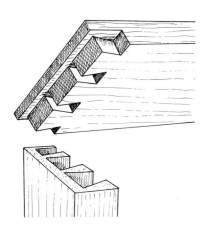

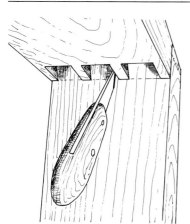

These are a variation on the lapped dovetail, and can be found holding down the tops of good quality carcass furniture. The pins are marked and chopped out first, and the top which will have the dovetails is then positioned over, or under, the pins (depending on which is most convenient) and marked. The reason for this is that the chopped-out space for the dovetails provides ample room for the scriber or knife, whereas there is very little room to move a scriber between the sides of a dovetail. Remember that, unlike the lapped dovetail, the dovetailed part will have to cover the entire face of the pinned part, but that a rebate has to be worked with a shoulder plane across the top of the dovetails to provide the overlap. In practice it is best to cut this rebate before marking the dovetails.

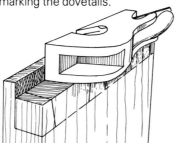

Dovetails to curved drawer front

Plane a flat at each end of the drawer. The flat should be set at right angles to the line of the drawer side. Cut and fit the dovetails to this, as with normal dovetailing.

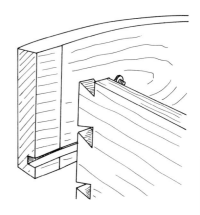

DOWEL JOINTS

Surfaces to be dowelled should be flat, clean, and close-fitting. Brad point drills with a centre pin and spurs should be used to bore the hole for the dowel. For shaped joints, scarfs and patches, where a dowel is required, its position can be marked on both pieces by taping a pin to one face, and gently pressing the other face to it. The indentation caused by the head should be used to guide the centre of the brad point drill.

Hold the drill vertically over the face, and control the angle of the drill by watching the marks made by the spurs on the edge of the drill. The spurs should describe an even circle

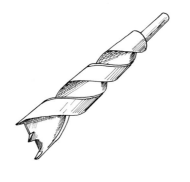

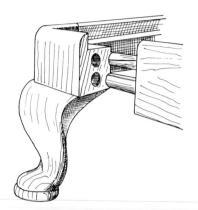

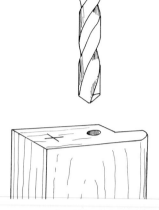

around the point of the drill. The dowel does not need to penetrate more than four times its diameter into either face. Drill both faces. Cut a dowel to length, cut a groove down its side to allow air and excess glue to escape, and assemble the joint.

Subsequent dowels can be marked and fitted after the first one is fitted and in place. Dismantle the joint, glue and clamp it together. Do not use P.V.A. glue where the dowel is less than ¼ in. (4 mm).

The end grain should be bored with a morse drill rather than with a brad-point drill

Dowelled edge joints

A dowelling jig should be made for this operation. This need only be a very simple affair. Bore two holes in the jig, perpendicular to its face and set in from the fence nailed to its side. Place the pieces to be joined edge up, face sides out, in the vice. Adjust the ends until they are in perfect alignment. Use a marking gauge to set a line down the centre of the edges at one end. Mark across the boards at the end with a set square. (If the boards are tapered or uneven, mark down the centre line with dividers). Drill the first two dowel holes where the gauge marks cross the line made by the set square (or dividers).

Place a short stub of dowel in one hole, and locate the hole in the dowelling jig in place over the board's edge, and clamp the fence against the face side of the board.

Drill the second dowel hole. Remove the clamp, place the dowel in the second hole, relocate the jig, clamp and drill again. Repeat this

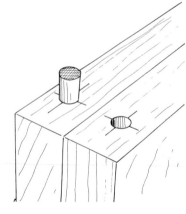

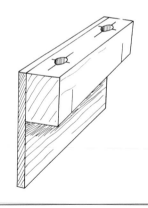

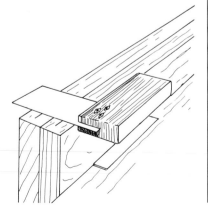

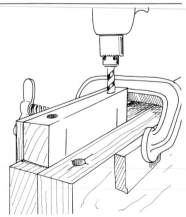

process until the end of the board is reached. Start the second board at the same end, using exactly the same technique. If the setting up of the jig and the drilling is performed carefully the piece will come together well. This is a joint that cannot be pre-assembled before final glueing. Cut and fit dowels to one edge, glue them in place, and chamfer around their heads. It is a help to vary the length of the dowels slightly, so that each dowel can be inserted individually, as the boards press together. Glue the other board, and assemble. P.V.A. glue should not be used in this operation as it has a tendency to grab the dowels, making it absolutely impossible to separate the joint if it fails to come together properly. A glue like Cascamite has the advantage of slightly lubricating the dowels, making the separation somewhat easier.

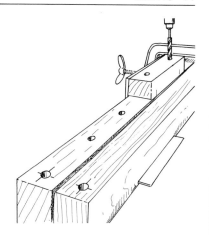

MORTICED EDGE JOINTS

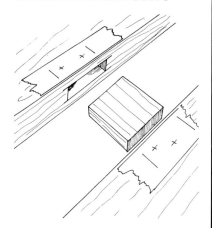

The tops of old tables are frequently morticed together. This is a straightforward operation, except that, in order to be able to peg the loose tenons, the restorer must mark their position before clamping the joint together.

NAILED EDGE JOINTS

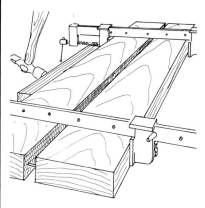

Pieces should be clamped face out in the vice, as for dowelling. A marking gauge should mark a line down the centre of each edge, resting the fence of the gauge against the face side of the piece. A set square is used to transfer marks across the boards. The intersection points will be the positions for the nails. Centre punch each point, and drill each pilot hole with a drill slightly smaller than the diameter of the nails to be used in the joining. Hammer a nail in each hole on one edge, and remove their heads. Glue one edge and bring the pieces together. Clamp and hammer the pieces together, taking up the slack and exerting slight pressure as the edges are struck.

CROSS HALVING JOINTS

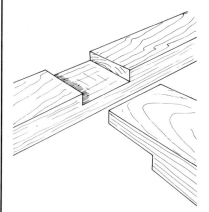

These simple joints can be marked by laying the jointing pieces across each other and scribing down their sides. Set a cutting gauge to half the width of the timber, and mark the depth of the recess in each piece. Relieve the lines for the sawcut with a paring chisel, and saw down to the cutting gauge line on each piece. If the joint is wide, or the grain curly and difficult to chisel, weaken the wood by making other saw cuts down to the line, a little further apart than the chisel width.

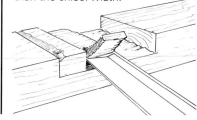

HOUSING JOINTS

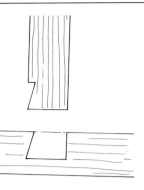

These are used for joining shelves to solid wood sides, and for fitting the drawer rails to the sides of a chest of drawers.

Marking the joint is very straight-forward, except in the case of the dovetail housing, where the slot for the dovetail must be less than the overall width of the board to allow for the cutting of the dovetail.

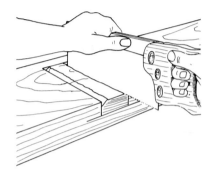

Cutting the joints

Use a router to cut housing joints, working it against a straight edge clamped to the face of the board. If a router is not available, relieve the sides of the housing with a paring chisel, slot a tenon saw against the line and saw down. Rest the left hand at the tip of the tenon saw, so that firm downward pressure is exerted along the entire length of the blade.

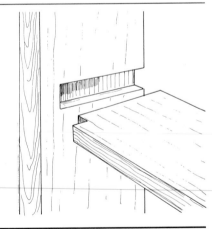

Cutting a stopped housing

It is possible to saw stopped housing in the same way, but where the wood is hard, or the housing is more than 6 in. (150 mm) long, it is worth-while chopping out a section of the housing at the stopped end, and running the saw into this. Remove the waste and cut the dovetail with a paring chisel.

7 Dismantling Furniture

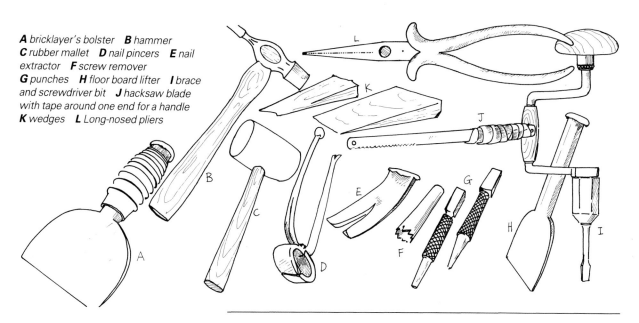

A *bricklayer's bolster* B *hammer*
C *rubber mallet* D *nail pincers* E *nail
extractor* F *screw remover*
G *punches* H *floor board lifter* I *brace
and screwdriver bit* J *hacksaw blade
with tape around one end for a handle*
K *wedges* L *Long-nosed pliers*

Dismantling furniture is an extreme
option and should not be undertaken
lightly. Bear in mind that the piece is
likely to be damaged in the process,
and also in the storage of the parts.

In some cases, nature and age
have already completed a major part
of the task. Where joints are all loose
or broken, it is a simple matter to
ease the piece apart, and in these
conditions this is the simplest way to
begin a restoration job. There are
other occasions when the carcass of
a piece is sound but when it seems
impossible to repair a weak or broken
part without dismantling. In these
circumstances consider very carefully any alternative methods of
tackling the job before undertaking
the step of dismantling.

If it is decided that dismantling the
piece is unavoidable, the tools
illustrated here are likely to be useful.

Before starting, assess the piece

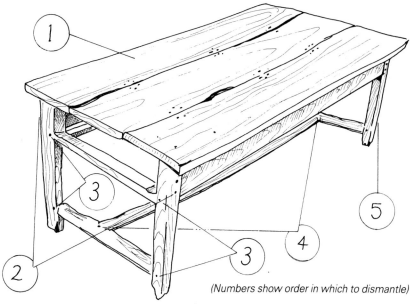

(Numbers show order in which to dismantle)

very carefully. Try to discover the
logic of its construction. This will
provide a key to the secret of
dismantling it. Minimum force

should always be used. When the
work becomes heavy or noisy, stop
and reconsider what you are doing.

There are certain to be joints that

won't move, or screws and nails that refuse to come out. Worst of all, there are likely to be bad repairs that have to be undone. The following sections give suggestions for coping with some of these problems.

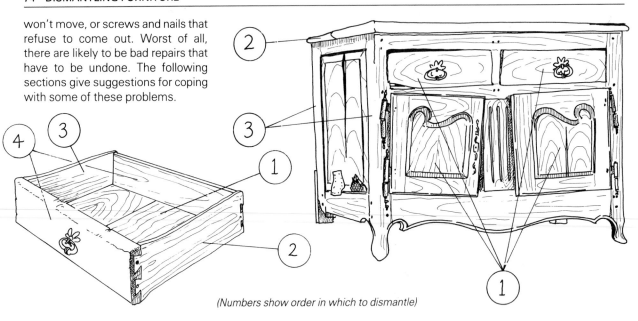

(Numbers show order in which to dismantle)

REMOVING FASTENINGS

Nails

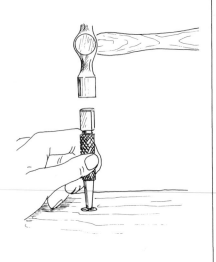

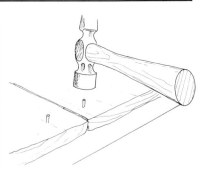

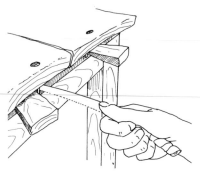

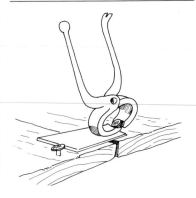

It is often possible to loosen a nail by simply punching it down with a hammer and punch. This breaks its grip in the wood, and the pieces can then be separated by levering them apart with a bricklayer's bolster or with wedges.

Where it is impossible to shift a nail, wedges can be driven into the joint. Once there is sufficient room, slide a hacksaw blade between the pieces and saw through the nail.

Nail heads can be removed by inverting the board over a piece of soft pine and punching the sawn shank. The softwood block absorbs the head, and also prevents the surface around the nail head from splitting as it is forced out.

Remove the head with pincers or pliers, protecting the wood surface with a pad.

Wooden pegs

Centre-punch and then drill out wooden pegs. Lever the joint loose, and peer into the hole. Remove any remaining slivers of peg with a pair of long nosed pliers before driving the joint apart.

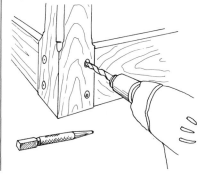 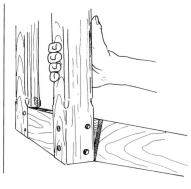

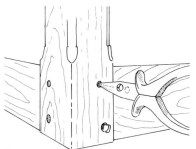

Screws

Screws can be released by giving them a smart blow with a hammer and punch. Heads that are rusted or damaged can be reslotted using a chisel ground from a broken machine hacksaw blade. Tighten the screw to release its bond in the wood before withdrawing it.

Where the screws refuse to turn, centre-punch and drill down into the screw head and the shank. Sometimes the heat and vibration of the drill is sufficient to release the

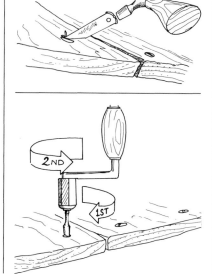 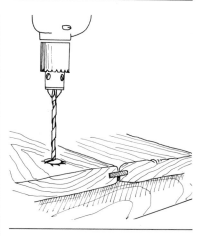 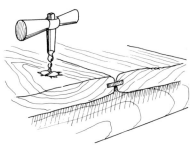

screw; otherwise, insert a screw extractor into the drill hole and twist the screw out.

Scotch-glued mortice and tenon joints

Sometimes it is possible to drill into the mortice and inject methylated spirits into the mortice to release the glue join. If this fails to loosen the joint, continue to apply methylated spirits and resort to levering and forcing it apart with hammer and wedges. In the last resort, it is possible to drive most joints apart using a heavy hammer and a protective wooden pad.

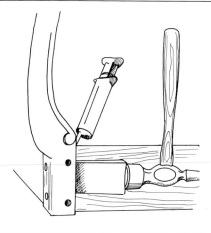

Dovetails

These can usually be released by hammering the joint apart. The glue join can be weakened by cutting down the pins using a fine dovetail saw. When reassembling the joint, a sliver of veneer will need to be glued into each saw cut.

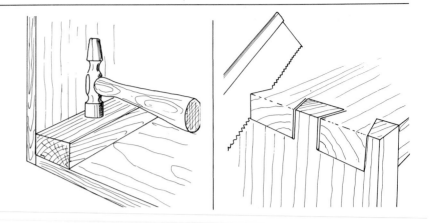

Glue blocks

Remove glue blocks by striking a chisel placed at the base of the glue block. If the chisel is placed correctly the glue block will be released in one blow.

Removing riveted metal brackets

Centre-punch and drill out rivet heads. Remove the bracket and punch out rivets.

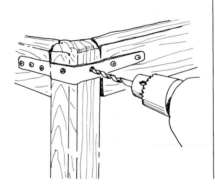
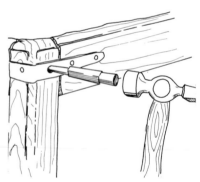

Removing broken rail or dowel

Punch and drill into the broken stub. Work both sides of any nails which hold the stub in place. Change drill to a larger one, use the same holes and redrill them. Remove the remains with long nosed pliers.

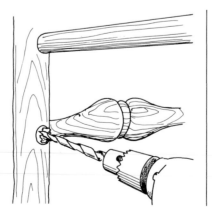
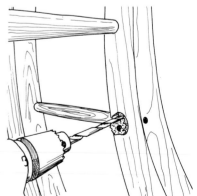

Removing a broken tenon

Punch and drill the full length of the tenon. Use a mortice chisel to chop out a centre wedge of the tenon. Work the chisel into the ends to remove the rest.

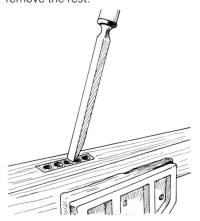

Bad repairs

Where wood is badly fractured, remove the damaged part and scarf a new piece in place.

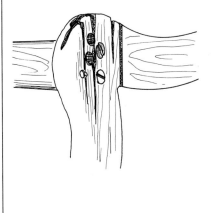
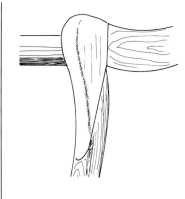

DISMANTLING CARCASS FURNITURE

Carcass furniture is made from solid planks of wood, or from sheets of composite board, edge-joined at the corners. Diagonal strength is usually supplied by a solid or boarded back. When the back is loosened or damaged, the carcass joins become weak. Stress may also result from distortion caused by uneven flooring or worn and missing feet.

Carcass furniture is easily weakened but is very difficult to dismantle. Considerable damage often results when this is attempted; however, if the situation demands that a piece be dismantled, the procedure is as follows.

Inspect the piece for any mouldings, beadings and banding that cross a joint which is to be separated. These should be loosened, using a steel table knife, and any pins should be sawn through.

Remove glue blocks with a sharp chisel, struck with a mallet. Any previous repairs should be inspected closely for evidence of nailing or screwing that may prevent the piece from separating. These should be removed before they cause damage by splitting out.

Remove the back of the piece, and replace it with a couple of light, diagonal battens. This is to provide the structure with a minimum of stability as the joints are loosened. Any pieces that were originally nailed to the back and need support should be tacked lightly to the battens.

When dismantling carcass furniture, always apply the hammer blows as close to the join as possible. Use a piece of hardwood between the hammer and furniture to carry the shock across the full width of the join.

Rest the piece with its bottom boards on the floor. Check the joints to ensure that a few smart blows to the bottom planks will cause them to

An exciting piece of furniture to repair. A broad range of skills is needed to restore this to its former glory

separate from the sides. Weaken the joins if necessary. With one hand, lift this side slightly (½ in., 1 cm above the floor is sufficient) and strike the hardwood smartly with a medium-weight hammer. Rest the carcass on the floor and inspect the join. As the joint begins to separate it will not need to be lifted quite so far from the floor.

Before the join is completely released, use the same process on the other corner, until the bottom is completely loose and easily removed.

Turn the piece over and use the same method with the top. It is inevitable that these joins will be damaged. All damaged dovetails should be replaced.

Once the top and base of the piece have been removed, shelves or partitions should present no

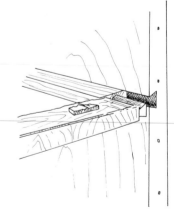

problem. However, in good quality furniture the rails dividing the drawers – and sometimes the shelves – are joined to the upright sides with a dovetail housing joint. If this is the case, they will have to be withdrawn with great care. If the

front edges of the carcass have applied edge-pieces these will have to be removed, and the shelf or rail pulled out from the front. It may be necessary to do this before the top and bottom are removed.

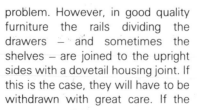

DISMANTLING FRAME FURNITURE

Before dismantling a piece of frame furniture, inspect it carefully to determine how much of the frame needs to come apart. Quite often the sides can be removed and repaired without dismantling the entire piece. If the legs and the end panels are the parts that need attention, then as long as one end is removed, repaired and replaced before the other end is dealt with, a fair amount of unnecessary work can be avoided. This possibility should be borne in mind when assessing the task of dismantling. If, in the process, tenons are broken or found to be rotten, it will be best to continue and dismember the piece completely.

All uprights and horizontal frame members should be clearly marked on the inside of the frame with their piece and side number. Marking should be in pencil, or with clear V-parting chisel cuts. Marks should be unambiguous. Quite often the original marks can still be found and, provided that they are adequate for the purpose of speedy information and assembly, they should be used.

Every piece of a panel should be marked with its position and orientation.

Once drawers and doors have been removed, dismantling can begin. The top usually comes off first, followed by drawer runners, shelves, side, back, and bottom.

The sides and back panelling can then be knocked apart (if necessary) after they are separated from the main framework.

Often, with old pieces of furniture, the joints will be pegged and not glued, and all that is needed is for the pegs to be removed. Pieces that are less than 150 years old will probably be glued, and these joints sometimes cause problems.

However, there should be at least one joint in the framework that is weak. If so, it is likely that others will also have been weakened. Tackle

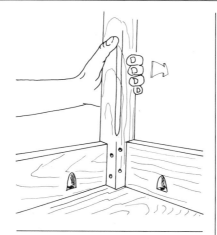

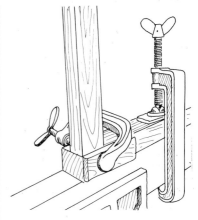

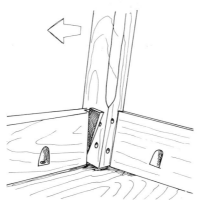

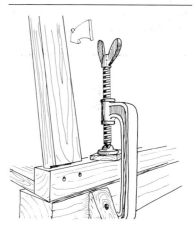

the weakest first, gradually working the joint to increase the movement between the pieces. Apply methylated spirits to the joint if it was scotch glued. As the amount of movement increases, small hardwood wedges can be placed in the shoulder of the tenon, which will cause the joint to pull apart as the rocking continues.

It is very important to control the amount of force used. Joints should not be struck apart unless you are absolutely sure that there is no glue or nail holding the joint. If there seems to be a danger that the mortice will split in the process, a clamp should be used to add to its strength. Mortices are much more difficult to repair well than tenons.

If everything short of violence fails to move the joint, the mortice should be clamped very firmly and the joint bent sideways, out of true. Clamp

For clarity, the joint is shown without the clamp across the mortice. Slip the dovetail saw into the crack and saw through the tenon

the frame in this distorted position, and saw the tenon free with a dovetail saw inserted between the shoulder of the tenon and the frame member. Provided that the touching faces of the mortice and tenon are unmarked in this treatment, it is a simple and effective solution to the problem.

It may sometimes be possible to dissolve the glue holding a join, or to liquefy it, by injecting boiling water into the mortice, continuing the process for several hours. Acetate injected into a join held by woodworker's white glue may also work. However, I find these methods time-consuming and often unsuccessful.

DISMANTLING CHAIRS

Only rarely do chairs need to be completely dismantled. Joints can be injected with gap-filling urea formaldehyde or epoxy glues, and new pieces spliced into place. Should it be necessary, however, the same general principles apply to the process as have just been described for the framed and panelled furniture. As chairs are a delicate combination of strength and grace, every join must be sound. Great care should be taken to avoid splitting mortices. Always opt for sawing away the tenon rather than risk damaging the mortice.

Occasionally, the back splat of a quality chair will need removing for repair. If the joints at the top of the chair frame (usually mortice and tenon joints) can be knocked apart, this is a simple matter, as the splat is never glued into its groove. Where these joints do not readily separate, the best technique is to work at one of them in an attempt to lever one side of the top sufficiently high to remove the splat. Here, it is particularly important for the force to be controlled. Levers and wedges should be used, never sheer muscle power.

8 Common Faults and their Remedies

LOOSE JOINTS

Loose dovetail joint

This is a common fault, often found in drawers and other lightly constructed pieces. The simplest solution is to tap the joint gently apart until it is nearly free, and to insert P.V.A. glue between the joining faces. Surface glue should be wiped off with a damp rag. For good quality work, use slightly thinned scotch glue. When using scotch glue, make certain that the joints are well together and cramped before the glue chills. If the row of dovetails is quite long, or if there is a possibility that the glue will have chilled before the joint is together, use P.V.A. If possible, insert glue blocks to support the joint; scotch glue should be used for these.

If the piece of furniture is rather delicate and the above methods are inappropriate, make several cuts with a tenon saw at 45° to the faces of the piece, and insert and glue slivers of veneer or slightly thicker pieces of hardwood. (P.V.A. glue should not be used for this as it has a tendency to prevent close-fitting pieces from sliding together easily.

Thinned scotch glue or a resin glue is better.) These slips of wood should be allowed to dry before being trimmed with a paring chisel.

All of the above methods are effective and very simple operations. Frequently, however, dovetail joints are so badly worn and weakened by constant movement and poor repair work that they will need to be replaced. For this it is best to separate the joints, and a certain degree of dismantling will be necessary.

When the boards have been separated, take one and place it, edge up, in the vice, with its top edge about 4 in. (100 mm) above the jaws. Identify which dovetails need replacing and, using a saw guide, cut down each side of the dovetail. The saw cuts should converge to a point about 2¼ in. (60 mm) below the shoulders of the dovetail. Repeat this operation with the pins that need replacing on the other side.

Select a suitable piece of similarly grained timber for the repairs. Cut cardboard templates which fit the V slot, align them on the timber, and mark round them. To allow for fitting, make each patch at least ⅞ in. (20 mm) higher than needed for the dovetail. These V-shaped pieces should be sawn out and planed to fit.

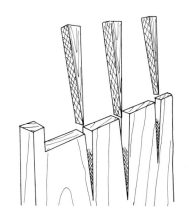

It is best if the angle of the V is slightly greater than the angle made by the initial sawcuts in the board, so that the patches can be secured in place by tapping them with a hammer. Before glueing, the faces of the inserts should be scored with a toothed plane or an old hack saw blade.

Once this is done, the joint should be recut.

Where lapped dovetails have failed, a similar method of repair is employed, except that the notches to hold the new dovetails should not show on the face side of the board. In this case, they need not taper, but can be squared and cut out with a router, or a saw and chisels. When repairing secret dovetails, remember that the pins should be marked and cut before transferring their shape to the dovetails.

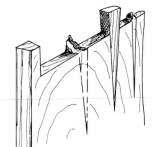

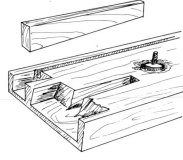

Loose mortice and tenon joint

The obvious treatment for a loose mortice and tenon joint is to separate and reglue them. The process, in fact, is seldom as simple as this, and may entail separating other well-glued joints. To avoid doing this, inspect the tenon to see if it appears sound; if there are no signs of breakage or rot in the part that is visible, it will be possible to inject glue into the mortice.

Hypodermic syringes (without needles), a drill, and either some urea formaldehyde or some epoxy resin gap-filling glue are required for this operation. Select a drill bit that is just slightly larger than the syringe

nozzle, and drill from under the mortice up towards the side and end of the tenon. It is easy to sense when the drill reaches the space at the head of the tenon, and the drill should be withdrawn. Follow the mixing instructions, where a hardener is used; inject it into the

hole before following with the thicker glue. Move the tenon to facilitate the flow of the glue, and ease the syringe pressure when the glue begins to ooze around the tenon, or from worm holes elsewhere in the timber. Clamp the joint and leave it to dry. If a P.V.A. glue or Cascamite is used, it needs to be left for several days before being unclamped. Wipe the joint clear of any surplus glue, and plug the hole with stopping.

Once the glue has begun to set, leave any trickles or runs of glue to dry before wiping them clean; it is easier to remove the solid mass of brittle glue than to remove a very thin film.

Loose tenons

Where the tenon has been broken, or eaten away by worm, it will be necessary to replace it with a loose tenon. This is a simple procedure which results in a very strong join.

Separate the piece needing the tenon from the frame, and set a mortice gauge to the tenon setting.

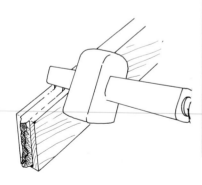

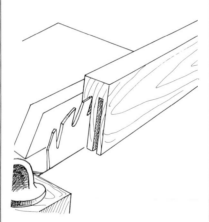

Saw off the remains of the tenon, and mark the end and underside of the workpiece with the gauge. If you have a circular saw, set it with the height of the blade a fraction less than the depth of the tenon, and set the fence so that the wood inside the marks left by the marking gauge is

cut away. A distance stop should be clamped to the saw table to prevent the saw from running too far into the length of the workpiece. Feed the piece into the saw, and reset the fence to make another cut against the inside of the marked lines. The saw, or a chisel, can be used to cut out the waste between these lines.

If no circular saw is available, a handsaw should be used to make the sawcuts, and a chisel to remove the waste and to deepen the cut at the end of the tenon slot.

Select a piece of straight-grained wood for the new tenon, and cut it to

shape to fit the slot in the workpiece. If the circular saw was used to cut the slot, then the shape at the end of the piece can be established by holding the loose tenon against the circular saw blade, and drawing around it.

Once the loose tenon is made and fitted, it can be glued in to the workpiece, and fitted into the mortice later, or both operations can be done together. Both the sides of the loose tenon, and the mortice and tenon joint, need to be clamped securely.

Where both the tenon and mortice are very badly split or weakened by rot or worm, a thickened epoxy resin glue can be used to add strength to the joint. When doing this, it is best to glue some reinforcing dowels into sound timber to help distribute any load that may occur at the joint. When a seriously weakened piece of wood is strengthened locally the

area where it is likely to fail is where the old and the weak wood meets the strong. The dowels will help to graduate the change.

If a mortice has been so badly damaged by stress, rot or poor repair work that it has caused splitting down the grain, it is probably best to

saw off the old joint and scarf on a new piece. For detailed descriptions of this operation see pp. 84-6. Where the joint is not load bearing, small dowels can be glued across the joint, both above and below the mortice, to hold the wood together and prevent further splitting.

DAMAGED LEGS

If people are to sit comfortably at a table, there needs to be at least 24 in. (610 mm) between the floor and the under rail of the table. Small additions to the height can be achieved by nailing a tap washer or a furniture glide to the bottom of the

leg. For legs that need additional lengthening, alternative methods are described in the following pages. When working on table legs, it is easy to damage the top or weaken the framework. Great care must be taken to protect the surfaces of the table, and to prevent stressing the structure.

Straight tip

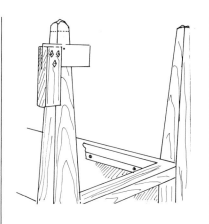

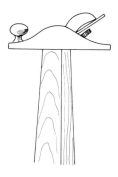

The strength of this tip is dependent on the width of the table leg at the join and the length of the tip. No leg narrower than 1½ in. (40 mm) can be tipped in this way, and no tip should be longer than 2 in. (50 mm). This repair is not appropriate for chairs, or where sideways stress is put on the leg.

If more than one tip is required, a production line method can be used, bringing all the legs to the same stage together. Mark cutting lines around the leg at the point where the join is to be made. Cut off as little as possible. The saw cut should reveal sound timber. Using a shoulder plane with the mouth set at a minimum opening, level the saw cut. It is more important for the surface to be flat

than square. Flatness can be checked by placing a plane sole across the surface and inspecting for wobble.

Measure carefully the length and width of the tip required. Allow ¼ in. (5 mm) overlap all round for misalignment. Select appropriate timber, mark it, and cut it out. Hold the roughly cut tip in place, and rotate it to match the grain patterns on the leg. Mark its orientation on the leg, and side of the tip. Smooth the jointing faces with the shoulder plane, and replace the tip to check vertical alignment. The tip can be planed to make any necessary adjustments in angle. When the tip sits well on the leg and is correctly oriented with the grain patterns,

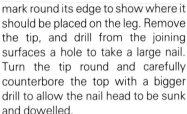
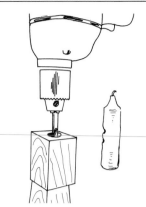

mark round its edge to show where it should be placed on the leg. Remove the tip, and drill from the joining surfaces a hole to take a large nail. Turn the tip round and carefully counterbore the top with a bigger drill to allow the nail head to be sunk and dowelled.

To provide a key between the surfaces, take four 1 in. (25 mm) panel pins and partially tap them into the leg at the corners. Cut the heads off at ¼ in. (5 mm) above the surface of the join, and carefully place the tip, correctly aligned, on these. A tap with a light hammer should be enough to locate the position of the nails on the tip. Use a bradawl to deepen the holes, and tap the tip and the leg together. If the tip is out of position, withdraw three of the pins,

and try again with new ones in new holes, pulling the remaining pin a little further out to help in relocating its position.

With the tip in position and using a narrower drill, drill through the tip into the leg for the full length of the nail. Remove the tip, clean away any dust on the glueing surfaces and apply a strong glue to both surfaces. Tap the tip into position, check its alignment, nail it and punch the nail home. Fit and glue a dowel to cover the nail head.

When the glue is fully dried, place the table, right side up, on two trestles. At a point just above the tip, wrap masking tape around the leg. This starts the saw a fraction away from the finished line and protects the original leg. Use a sharp hand

saw held against the table leg, and cut away the waste from the tips.

When the waste is removed, the table can be inverted, and the new tip smoothed with a plane. Before finishing with block and sandpaper, fill any cracks in the join with a two-part filler, round off the base of the foot, and simulate any ageing marks – cracks, worm holes, etc., before staining and finishing.

If difficulty is experienced in acquiring drills long enough for this operation, take a normal morse drill to an engineering workshop and ask them to weld an extension bar to its end. When using long drills, hold the side of a wax candle against the rotating drill to lubricate it as it drives into the wood, and withdraw and clean the drill frequently.

Scarfed and built-up repair to legs

This type of repair is very strong and simple to do well. It is ideally suited where table or chair legs have been badly worn away on one side, or where rot is so extensive that major rebuilding is necessary. The disadvantage of this method is that a lot of new wood is always left showing, which makes it more difficult to colour in and age.

Using the sawing guide clamped to the leg, and angled to give a join long enough to be strong – but not so

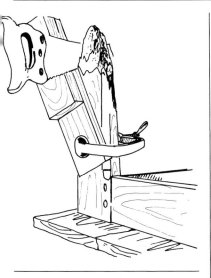

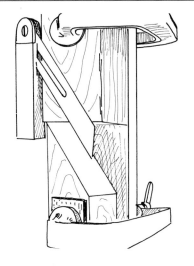

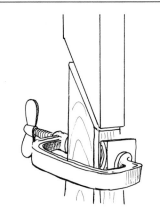

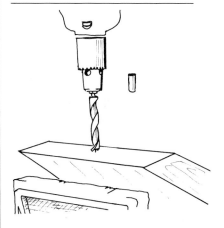

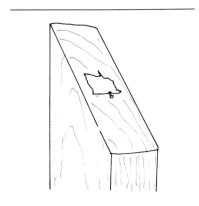

long as to cut away too much good wood – saw away the waste wood.

Flatten the face of the scarf with a plane, checking its level with the sole of a large plane. Select a piece of timber with a grain pattern similar to the leg for the tip, and clamp it to the edge of the sighting board. Clamp the sighting board to the neck and mark the cutting angle on the tip with angle bevel and pencil. Saw and true this up.

The leg and tip should fit perfectly. If they don't, rub blackboard chalk onto one surface to highlight the high spots on the face when they are touched together. Ease away the high spots with a shoulder plane.

When both faces fit snugly, tape a pin to the centre of the scarf and press the tip firmly in position over it. The head of the pin should make a clear mark on both surfaces and this mark can be used to centre the drill bit. A block can be temporarily clamped onto the leg to help locate the tip.

Drill each face in turn, at right angles to the scarf, using a brad point

drill. It is not necessary to drill more than 3/8 in. (10 mm) into each surface. Cut a dowel to fit and place it in one hole, and place the other scarf over it.

Use a G clamp to tighten the two together. If they align well separate the scarf and score both surfaces with a toothing plane or an old hacksaw blade. Use a urea-formaldehyde or epoxy resin glue to

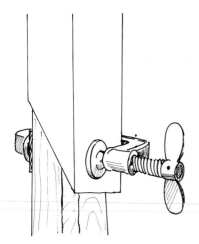

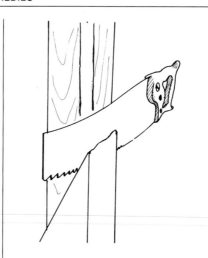

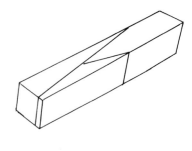

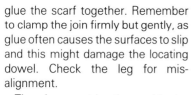

glue the scarf together. Remember to clamp the join firmly but gently, as glue often causes the surfaces to slip and this might damage the locating dowel. Check the leg for mis-alignment.

The glue must be thoroughly dry before the waste wood is removed. Use a hand saw pressed against the old leg to help guide the saw through the new wood. Plane the surfaces smooth and check frequently with a straight edge for accuracy.

If the leg is badly worn, other

pieces can be scarfed on to replace the missing timber. If the piece of furniture is of good quality, the scarves should all be cut from the same timber in the pattern in which they are going to be used on the leg. In any case, the grain should always be carefully matched.

V-angled join

This method of joining a tip to a leg is the strongest, and the easiest to fade in. It is also the most difficult to do well. The V-angled tip, when inserted into the old leg, usually reaches sound timber, even when the out-side of the leg is badly worn or worm-eaten, and it has its own inherent stability apart from the glue adhesion.

There is no great advantage in removing the legs from the carcass of the table, but a means of holding a leg firmly in a vice for sawing, and a way to clamp the tip in place, should be tried before this method is used.

A saw guide, illustrated and described on p. 13, will be needed.

Wind masking tape around the leg at the point where the apex of the V will come. Mark the centre point of the leg on each side. Hold the table leg in a vice, or clamp it against a trestle below the masking tape.

Clamp the saw guide to the leg, adjusting the angle so that the guide intersects the centre point on the masking tape and forms part of an acute-angled V to the tip of the leg. Hold a sharp rip saw against the saw guide and saw down, without using downward pressure (which might

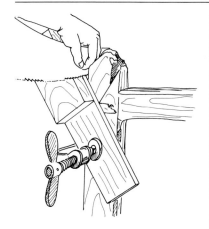

cause the saw to twist or wander), until the centre point at both sides of the leg is reached. Don't saw beyond the centre line; it doesn't matter if the cut reaches the centre line on the reverse side of the leg before it reaches the masking tape, as the tip can easily be planed to fit.

When one cut has been made, the saw guide is switched to the other angle and a cut made which should release the V waste.

Clamp a sighting board in vertical alignment to the leg. The timber which is to be used for the tip should be rotated to match the grain, clamped on the board, and aligned to it. With an angle bevel, or a parallel-sided card, transfer the line of the V to the tip. Remove the tip and, using the saw guide again, saw the V.

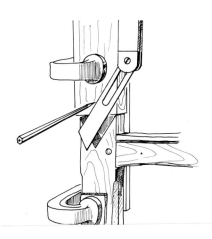

If the sawing and the marking have been accurate, the tip should fit perfectly into the V. In practice it sometimes does not. A close inspection will usually reveal the reason. The most likely is that the saw cuts on the V are not parallel. The tip must be adjusted to fit the V. Run a pencil line down the two facing edges of the tip. Shave the surfaces with a plane, avoiding the pencil lines, which act as a reference and prevent the angle from being altered. Carefully reduce the sides until the tip fits. Never trim the V slot in the leg unless there is an obvious and easily remedied error.

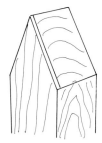

If the tip still fits badly, rub blackboard chalk onto the tip, and shave away on the V where it leaves a mark on being inserted.

Errors in sawing are often caused by badly set or blunt saws. For instructions on setting and sharpening see pp. 45–6.

When the tip fits so that gentle pressure is needed to remove it, it can be glued. Before compressing the join with a cramp, place a G clamp against the V (with blocks to prevent it marking the leg) and tighten it slightly. When the end pressure is applied, this will prevent

the tip from splitting the leg. Tighten the G clamp after the leg has been cramped up.

When the glue is dry, the waste can be removed by saw, wrapping masking tape just above the apex of the V before sawing. Plane and sand to finish. Ageing and rounding should be completed before finishing.

It is often difficult to find the exact angle of the V on a turned leg. A carefully fitted cardboard template, cut to fit the V and showing the centre line of the leg, can be used instead of the sighting board.

Shaped legs

If the leg to be tipped is shaped, it will be necessary to tip the leg with sufficient timber to accommodate the extra shape. It is probable that only one template will be required when repairing a shaped leg. Even a cabriole leg, which looks so complex to mark and saw, is marked using a single template, used twice on adjacent faces of the timber. Simpler designs use the template only once.

A template is made in the following manner. A flat board with white card taped to it is positioned firmly against the leg to be copied. It must be aligned parallel to one of the sawn faces of the leg and firmly clamped in place. The shape is then transferred, using a pair of dividers locked to a convenient setting. Allow room on the card for the full thickness of the leg to be marked in. Once the back or front line of the leg has been marked, the thicknesses can be measured with a pair of calipers, and transferred to the card. For a fuller description of the use of dividers see p. 48.

All that remains to be done now is to ensure that the tip is big enough for the shaping, and since its size and shape can be checked against the template this is not a difficult task. Never try to economise on wood by fixing the tip at an angle to the plane sides of a cabriole leg. This makes the marking and shaping of the leg very difficult. Reject any knotted or split wood because, although the tip may appear to be very substantial, the shaping and carving whittles away at its strength, and con-

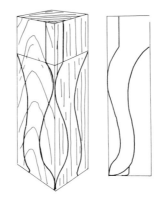

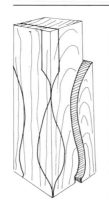

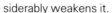

siderably weakens it.

The scarf joint is the best type to use here as it is a simple process, and does not require any end clamping.

If the tip needs to be sawn on two faces, mark both adjacent sides with the template, and saw the first with a bow saw or a bandsaw. Stop the saw cut before the waste wood is quite free. Tape the loose end back against the leg, and saw the second face of the stock. When both saw cuts are nearly complete, the waste pieces can be removed.

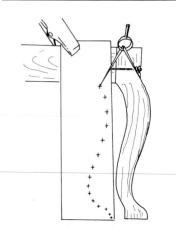

Turned tips

If the tip is very short, or simple in design, it may not be necessary to use a lathe to lengthen the leg satisfactorily. The tip should be glued on, preferably using the V joint described on p. 86 and the centre line established (see below). If great care

is used, a very convincing turning effect can be achieved by carving and then sanding the tip. Back the sandpaper with plastic tape to give it greater strength. The advantage of this method is that the table does not need to be dismantled; however, the

resulting finish lacks the crispness of a turning, so is inappropriate for shaped or long tips. A jig for roughing down a turned leg, without dismantling the piece of furniture, is described on p. 60.

If the leg requires turning, it must

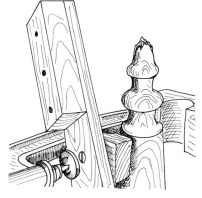

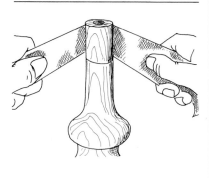

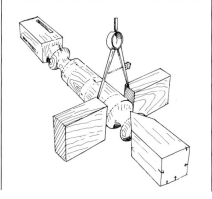

be removed from the carcass of the furniture.

Any of the previous methods for joining a tip to the leg can be used. The best is the V join, but in order to use the saw guide a little ingenuity will be needed. Do not start to saw the V if there is any chance that the saw guide might slip.

When the tip is glued in place, the corners of the tip can be roughed round with a chisel, but do not attempt to shape the leg until the centres have been found. Two methods can be used to find the centres on a turned leg. The turning marks are often easily visible at the top of a leg, and should be re-used. If they are not visible and the leg is turned from rectangular or square stock, diagonals from the corners might give the centre, but should be checked when adjusting the centre on the lathe.

A straightforward means of finding the centre of the tip when there are no marks or clues to follow is to wrap some bands of masking tape around the leg. At least three bands are necessary, one at each end, and one approximately at the centre. With the leg horizontal on the workbench, consider and mark a centre line at each band. A pair of wooden blocks pressed against the sides of the leg will help to establish the width of the leg, and dividers can be used to halve the measurement and to locate the midpoint at each band. When all of the marks have been pencilled onto the face of the leg, hold a straight-edge to them, and mark off the centre line at the end of the tip. Repeat this at opposite faces and then mark across the end, joining the points. The marks should intersect at the centre of the leg.

A simpler method involves using a centring guide, which can be easily made up, and is described on p. 165. Fasten this to the end of the tip with short screws, the outer ring holding the inner disc firmly against the tip. Place the leg between lathe centres.

(Approximate one end if both centres are unknown; transfer the guide to the other end once the first centre is established.)

Place the edge of the tool rest close to the leg and, after checking that the centre guide is correctly adjusted so that a light tap with a hammer will move it, rotate the leg by hand, tapping the leg at the end until the leg runs true. It may be impossible to eliminate all wobble in the leg, because the leg may have warped or shrunk across its width.

When the leg is running true, or nearly so, tighten the centre-guide screws, and remove the leg from the lathe centres. Use a veneer pin to tap through the special hole in the guide to mark the centre, and remove the guide. Punch the veneer pin mark, and replace the leg in the lathe.

Use a slow speed for the initial roughing out into a cylindrical shape; higher speeds can be used for the shaping.

Finding the shape of the leg

It is usually sufficient to place a leg to copy parallel to the lathe bed, using calipers to take off its important diameters, and judging the rest by eye. However, if the furniture is of very high quality, or the legs very close together, make a template of cardboard and hold it against the leg.

Do not try to turn a finished tip right up to the end of the V, as any slight wobble will cause the lathe tool to mar the original surface of the leg. From the point where there is more old wood than new at the V, turn it roughly, and finish with hand chisels. When the rest of the leg has been turned, finish by hand with chisels and sandpaper. When all the shaping has been completed, replace the leg in the lathe, and use sandpaper strips backed with plastic tape to sand the new wood.

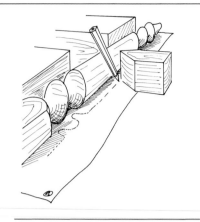

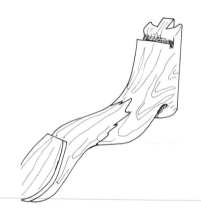

Great care should be taken when staining turned woods. It is best to use chemical stains if possible, as oil and water stains tend to penetrate deeply into the end grain, making it too dark. If oil or water stains are used, first brush dilute shellac onto the leg. When it is thoroughly dry, replace the leg between centres and sand it. This will help seal the end grain.

If difficulties are still experienced, sand the leg, and apply two or three thinned coats of shellac to the leg. When dry, stain the new work with spirit-soluble aniline dye, with a dash of water added to inhibit its bite. This is best applied with an air-brush, the spray line controlled by holding a cardboard mask against the join in the leg.

DAMAGED FEET

Occasionally it is necessary to repair the broken foot of a shaped leg. This problem sometimes arises with the legs of tripod tables, where accidental pressure at the edge of the table can easily snap off a foot at its weakest point, just above the pad.

The first operation is to try to remove the leg. With a tripod table this is often fairly straightforward. The top is removed (if necessary by removing the wood plugs that cover the screws and unscrewing the screws holding the top to the bearers) and the pedestal is inverted and held in a vice. The metal tie-bars screwed across the base of the piece are released, and the broken leg is then gently tapped clear. The joint holding the leg is usually a stopped dovetail and is normally freed without trouble.

If it is impossible to remove the leg, the following processes should still be followed, although provision will have to be made for the added

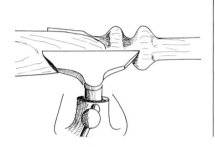

complication of the pedestal and other legs being in the way.

Take the broken parts of the leg and inspect them closely. Any evidence of previous repairs should be probed, nails and screws and metal bands removed. Clean away any remains of old glue. When this is done, hold the broken pieces together, to see how they align. Although there is likely to be a considerable amount of surface damage, there should be plenty of contact between the broken faces,

sufficient to make a temporary glued repair.

Use a fairly thick mix of scotch glue, and apply it to the joining surfaces. Hold the pieces together in place and in perfect alignment, until the glue chills. When the glue has begun to set, the piece can be put down to dry, with all parts of the leg supported by wedges.

When the piece is dry, place the leg in the router box (the top can be cut to the shape of the leg, if this is thought necessary) and clamp it firmly in place. Set the router so that its cutter runs parallel to the side, and up the centre of the underside of the leg. A slot, slightly wider than a third of the width of the leg, should be routed out. It should be taken well beyond the break in both directions. Cut the slot as deep as possible, without breaking through on the top side of the leg at its thinnest part.

If a router is not available for this operation, the slot can be marked with a mortice gauge and cut out using a bevel-edged chisel and a light mallet. Before cutting, the shaped side of the leg should be supported and protected by a piece of waste wood, cut to fit the curve of the leg and covered by a layer of carpet underlay or felt.

Cut a straight-grained wooden fillet to fit the slot. Let the edge pro-

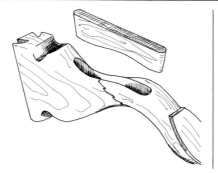
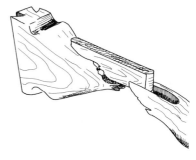

trude above the underside of the leg.

Separate the temporary join by wrapping the leg with very hot wet towels. Residual traces of the temporary glue should be washed off, and the pieces allowed to dry. Use a gap-filling epoxy glue to make the final repair. First glue the leg to the fillet and clamp it in place. Then move the pad into position, glue it,

and clamp it. The underside of the fillet which was left proud when it was fitted can be used to support one face of the G clamp. The other side must be padded to prevent marking of the leg.

When the glue is dry, the fillet should be shaped and the surface damage around the edge of the join filled with wax stopping.

Repairing bracket feet

To increase the height of a bracket foot, saw across the foot and then carefully level the saw cut with a chisel. New pieces can be glued on with scotch glue. The pieces must fit exactly at the line of the mitre, but can be trued up elsewhere once the glue has dried.

A failed glue join holding the feet to the frame may cause the bracket feet to be loose rather than broken. In this case, the repair is simple: remove the foot and reglue it.

Looseness may, however, be the result of a weakness in the foot supports. The foot often rests on a moulded bearer, which is nailed and glued to the bottom edge of the carcass. This may become loose and should be refastened before the feet are attended to. Once the feet have been put in position, fit glue blocks to the inside of the mitre and along the back of the feet. These should bear on the carcass, and not on the bottom boards or edge moulding of the piece.

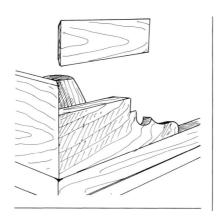

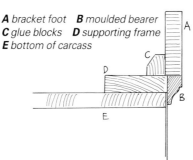

A bracket foot   B moulded bearer
C glue blocks   D supporting frame
E bottom of carcass

If a completely new bracket foot is needed, its shape can be obtained by drawing around an existing foot. Cut it out with a jig saw or a bow saw. Next, plane the top edge of the foot

where it bears against the moulding and check its alignment by sighting down the side of the piece. Saw, and then, if necessary, plane the mitre at the edge of the foot until it sits snugly

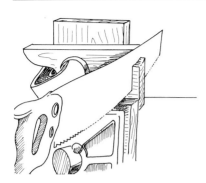

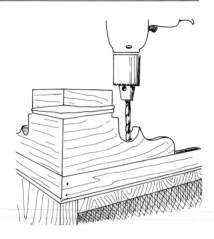

against the existing foot. Any alterations in shape can be made at this point. Use a veneer or panel pin to hold the foot in place at the inside of the piece, and stretch a strong rubber band around the two parts of the foot where they join. Drill and countersink a hole to take a single screw. Remove the foot, and then glue and screw it into position.

When the glue is dry, the foot should be supported with glue blocks and the inside faces rounded with a rasp to give the effect of wear.

If the foot needs to be veneered, it is best to veneer both sides of the timber before the foot is cut from the board. This avoids the sometimes difficult task of trimming the veneer from the shaped insides of the foot. A foot that is veneered on both sides will not curve as the veneer dries.

SPLIT SURFACES

Splitting within a panel

This usually occurs around knots, vigorous grain patterns, and (in poorly made furniture) in panels made from tension wood. Cracks can be very tightly curved, may radiate across the board, and are often associated with distortions in the surface. It is quite likely that these disfigurations occurred shortly after the piece was made, so that the cracks are full of dirt and wax.

They are the result of differing rates of shrinkage present in a single piece of timber. Dense wood, having shrunk less than the soft wood, has separated from it, weakening the board and spoiling its appearance.

Before attempting to fill these cracks, the piece must be thoroughly dried. Clean the cracks with a penknife, and screw a board behind the cracks for support. Insert a sheet of newspaper or polythene between the board and the panel to prevent the filler and glue adhering to the board.

Cut small fillets of hardwood, and fit them neatly into the crack. If the panel is decorative, it is often a good idea to place them with the end grain showing. This tends to break up the

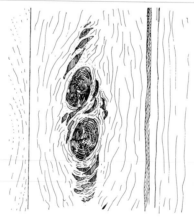

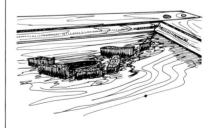

line of the crack, whereas a straight grained fillet will appear to emphasise the fault. Once these are in place, pour thickened epoxy glue over the repair. Scotch glue and P.V.A. can be used, provided it is certain that they penetrate the full thickness of the repair.

When the glue is dry, filling pieces can be sawn to length with a hacksaw blade, and then planed and scraped smooth. The inside board should be unscrewed and the paper sanded away from the inside of the repair.

Splitting due to poor construction

As a piece of timber dries, it will shrink more across its grain than along it. This tendency is catered for in most pieces of furniture: large panels are set in grooves and allowed to move freely, table top planks are often cleated and so permitted sideways movement. Where this movement is prevented, splitting will occur.

Where provision for movement has been made, the solution is often very simple. An old plane iron can be used to lever the pieces together. This should be done on the underside of the plank, or the inside of the panel. Considerable grip can be obtained with the iron if it is dug into the side of the wood, and very little damage results.

If this fails, move the pieces farther apart, and clean the groove of any debris that may be preventing the pieces from coming together. Inspect inside to see if any later additions – shelf supports, or drawer guides – or any fastenings, are preventing the pieces from sliding together. Once this has been done, screw wide blocks about ⅝ in. (15 mm) thick to each side of the split on the inside of the panel. Ensure that the screws are firm and strong;

however, they should not penetrate through the face side of the panel. These blocks can then be clamped together. A simple wedged clamp will serve if there is difficulty in applying a sash cramp or G clamp to the blocks. If the two pieces come together, inspect at the sides to ensure that the panel has not pulled completely away from the frame groove. If it has, it may be possible to move the whole panel across to cover the gap. When this is done, remove the clamp, run glue into the crack and reclamp it.

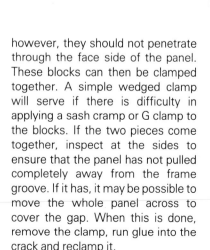

A French wine-tasting table. Very little work is required to turn this into a beautiful dining table

Solid tops

Shrinkage is bound to occur in wide pieces of solid stock, and particularly where old furniture is taken from cool damp conditions into a centrally heated home. Shrinkage is often evident in plank topped tables and in the sides of carcass furniture.

It is sometimes possible to remove the shrunken planks and replace them after reshooting the joins. If the piece is warm and thoroughly dry when this work is performed, the problem of shrinkage will be overcome. Unfortunately, in carcass furniture this is either impossible or impractical. Also – with drop leaf tables for instance – a small loss in overhang (due to shrinkage) will prevent the leaves from hanging vertically. Joints in round or oval

tables cannot be reshot either, or else the perimeter of the table will become misaligned.

In these circumstances, as with the panel that is shrunken until it is too small for the framework, it will be necessary to insert a fillet into the crack to make up for the loss of wood from shrinkage.

The gap must first be straightened as much as possible. This is accomplished by using a special, easily made tool illustrated here. The blade is sharpened at both leading and trailing edge, and the size of shavings cut by the tool is controlled by the offset prongs placed both in front and behind the blade. The tool, which can cut on both the forward and return strokes, should bear against a straight edge for the final straightening cuts.

When the major irregularities in the crack have been evened out, a fillet of wood similar to the panel and, if possible, with a similar grain pattern, is cut to length and given a slight taper so that it can be driven into the crack. Glue one side of the fillet. (If both sides are glued, further

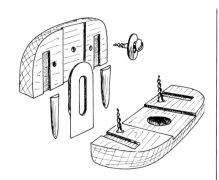

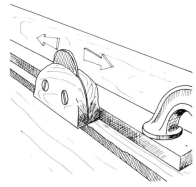

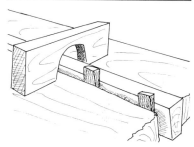

shrinkage may cause the fillet to unglue itself on alternate sides, and make it appear to snake up the crack.)

P.V.A. glue is ideal for the purpose, and it is handy to have a supply of thin softwood wedges to force the fillet sideways into the hollows. Before the glue has dried, the join should be checked to see if the wedging has misaligned the two edges of the crack. A straight-sided piece of wood with a bridge cut to pass over the fillet can be used to check this. Any piece that is out of true should be tapped back into position.

When the fillet is dry, it can be trimmed down with a paring chisel and cleaned with a scraper and sandpaper. Always remember to clean the underside of a repair, as well as the outside.

Dovetail keys

Where the ends of a board are split, and considerable pressure is required to press the split parts together, a key can be inserted to bridge the split and to help prevent the board from splitting further. This is a mechanical repair, which takes its strength from the inlaid tapered dovetail key which resists the opposing pulls of the board.

The dovetail key should be placed on the underside of the wood where it will not be seen. Its fitting is the same as for any patch, except that it needs to be recessed between about a quarter and a third of the thickness of the board. Bevel the

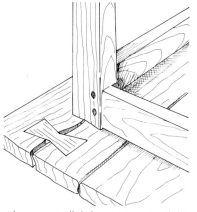

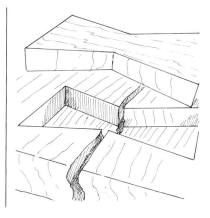

edges very slightly to ensure a tight drive fit, and glue the key in place. Insert a sliver of a suitable timber to fill the crack in the board on the face side.

It is convenient to keep a store of dovetail keys in the workshop, and one of the best ways of keeping them is to make up lengths of key moulding taken from offcuts from the ends of oak or elm boards. The dovetail shape is first cut with a saw to the waist of the key, and the sloping sides are cut with a paring chisel. When a key is needed, the appropriate size is selected and a key is sawn from its end.

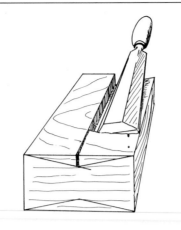

WARPED AND TWISTED TOPS

This problem is quite frequently encountered when working on rather poor-quality furniture. The reason that the plank has cupped is that the top of the boards have shrunk, while the underside has absorbed moisture from the atmosphere. The movement of the wood often pulls the fastenings away from the holding framework. Only drastic treatment will remedy this, unless the framework is very strong and the planks relatively flimsy. Where this is the case, it should be possible to warp the timber flat in the method described

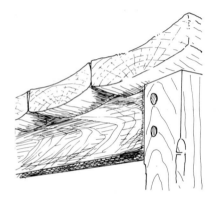

below, and then to refasten it using heavier gauge nails or screws than those used before.

If, on the other hand, the top is more than about 1¼ in. (30 mm)

thick, it may be impossible to do anything at all, in which case the rails should be shaped to fit the cupped planks, so that they can be bedded down securely in their curved state.

Method for flattening a cupped plank

The top must be removed for this operation, and the pieces marked, and checked for any nails or screws that may be embedded in the wood.

The planks are then flattened. This is only a temporary cure, but it greatly assists the restoration process. The technique is to dampen the hollows, to swell that side, while the bowed side is dried. A temporary rack over a radiator is the best means of storing

the pieces while they resort to their original flat state.

When the pieces have been flattened, set the circular saw to cut a depth of three-quarters the thickness of the planks. The underside of the planks are then run through the saw at intervals of not more than 1 in. (25 mm).

Stop the saw cuts before the ends. The saw should not cut right through the plank, but will relieve the tensions within it which caused the cupping.

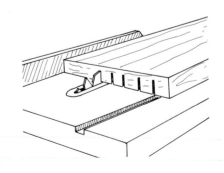

An attractive, but unusually twisted, pine table

Glazed pine dresser, after sympathetic restoration

Wood identification

old pine	pine	ash
elm	Honduras mahogany	yew
wych elm	Honduras mahogany	walnut
beech	sweet chestnut	walnut
teak	holly	satin walnut
newly-sawn oak	quarter-sawn oak	sycamore
very old oak	English oak	sycamore (figured)
cherry	Western red cedar	rosewood

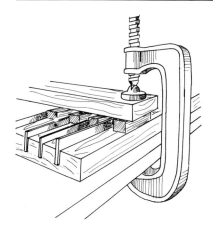

When all the planks have been grooved, glue thin slivers of similar wood into the grooves and clamp each plank against a flat board until the glue is set. The inserts will restore strength and stability to the planks, which should then remain flat.

When the glue has dried, the underside of the planks can be cleaned up, stained and replaced on the frame of the table.

Twisted tops

This may be the result of uneven legs causing the top to sag, or of a poor choice of wood when the furniture was made. The top must be removed, and each piece inspected for twist. Those pieces that have twisted should be treated in the same manner as the cupped timbers, but before they are clamped to dry, they should be given a degree of opposite twist to compensate for the inevitable spring-back of the timber as it is released from the clamps.

PROBLEMS WITH DOORS

Sagging

Evidence of sagging will be seen on the underside of the door and on the doorframe. The joints will appear to flex as the door is lifted slightly. Often the mortices will be cracked and slightly swollen.

The door must be removed from the piece of furniture and dismantled. The joints should be cleaned and the whole piece re-assembled and fitted into the doorway. If the door fits, it should be glued together and clamped up. An epoxy gap-filling glue should be used where joints are badly worn and weakened. If the door does not fit the frame, the frame should be checked for any broken or weak joints which will need to be repaired. If the problem is one of distortions due to age and stress, rather than weakness, the door should be glued together and put in place, resting on a piece of thick card and wedged against the verticals to keep the joints together. The cardboard ensures that there is sufficient working clearance for the door to close when it is screwed into position.

Wide very heavy doors will sag, and the only cure is to screw a diagonal in place against the back of the door from the bottom hinged side to the top outside. This should be notched into the frame of the door at the top and bottom and fumed and aged before being fastened.

Swollen doors

This is a very common problem with furniture that has been kept in damp conditions, and sometimes the solution is simply to let it dry out.

However, if the piece does not appear to be damp, then the hinges should be inspected carefully. Look for signs that the hinges have pulled away from the door post. There may be an accumulation of dirt between the flaps of the hinges which is preventing the door from closing. Also check the screwheads to see that they are flush with the flaps of the hinge.

If these have been checked and the door still fails to shut properly, the positioning of the hinge should be tested by opening the door and slipping a thin piece of paper between the door and the door frame on the hinge side. Shut the door and see if the paper can be withdrawn. If it is held fast between the door and the frame it may suggest that the hinges have been placed too deeply into the door frame and that a sliver of veneer inserted behind the hinge may cure the problem.

If all of these checks prove negative, the door should be planed to fit the doorway. This should be done with care, with the cut slightly angled to allow the door to swing into place.

Warped doors

This is a nuisance, but not difficult to correct. A warped door will not lie flush in the doorframe, and will tend to spring out when it is forced into place. First check that the fault does not lie in the frame itself. If this is flat and true, the door will have to be removed from its hinges, and dismantled.

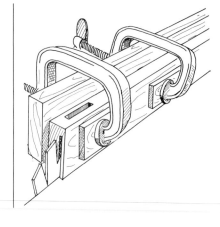

When the door is apart, inspect each part of the framework carefully for distortion. Warping may be quite localised, and present in only one of the four pieces of the framework.

Once the offending piece has been identified, it should be clamped tightly to a straight-edged piece of strong timber, and the circular saw used to make two cuts down to, and a little beyond, the warped part of the frame. The face side of the doorframe should rest against the saw fence and the blade should cut a slot only fractionally less than the frame thickness. The saw cuts are best if they can run each side of the mortice or tenon at the end of the frame member.

Release the door frame member from the clamps and insert thin pieces of timber into the saw cuts. Glue them with epoxy resin or urea formaldehyde glue. When they are in place, clamp the frame against a strong, straight-edged board. The saw cuts minimise the tendency of the wood to distort, and the glued inserts should hold the wood straight.

When the glue is dry, remove the frame from the board, clean up and stain the new inserts, fit the joints, and reassemble the door.

Joints out of true

If a close inspection of a door reveals no twisting of the framework, then the reason for the warping may be that the joints are out of true with the piece. Tenons can be checked by being sighted (as illustrated) and mortices checked by inserting pieces of parallel-sided stick into each mortice and sighting down them. If these sticks reveal a difference in line between the mortices, the cause of the problem will have been found.

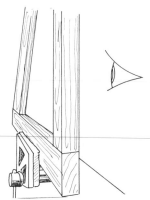

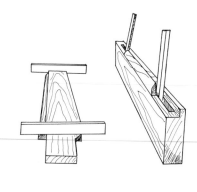

Always make corrections to the mortice, and not to the tenon, as the latter is the least substantial part of the joint. A wide bevel-edged chisel should be used to pare away the side of the mortice, until the door can be assembled and lies flat against a board.

Dismantle the door, and glue it

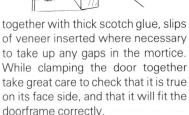

together with thick scotch glue, slips of veneer inserted where necessary to take up any gaps in the mortice. While clamping the door together take great care to check that it is true on its face side, and that it will fit the doorframe correctly.

For further information concerning the hinges and locks see pp. 99-102, 122.

PROBLEMS WITH HINGES, PIVOTS AND KNUCKLE JOINTS

Loose or damaged hinges

It may be possible to tighten the screws holding a loose hinge; if the screws cannot be tightened any further, remove them and use longer screws.

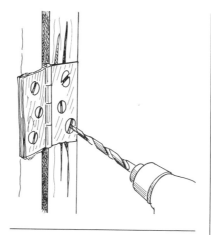

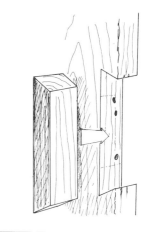

Screws holding a hinge sometimes weld themselves into the timber framework, and a slight shrinkage in the timber, coupled with the constant use of the hinge, wears the hinge loose from its bed. It will be impossible to release the screws and they must be drilled free. There is no advantage to be gained by forcing the hinge away from the screws, as this often damages the hinge. Remove the damaged screws from the timber by drilling deeply into the screw, until the heat and the vibration of the drill cause it to break free. A depth stop should be set to prevent the drill from sliding off the screw and cutting through to the surface of the timber. Once the screws are extracted, it will be found that the wood is so decayed by the reaction between the screw and the wood that it will be in no condition to hold a replacement screw.

The bedding of the hinge should be inspected for signs of splitting. Where this has occurred, the faces of the crack should be cleaned, and P.V.A. glue squeezed into it. Clamp the crack together and insert thin glued dowels to hold the crack together.

Once the bedding is sound, the hinge can be replaced. Drill new holes in the hinge and use replacement screws. Where this will result in a serious weakening of the hinge, an alternative method must be adopted.

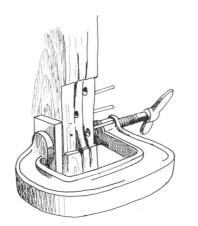

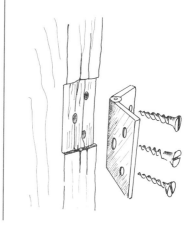

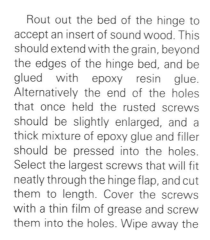

Rout out the bed of the hinge to accept an insert of sound wood. This should extend with the grain, beyond the edges of the hinge bed, and be glued with epoxy resin glue. Alternatively the end of the holes that once held the rusted screws should be slightly enlarged, and a thick mixture of epoxy glue and filler should be pressed into the holes. Select the largest screws that will fit neatly through the hinge flap, and cut them to length. Cover the screws with a thin film of grease and screw them into the holes. Wipe away the

excess filler, check the positioning of the hinge, and place a pad and clamp over the hinge and screws to hold them in place until the resin cures. Self-tapping screws can be used instead of ordinary wood screws with the advantage that the thread extends right to the head, but do not choose screws that are difficult to age. The grease film on the screw thread will enable the screws to be withdrawn from the epoxy filler, so that the same procedure can be carried out on the other flap of the hinge.

Centre hinges

These rarely fail completely, but they often work loose. One part of each hinge is screwed to the top or bottom of the door while the other part is screwed to the framework.

When the pivot wears, or the screws work loose, the door will tend to wobble in the door frame. Screws should be replaced with longer ones. This may be rather difficult as the screws, particularly those holding the top hinge, are often inaccessible. However, of the four separate parts to the two hinges, only one part needs to be released for the entire door to be removed. Turn the piece on its back, and try to unscrew the fitting on the underside of the door. This hinge is quite accessible, and often loose because the bottom hinge takes the entire weight of the door. The remedy is to remove the door and to slip small washers over the pivot to raise its bearing surface. If the pivot is seriously worn, it should be removed and drilled, and a replacement pivot riveted into place.

If, on close inspection, the hinges seem to be in a sound state, and yet the doors still stick, then the framework of the piece should be checked for distortion and shrinkage, and the doors for sag.

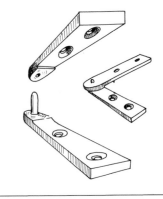

French hinges

These, like the centre hinges, often suffer from wear.

If the hinges are not seriously worn, the door should be lifted from its hinges, and hard car body filler pushed up the tube of the hinge. Before the door is replaced, pin a shim of ply to the front bottom edge of the doorframe so that the rebate of the door rests upon it, thus providing the door with clearance when it is removed. Replace the door, wipe away the excess filler, and leave it to set. Before the paste is fully hardened, open the door a few times to free the hinges.

This solution can only be used where there is a very small degree of wear, as a gap will be created between the top and bottom barrel of each hinge. Where this is more than 1/4 in. (4 mm) the hinges will need to be moved.

French hinges are morticed into the frame and door with tangs which are cast with the barrel of the hinge. These are then secured by pins nailed through the hinge from the inside of the door or into the side of the doorframe. To remove the hinge, these pins must be released. A

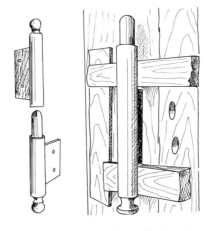

hollow cutter will probably be needed for this (described on p. 16). Only one part of each hinge needs to be moved, and the one to choose is the part that is easiest to remove. If they are all intractable, then work on the ones in the doorframe. The wood is more substantial, and there will be no danger that new fastenings will break through to the front of the piece.

Once the pins holding the hinge have been withdrawn the hinge can be pulled out. If this is difficult, softwood wedges can be forced behind the barrel of the hinge to prise it out.

A new slot, or an extension of the existing slot, will have to be cut into the door frame to accept the tang. Chisel this out using a narrow mortice chisel, or the specially made chisel described on p. 103. Never saw away part of the tang to allow it greater vertical movement. Once both hinges have been moved, place a strip of ply along the front of the framework for the door rebate to rest on, hook the door onto the hinges, and close it. If all the bearing surfaces seem to meet and the hinges are nicely aligned, the door can be removed, and a small amount of hard car body filler pressed into the enlarged hinge mortices. Lightly grease the tangs, and tap them into the slots. Wipe away any excess filler, and replace the door. Check for alignment and place a clamp at the top and base of the door to make sure that the hinges stay deeply embedded in the slot.

When the filler is set, check the door for free movement. Drill through the doorframe and through the tang, and insert screws to hold the tangs in place. Screws are better than nails, as they are easier to remove and replace.

Knuckle and finger joints

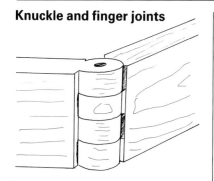
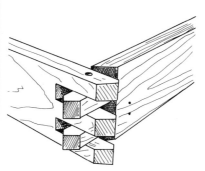

These are wooden hinges that rely on close contact between the faces of the joint for a satisfactory hinge. Once the bearing faces of the joints have worn, the hinge will become sloppy and the rigidity of the piece will be affected.

Temporary relief may be obtained by replacing the pivot pin. This will decline into the previous condition and is not a proper repair for a joint that is used frequently.

To make a thorough repair, at least one side of the joint will have to be removed from the carcass, and the bearing faces rebuilt. The quickest way to do this is to mount the joint on the circular saw, clamping a stop to prevent the saw cuts from running too deeply into the joint. Rest the edge of the joint against the fence, and cut back the bearing surfaces. Continue the cuts about 1 in. (25 mm) into the solid wood behind the join. Only one side of each knuckle or finger join will be a bearing face. Slivers of hardwood should be cut, and fitted and glued into position. Use an epoxy resin glue and wedge the pieces in position. When the glue has dried, the shims can be trimmed and offered up to the other part of the joint. They may need paring down in order to make a sliding fit. A chisel can be used for this, but a more satisfactory method is to place the join on the circular saw table, bracing the piece against the saw fence, and make tiny shavings with the edge of the saw blade until the two pieces fit. This guarantees that the faces are true and square with the rest of the joint.

When the pieces fit together, the pivot hole should be drilled. This is best done with the two parts of the join clamped together and held in alignment by a board. The pin must be a drive fit, but should only require gentle tapping to insert it. Greater force may cause the knuckles to split.

Rule joint

Sides to drop leaf tables are often fitted with a rule joint. If the joint is well cut and the hinges fitted correctly, it is unlikely to cause any trouble. The rule joint will support the flap in the up position, and relieve the hinges of the weight of the flap. If the hinges are badly placed, however, the joint will bind. The following illustrations show a well fitted joint, and the causes and consequences of a tight rule join.

When fitting a hinge in a rule join, make sure that the pivot of the hinge is set exactly in the axis point of the two hinged surfaces. The simplest method of discovering this is to

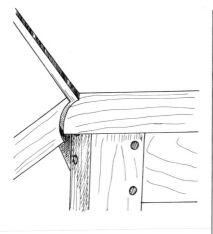

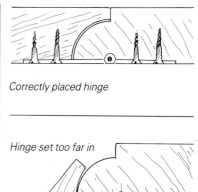

Correctly placed hinge

Hinge set too far in

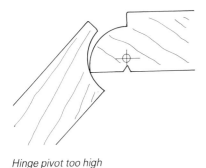

Hinge pivot too high

make an exact drawing of a section through the rule joint; from this the radius of the rule joint can be determined, which gives the position for the pivot of the hinge. Fix the hinge in place with both pieces of the rule joint placed together on a flat board.

Where difficulties in lifting the flap are the result of warping in the table leaf, it may be possible to remedy the problem by fitting one or two extra hinges along the length of the rule joint.

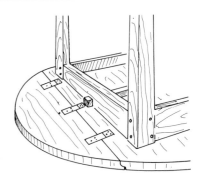

Fitting door hinges

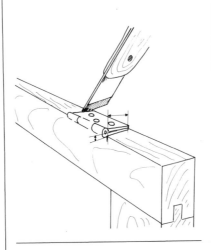

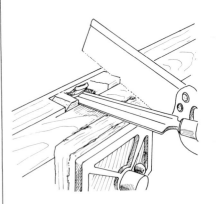

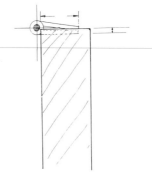

Fit the door in the doorframe and insert a thin piece of card under the door to give it adequate clearance. Use a marking knife to locate the position of the top of the hinges on both the door and doorframe.

Remove the door, place the hinges on the edge of the door, and mark in the length of the hinge. Establish this line cleanly with a set square and marking knife. Use a marking gauge to mark the depth of the hinge, and the cutting gauge to mark in its width. The correct position of the hinge places the pivot of the hinge just clear of the corner of the door. Remove the waste with a dovetail saw and bevel-edged chisel.

Replace the door in the doorframe, with the card beneath the door as before, and mark across the position of the bottom of each hinge on the door frame. Remove the door again, and mark out the slot for the hinge in the door frame as for the door. Remove the waste as before, and screw the hinges in place. (It is usually best to fasten the hinge to the door before fastening it to the frame.)

Hang the door before marking the position for the hinges on the second door. When positioning the second door, ensure that the hinges, door tops and escutcheons are all level with those on the first door.

Marking and fitting French barrel hinges

These are best separated before being fitted. Measure in on the framework of the piece the overall length of the hinge (when the male and female parts of the hinge are both together). Stick a short strip of masking tape to the doorframe at the centre point of each hinge, and on it mark the exact position of the pivoting point of the hinges.

Hold the doors in place, rest the barrel of the hinge against the side of the door, and mark its width on the masking tape. Set a marking gauge to measure from the tang (probably the centre of the barrel, but check) to the inside edge of the doorframe. Use the gauge to mark in the slot for the tang.

Repeat this operation at each hinge, holding the part against the frame with its bearing face level with the marked line, and scribing off the position for the tang. Cut the slot for the tang with the specially made chisel. Fit and screw the lower half of the hinges in place in the doorframe.

Hold the doors in place, resting them on some card or ply tacked along the lower edge of the frame to give adequate clearance, and mark across the location of the bearing face of each male part fixed into the doorframe. Remove the door from the framework, and mark in the slots for the other part of the hinge. Take great care when marking the position for the tang, as some hinges vary,

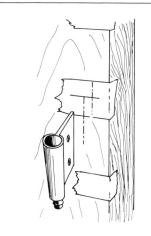

Masking tape shows overall hinge position, and the location of the pivoting point at each hinge

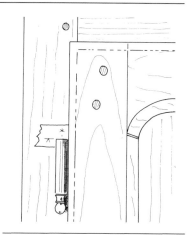

This chisel is cut from ⅛ in. (2 or 3 mm) or thinner section tool steel, and through-riveted to the wooden handle. Temper the blade before fixing the handle in place

and the tang may be off-centre to allow it to pass against the edge of the door rebate.

Cut the tang slot and assemble the hinge. Vertical adjustment (where necessary) can be achieved by lengthening the slot, and placing shims beneath the tang. When the hinges run freely and the doors are properly aligned, fasten the hinge in place with two screws per tang.

DRAWERS

Repairing worn drawer sides

Drawers that are lightly worn at the sides are simple to repair. Worn parts are planed off and new shims glued in place. Avoid using nails or pins to hold the replacements because, as the wood wears down, the nail heads will tend to score the runners and may chip the front rails as the drawer is pulled out. Scotch glue should be used, and the repairs held by spring clamps.

Where drawers have been badly worn, a considerable amount of replacement wood will need to be

inserted. This is best done with a router, although the same job can be performed with a chisel and a bull nose plane.

Clamp the drawer in the vice, with its worn side uppermost. Fit a ⅜ in. (9.5 mm) tungsten-tipped cutter into the router. If the drawer front juts above the sides, a piece of thin, level board should be rested on the drawer side to bring the side and front to the same level. Place the router with the cutter over the worn side, and move a straight edge against the fence of the router. Clamp the straight edge. Move the router to the other end of the drawer side, position it as before, swing the end of the straight edge against the fence and clamp its end. Tack or clamp an end stop to the edge of the straight edge to stop the router cutting through the drawer front. Move the router along the straight edge, increasing the depth of cut until the rebate holding the drawer bottom is reached.

The router will make a perfectly straight cut, releasing the worn side at all points except where the side meets the drawer front.

Remove the straight edge, levelling piece and router from the side of the drawer, and free the remaining piece holding the worn part to the drawer front with a dovetail saw or bevel-edged chisel. A replacement drawer side should be

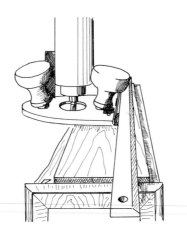
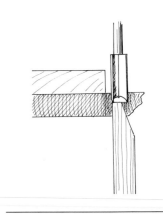

cut out to size, grooved to hold the drawer bottom if necessary, and located over the dovetails at the front of the drawer. These should be scribed in place; alternatively, a cardboard template can be made up and the dovetail transferred to the new side and cut out.

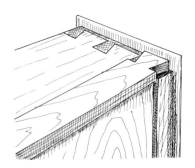

Glue the replacement in place with scotch glue and clamp it with spring clamps. Reinforcing pieces can be glued in place beneath the drawer, but they should be glued only on the side, and not to the bottom boards of the drawer. Clean up the sides, and stain and finish once the glue has dried.

Where new wood is used for the replacement to an old drawer, it is worthwhile fuming it to colour before glueing. This saves a lot of faking once the repair is in place.

Repairing drawer runners

When these become rounded or worn they should be replaced. They can often be removed by simply tapping up the end join at the backboards and freeing the small tongue from the front end of the runner. It is rarely worthwhile repairing worn runners, but an attempt should be made to colour the new wood to match the tone of the wood on the inside of the piece.

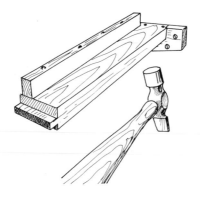
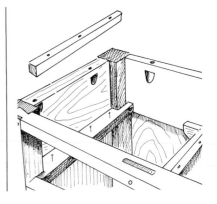

If possible, drawer guides should be positioned and nailed after the runners are in place. The drawer is inserted and aligned to the front of the piece, and a guide tacked into place. The line for the other guide is scribed on the runner. Where it is difficult to see marks, a row of sewing or veneer pins can be used to mark the line of the drawer side: the runner is then pressed against them and tacked. The pins should then be removed.

Loose drawer joints may also cause the drawer to stick. This should be corrected in the manner described on p. 81.

Repairing damage to drawer fronts

When repairing superficial damage to the edge of the drawer front, it is essential to investigate the cause of the damage, and if the investigation reveals worn runners, guides, and missing drawer stops, these should be repaired or replaced.

Replacing damaged cock beading

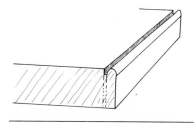

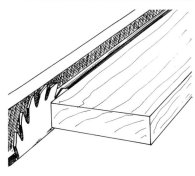

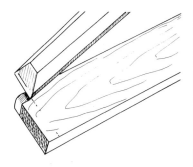

Detail of beading mitre join for the top and bottom edge of the drawer. Bevel width is set by marking gauge and cut with a chisel

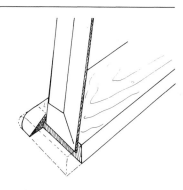

Detail of beading mitre join for drawer sides. Width of the bevel is set using the same setting on the marking gauge. All cuts are with a chisel; no sawing is necessary

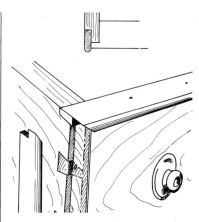

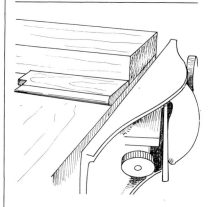

Assess the quantity of new beading necessary, and plane and saw it to size. Use a combination plane fitted with a beading cutter, or a scratch stock, to shape the beading, and then cut away the bead from the edge of the board with a circular saw. Always make up a little more beading than is necessary.

Remove the old, broken beading, cutting it free with a dovetail or veneer saw, and clean the beading rebate. Trim and fit the new beading. Cut the corners, and trim the bead to length at the butt joins between the existing beading and the new. Use a shoulder plane and bench hook, or very sharp paring chisel cutting down to a pine board for the fine trimming.

Fasten the beading with scotch glue and, where necessary, tack it in place with short veneer pins. After stain has been applied, a strip of hardwood, shaped to take the curve of the beading, should be rubbed along the beading to help the two pieces to merge together.

Repairs to drawer edge mouldings

Considerable damage can occur where drawer mouldings extend beyond the edge of the drawer. As the drawers are closed, the mouldings hit the carcass and are broken. These are usually simple to repair, except where the damage has occurred at the end grain at the sides. Here the damage often extends to the face of the drawer, and great care is needed in choosing and fitting a suitable replacement patch.

Where damage is limited to the top and bottom edges of the drawer, and to its corners, patching is a simple and quick operation. Where possible the patch should extend below the inside edge of the drawer front so that it is supported on two sides. As an alternative to hand tools, use a router to cut the seating for the repair. Where a number of such repairs are needed, a parallel-sided piece of ply or board, cut to the width between the router bit and the fence, will quickly give the line of cut, and position for the straight edge guide.

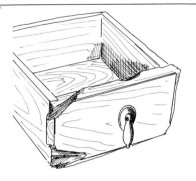

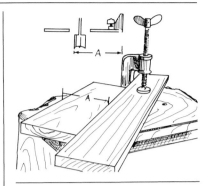

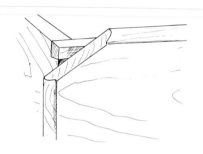

Glue the patches with scotch glue, and clamp them with upholstery spring clamps. They should be planed true to the outside of the drawer, the moulding marked with a cutting gauge, and shaped with a

delicately set rebate plane or paring chisel. The final shape should be smoothed with sandpaper held against a backing board carved with the negative shape of the moulding.

Repairing damage to end grain drawer mouldings

Where breakages have extended to the face of the drawer, great care should be taken in choosing a wood suitable for the patch. The drawer front should be cleaned and, if necessary, brushed with shellac so that the grain and reflective qualities of the wood are revealed. Once a piece of suitable timber has been found, the shape of the patch should be considered.

Patches which lie across the grain are very difficult to conceal. An unbroken straight line is almost impossible to hide, so the patch should have either a curved or a jagged edge. For straight-grained

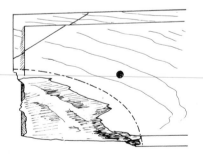

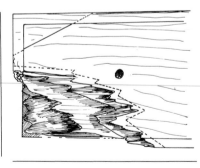

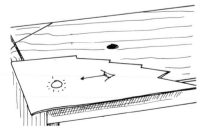

drawer fronts it is best to use a jagged patch.

The shape of the patch should be cut from clean white paper, and held against the broken drawer front. The direction of the grain lines and the spot where they pass beneath the paper should be marked on the paper.

It is then removed from the drawer and placed upon the selected wood, which has been positioned to display the same reflective characteristics as the drawer. The paper is moved about until the orientation of the grain is approximately correct, and at least some of the strong grain lines pass across the lines marked on the paper.

Cut out the patch; the joining edges should be finished very cleanly, and slightly undercut.

Remove the paper, place the patch on the drawer front, and spot glue it in place with superglue (cyanoacrylate). Cut the shape of the patch on the drawer front with a marking knife, and remove the patch. Excavate the area with a router, or chisel, and finish with paring chisels and gouges.

There is no second chance with a patch of this type. Either it fits, or both the patch and the recess will have to be begun again. Only very minor adjustments can be made, and these by rubbing the edge of the recess with blackboard chalk, pushing the patch into position and easing away at the high spots. Finishing and shaping is as for the previous patches.

In the unusual case that the edge moulding has broken away without damaging the front face of the drawer, the broken and damaged parts should be cleaned away with a chisel, and the router used to cut a seat for the patch behind the face of the drawer, and about ¼ in. (5 mm) deeper than the inside drawer edge.

When replacing damaged edge

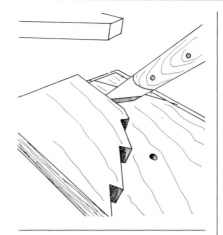
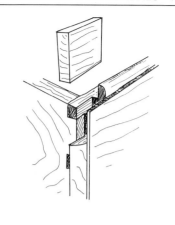

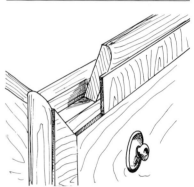

mouldings always ensure that the new part is in line with the rest of the overlapping edge. If it is proud, it will soon be broken away; if it is forward of the line of the moulding, it will tend to concentrate the shock of closing onto hitherto undamaged parts. When the repair work has been completed, check to discover the state of the drawer stops. If they are missing or worn, they should be replaced.

Eighteenth-century furniture often

has cross-banded drawer fronts, which hide a separate thumbnail moulding glued into a rebate in the drawer front and mitred at the corners. Where these edges are badly broken, and the banding has been lifted, it will be necessary to cut back and remove the banding before working on the damaged moulding beneath. Once the moulding is made good, the veneer banding can be repaired.

Stopping holes in drawer fronts

Most handles leave marks and holes in the front of the drawer when they are removed, but few make such a large hole as a Victorian wooden drawer knob.

To remove it, unscrew the knob

and tap it out, or, if necessary, break it free using a light chisel and a mallet.

Insert a taper reamer into the hole and bore the hole larger until the edges are clean and round. Cross-grained plugs should be turned on the lathe to the correct taper, and glued into place. On reflective woods

like mahogany, cherry or walnut, take care to position the wood pellet to reflect the light in the same direction as the drawer front.

Where the piece of furniture is of particular beauty, it is often best to apply a diamond patch over the pellet made from a well-matched and very thin piece of similarly grained wood.

This is a delicate, time-consuming operation, but the disguising of the patch will be easier, and the diamond shape will tend to distract the eye from the faint concentric rings remaining where the drawer knob was once fastened. Smaller handle holes are best filled with hard, coloured wax.

Repairing drawer bottoms

Drawer bottoms that are cracked or split should be removed and reglued. Reshoot the edges if they do not make a satisfactory join. Apply scotch glue to one surface, lay the pieces on a flat board covered by a sheet of newspaper, and rub the pieces together. A couple of battens should be put across the piece, and a weight placed upon them to hold the join together. If a drawer bottom has shrunk, is damaged, or has a part missing, a new piece will need to be made and fitted. Always stain or fume, and age the new piece before it is fixed into position.

Where a drawer bottom is particularly thin, and needs supporting at a join, a strip of calico or hessian, stained with an aniline dye and glued with scotch glue, can be stuck to the underside.

DAMAGED MOULDINGS AND BEADINGS

A small length of moulding in need of repair should be cut away, and a new piece fitted and trimmed to the correct width. The piece should dovetail into place and be glued with scotch glue. Hand tools can be used to cut the moulding to shape. Check for alignment of the original moulding to prevent unsightly kinks. The new piece should be sanded to its exact profile with sandpaper backed by a block specially carved to shape. Stain it, and then rub the moulding with a hardwood stick to define and harden the edges. This is important, because mouldings reflect the quality of a piece of furniture, and should be clean and sharp edged; a moulding that is carelessly sanded and left looking approximately right does more to disfigure a piece than its absence would.

Where a large amount of moulding is needed, perhaps for a new cornice, the new piece should be made in the following manner.

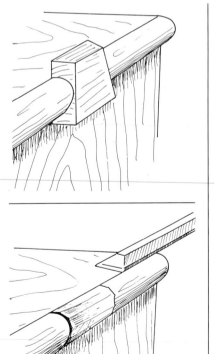

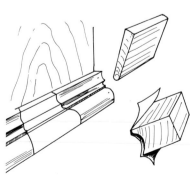

Cornice moulding

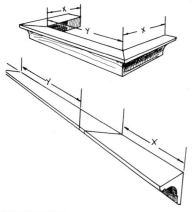

Ascertain how much stock is needed. Remember that mitred joins take up a considerable amount of extra moulding. Add a small amount for adjustments in saw cuts.

Decide on the profile of the moulding. If there is a sample available, then this is no problem. Where there is nothing to copy, then the restorer must adapt the moulding shapes that are used elsewhere in the piece. They can be enlarged, and combined to create a pleasing effect. Mouldings,

particularly cornice mouldings, have a purpose. The restorer must take his time to consider what effect is needed. Some cornices have the effect of compressing a piece, others give it a sense of grandeur. Some can lighten a heavy piece, and others can promote a solid and formidable appearance. Above all, the cornice should be in style and keeping with the piece. This is why it is best to make variations on the mouldings already present, rather than introduce new shapes.

A simple pine dresser, requiring replacement back and bottom boards, new glass, cornice return, feet and complete refinishing and polishing. (Two to three days' work.)

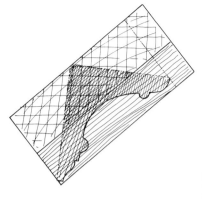

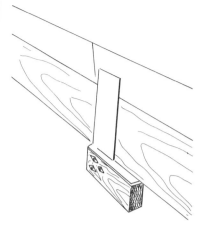

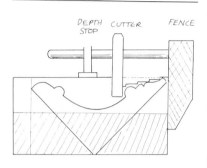

DEPTH CUTTER FENCE
STOP

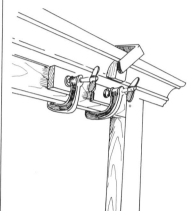

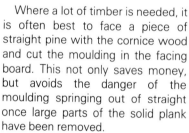

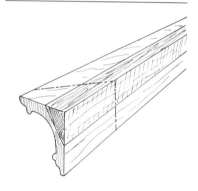

Where a lot of timber is needed, it is often best to face a piece of straight pine with the cornice wood and cut the moulding in the facing board. This not only saves money, but avoids the danger of the moulding springing out of straight once large parts of the solid plank have been removed.

Trace the profile onto card, and draw this at each end of the board. Clamp this to the bench or hold it tightly in the vice, well supported at each end. A combination plane with a straight cutter fitted to it is used to rough out the shape of the moulding. The cutter should first work the edge closest to the fence and work inwards. Adjust the cutter to fit the varied depths of the moulding across its section. This operation creates vast quantities of shavings, which should be swept up before the next operation.

Use a gouge to remove the edges and corners that will not be required in the final shape. A chair scraper is

then sharpened to the desired profile and fences tacked on both sides of the cutter. Draw the cutter gently along the face of the moulding, and rock it deeper into the cut as the moulding is worked.

Once the moulding has been made and sanded (if necessary) it should be fitted to the carcass. Inspect the top of the piece of furniture to discover the kind of fitting needed. On some, the cornice is glued to the carcass and secured with glue blocks. On others it is made to be detachable and is held in place by small tenons. If the cornice needs to have a rebate worked into the base, it should be done at this stage.

Fit temporary clamping blocks to the carcass, and hold the moulding in place. Check that it is at the correct angle to the face of the piece, and mark at the base of the moulding the exact location of the corner of the carcass. If the reverse side of the moulding is parallel with the face of

the piece, this line can be scribed up the back.

Remove the moulding and hold it against a vertical plank clamped to the vice. The mitre should be marked and cut with a cross-cut handsaw, held with very little downward pressure.

Return the moulding to the

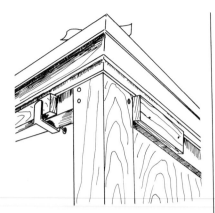

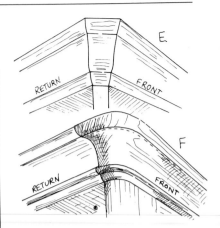

carcass, and assess your work. The line of the mitre should appear to spring from the corner of the piece. Adjustments to this should be made with a shoulder plane before any wood is cut from the other end of the cornice moulding.

Once a satisfactory cut has been made, remove the moulding. Cut to length a piece a little greater than the return moulding. Mark and cut this in the same way as before until it fits perfectly to the front piece. The other end of the main moulding should now be cut in exactly the same way. Any difficulties in marking or sawing should be ironed out before attempting this most important cut. Mark it accurately, but saw a little on the waste side, and leave it for final adjustment.

The second return is now cut and the mitre planed to its correct angle. This should be moved into the front mitre which should be carefully trimmed to meet it. Take great care at this point, and at intervals stand back to assess the work. The mitres should be clean and vertical.

Once the moulding has been cut and fitted, and before it is assembled, it should be stained. For instructions, see pp. 182, 194.

Use scotch glue, or quick-grab P.V.A. glue, to hold the joins together. A single nail can be driven from the return into the moulding to hold the faces together while glue blocks are fitted.

Once the glue has set, and before

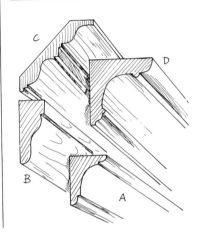

the cornice is removed from the piece, position glue blocks behind the mitres and (on large pieces) nail diagonals across the corners. Screw the locating blocks with the stub tenons in place.

Corner cupboards whose sides are angled at more than 90° require special attention. The correct angle for cutting the main centre part of the cornice will be half the angle that the sides make with the front. However, if the cornice is to be viewed from below, the returns must be angled down towards the back of the piece, otherwise they will appear to rise away and give the cupboard a slightly quizzical appearance.

A variety of cornice mouldings and corner joins are illustrated above (A, B and C). Note that the butt join can only be used where the moulding does not undercut itself.

Awkward problems can arise

*Cornice join **E** can be used where the corner of the framework is bevelled. The curve at **F** is carved once the return is butted and glued in place. Undercut mouldings **D** cannot be jointed like this, unless the joint is made before the moulding is cut to its full depth*

where a cornice moulding slopes at an angle, without any part of it vertical. This vertical face is necessary because it helps to determine the angle at which the face of the cornice leans from the vertical, and also affects the angle at which the saw cut is made. This can be overcome by glueing blocks at the corners to give a vertical, before cutting. Alternatively, a simple jig can be made which can hold the cornice moulding to any angle required while it is being sawn.

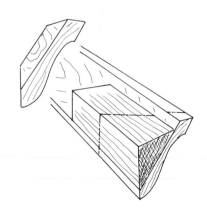

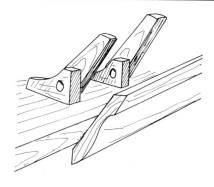 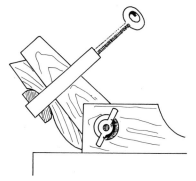 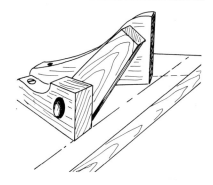

Two swivel clamp posts are screwed in the line close to the edge of the board. The cornice moulding is clamped to the posts and adjusted to

the desired angle. A mitre cutting guide is temporarily screwed at one end of the moulding and the moulding is sawn.

BLEMISHED SURFACES

This section refers to the wood-working task of making good a damaged surface. For remarks on

staining and faking in repairs, turn to pp. 186–8. Minor blemishes can be filled with a stopping compound. There is a wide variety of stoppings available, and the main types are as follows.

Coloured waxes

These have a semi-transparent appearance, and are useful in all kinds of repair work. They can be made to suit the requirements of the job, and tinted with dry powder colours. Melt beeswax and a little dry colour over a low heat. When the molten wax is coloured the correct shade, it should be left to cool in a foil mould.

Use the wax stopping by holding the stick of coloured wax against the tip of an electric smoothing iron. The wax will run down the iron and drip into the small surface hole or crack. It should be allowed to cool thoroughly and can then be pared down with a chisel. Final cleaning should be with fine wire wool held against a backing board.

For a more brittle stopping, a small quantity of tree resin and some flakes of shellac can be added when melting the wax.

Water soluble stoppings

These are very convenient paste-like compounds, but they tend to be friable and lack a strong adhesive quality. They are suited to filling small holes. They can also be used as a foundation onto which hot wax can be dripped. A smooth finish on the water soluble filler can be obtained by pressing the stopping with a wet knife blade.

Shellac sticks

These can be purchased from cabinetmakers' suppliers. A curved knife is heated over a methylated spirit flame, and a drop of melted stick picked up with the tip of the blade. Press the tip of the blade into the crack, and allow the shellac to run into the wood. Wipe the blade clean, and heat it again over the flame. Scrape the warm blade over the crack to remove the residue of the filler and smooth the finish.

Glue and sawdust

Very fine sawdust is needed, and it should be mixed well into the glue. Scotch and epoxy glues make a good binder for the sawdust, as they have a transparent quality which prevents the filler taking a dead appearance. P.V.A. should not be used; it is not brittle enough to allow satisfactory smoothing, and permits itself to be stretched as the timbers move; thus a well filled crack may soon become an area of unsightly fissures and small crevices.

Two-part commercial fillers

These are very simple to use, and come in a variety of colours. The hardener is added and mixed in prior to applying the filler. The compound is quick drying, and very hard when set. Different shades can be obtained by mixing the colours together. The disadvantage with these fillers is that the colours tend to be rather subdued, and it is often impossible to make a colour match with the existing surface. As the filler is impervious, it will not take a stain, and paint has to be resorted to in the finishing process.

Where a hard filler is to be applied to an area weakened by woodworm or wet rot, it is a good idea to saturate the area with unthickened epoxy resin glue before applying the filler. This increases the chance that the filler will bind well to the wood, and will not pull away with a thin layer of rotten wood sticking to it.

Masking tape around the hole will prevent the spread of the filler; the residue can be removed with stripper or sandpaper.

Patching

Large areas, or parts likely to be under close scrutiny, should be repaired by inserting a patch of wood over the blemish. If this is done well, the repair will enhance the piece of furniture. Two types of patching are generally used. Straight-sided patches (diamond-shaped, and variations of that shape) are quick and easy to do, and can be readily merged into the surrounding timber. They should not be used to cover areas of more than about half an inch square (two square centimetres) or the straight sides will be difficult to conceal.

For larger areas, curved patches are used. The sides of these can follow the grain pattern of the timber being patched, and the ends curved so that at no point are there straight joins crossing the line of grain.

Straight-sided patches

The shape of the patch should be cut from a piece of thin card. This should be a little larger than necessary to allow for the patch to be rotated to align perfectly. Mark the direction of the grain on the card.

Select a piece of timber for the patch. It should be of the same type as the piece to be repaired, lighter in colour, and have the same reflective qualities. This latter quality is less important on woods like oak or pine than on more iridescent woods. To help in the choosing of the piece, the face of the timber should be planed

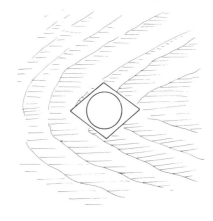

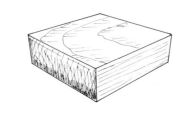

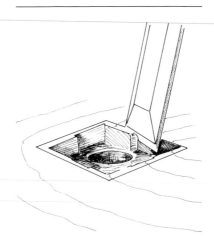

and covered with a thin coat of shellac.

Position the card on the board, and align it with the grain. Check the reflective qualities. Glue the card over the timber with a spot of scotch glue or shellac, and cut out the patch. Smooth and slightly undercut the sides of the patch with a shoulder plane. Remove the card and clean the surface of the wood. Position the patch over the blemish, view it from all angles to check its position, and tack it in place with superglue (cyanoacrylate). Cut around the edge of the patch with a marking knife.

Excavate the hole to take the patch with a small bevel-edged chisel and light mallet. The very edge should be left untouched until the centre and bottom of the area has been cleaned and levelled. The final ⅛ in. (1 mm) at the edge is then chopped away. In order to do this accurately, the chisel should be gently slotted into the knife cut, and a steady downward cut made. The line is followed by moving the chisel along and locating most of the blade in the knife cut, with the rest tilting slightly into the existing cut. Cuts should be started and worked into the corners from both sides. When the final cuts have been made, the patch should be placed across the hole to check for gross inaccuracies. Taking care not to rotate the diamond out of position, make a very slight bevel at the underside of the patch, and apply scotch or epoxy glue to the sides and underside of the patch. Tap it firmly into position.

Allow the repair to dry. Although the patch may seem firmly embedded in the timber, the action of the glue drying may tend to pull it deeper into the hole.

Use a shoulder plane to pare away the surface of the patch until it is flush with the adjoining surface. It is helpful to rub candle wax onto the sole of the plane to ease its path across the wood. This helps the restorer to sense how much wood is being removed at each pass.

A small strip of sandpaper held against a flat backing board should be used to level the patch. (For staining and finishing see pp. 172, 182).

Curved patches

These are made and fitted in the same way as the small patches. They should be designed to fit with the curves in the grain pattern of the timber. Sometimes the grain of the patch will suggest its shape. This is particularly so if the patch contains a knot, as the strong grain patterns swirling round the knot will easily hide a join.

Cut the patch with a bow saw or a coping saw, and finish the edge with a curved sole spokeshave. Rout or

chisel the space for the patch, and drill a small hole into the centre of the recess to allow surplus air and glue to escape as the patch is fitted.

For a final fit, blackboard chalk can be rubbed against the bevelled edge of the patch before it is lowered into place. High spots on the inside of the area can be pared down with a chisel or penknife, but great care is needed here, as it is easy to press the patch in too far, and then have difficulty removing it. If this happens, the best solution is to tap a small nail gently up the drill hole beneath the patch, head first, to push the patch out.

Epoxy resin, or Scotch glue, is best used for holding the repair in place. Glues that incorporate an acid hardener should be used with caution, as the acid may tend to discolour woods with a high tannic acid content. Finishing processes are exactly the same as those for the small diamond-shaped patches, although the larger patches can be levelled with a scraper for the final finish.

Some reference books describe a method of patching that involves sloping an edge patch into the timber. Thus the seat of the patch also becomes the join where it meets the surface. Because this join approaches the surface at an angle

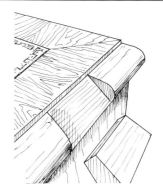

the glue line is exaggerated. This is not a good way of repairing, and should not be used, unless the glue line can be arranged to merge with a strong line already on the timber which may help to mask it.

ROT AND DECAY

Dilapidated old furniture that has been left to rot or has been badly infested with worms is now considered worth repairing.

The problem with such pieces is knowing exactly how strong they really are. Most old furniture was made with a built-in margin of safety. Once the structural members are weakened by rot or worm, the only certain way of discovering a piece's real strength is to test it until it breaks. This is, of course, absurd. The restorer must approach his work

with care and craftily replace as much of the rotten worm-eaten wood as he can while still keeping the original surfaces.

If a purplish fungal growth surrounds the decayed wood, the timber is probably infested with dry rot, and a specialist company should be consulted.

Wet rot only attacks damp wood and is not associated with the purple fungal growth. It can be cured by drying, after which a preservative should be washed over the infected part. The crumbled and weakened wood will have to be replaced. Old

timber should be cut back until sound wood is reached, and new pieces scarfed in place.

In areas that are not on view, it is sometimes easiest to replace the entire board or frame member.

Where damp and woodworm are combined, the wood will become spongy and impossible to work. Some parts can be cut out and replaced or, if the weakened part is not structural, it can be dried and injected with unthickened epoxy glue.

Allow the affected timber to dry slowly, and then place it, face side down, on a board covered in thin polythene sheet. Clamp the board to the timber.

A hypodermic syringe (without a needle) and a drill slightly larger in diameter than the syringe nozzle are needed. Set a depth stop to the drill to allow it to pass about three-quarters of the thickness of the piece and drill into the back of the affected area. The drilled pattern should be regular and comprehensive. Fill the syringe with unthickened epoxy resin glue (with its hardener mixed in) and insert the nozzle into each hole and pump firmly. The resin will flow readily into the wood and may emerge from distant wormholes or well up other bore holes.

When all of the holes have been filled, allow the resin to dry. If necessary, more holes can be drilled, with the depth stop set at half of the thickness and more resin pumped in. Before long the wood will have lost its sponginess, but it will not have gained much in strength. It can, at any rate, be worked, particularly with machine tools, and long reinforcing pieces or loose tenons can be inserted into the wood. (Plastic syringes can be cleaned out once the resin has dried).

Although the application of filler to a piece may increase its ability to take compressive loads, it will not increase its longitudinal strength. One should, therefore, be quite ruthless in dealing with badly weakened timber, and replace it where necessary. Where that is impossible, or thought to be too drastic, the insides of the timber must be removed and replaced by sound wood.

All pieces that are attacked by woodworm should be treated with worm-killer before refinishing. If this is not possible, a worm-killing wax, or a fumigator, should be used.

BAD REPAIRS

After the ravages caused by dry rot and woodworm, the bad restorer comes a close third. Generally speaking, a piece that is in its original derelict state is easier to repair than one that has been worked on by an incompetent restorer.

When assessing a job, it is important to look for signs of poor repair, as well as the obvious faults that need attention. If the repair is being done commercially, the owner of the piece should be notified that these bad repairs exist, and asked whether they should be redone, otherwise the owner may refuse to pay for the good work (because it is indistinguishable from the original piece) and accuse the repairer of the poor work.

There is an infinite variety of bad ways to repair furniture. Unfortunately, many of them result in a weakening of the structure of the piece as well as a spoilt appearance. A restorer will quite quickly develop an eye for such a piece, and the areas of dead colour, swollen joints and dramatic discolorations in the piece will be readily identified. Whether they should be allowed to remain is a matter of individual judgement. Sometimes a cosmetic job can be performed that can improve the piece's appearance. Once repair work is begun, it is often easier to re-do the work completely than to tinker with it.

The following sections outline some of the poor repairs frequently encountered, and suggest methods for correcting them.

Screws and nails

These have their correct uses, described on p. 127, but they are often used to strengthen loose or weak joints or to hold together pieces that have separated. Sometimes the same method of repair has been repeated over the years and the age of the piece can be judged by the number and type of the nails driven into the joint. Used in this way, nails, bolts and screws have the unfortunate effect of splitting and weakening the joint. All should be removed and, if possible, the joint clamped and glued with a thickened epoxy resin glue. Where the joint is badly damaged and weakened by the action of the nails, or in the dismantling of the piece, it is best to saw away the broken parts and scarf on new wood.

Metal straps and brackets

These may disfigure a piece but they are far less damaging than the indiscriminate use of nails and screws. All should be removed and the joint failure attended to. Surface damage can be remedied by slipping small pieces of replacement timber into dovetail-shaped housings.

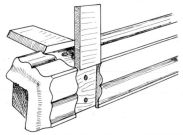

Unsound woodworking practices

Wherever these are identified, they should be rectified. Unsupported butt joins must be reinforced by inserting pieces to bridge the join. Legs that are nailed to the underside of a frame and wobble when the piece is being used should be removed or reinforced with glue blocks. Repairs that prevent a piece from shrinking should be released to prevent cracking. Where a repair has resulted in a distortion in the shape of a piece, it should, if possible, be remedied. This often occurs at the backs of chairs, where the backrest has broken from its supports. These are sometimes cut back to new

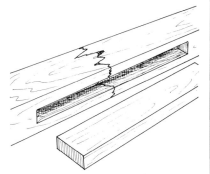

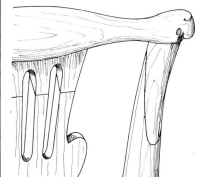

wood, and the centre splat lowered to fit. The proportions of the piece are ruined. Repairs are costly. Both the splat and the supports to the backrest have to be repaired with scarf joins which extend down the back of the chair. Colour the glue to

match the tones of the wood by mixing small quantities of dry colours into the glue mix.

Where moulding repairs are kinked, remove the offending parts and refit them.

REPLACING LEATHER DESK TOPS

Equipment

A packet of paperhangers' cold water paste, a small rolling pin, and an extremely sharp scalpel are needed.

There are companies that specialise in preparing, tooling, and posting leather writing-tops, etc. to restorers and furniture manu-facturers. Unless the restorer is prepared to invest a considerable amount of money in tooling wheels, gold leaf, and supplies of leather, I suggest that the services of these people should be used. (Some addresses are given at the back of the book.)

Technique

Initial preparation: all the old leather or oilcloth should be removed, and dents and cracks made good. Clean the recess right to the very edge.

The leather-tooling companies need precise dimensions of the shape of the leather. If this is a square or rectangle, the length and width are all that is required. For irregular or curved shapes a paper template will have to be made and sent. This is made by laying a piece of brown paper over the desk top and rubbing a pencil across the edge of the leather recess.

Cut out the template, and mark on

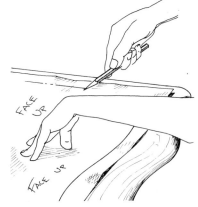

it the face side and the underside. Also specify the colour of the leather and the type of tooling desired. Roll the template into a cardboard tube and send it away.

Laying the leather

Mix up a sufficient quantity of cold water paste. Make a slightly thicker mix than one would use for wallpaper. Brush the paste evenly over the area, taking care that there is a covering of glue at the edges. Take the leather, and lift it gently into

place. Do not press it until you are quite certain that it is correctly aligned, with the tooling running parallel with the edges.

Press the leather flat; work air bubbles and accumulations of excess glue from the centre with a small rolling pin. Do not stretch or over-work the leather. If there are

difficulties, lift the leather and realign it, reglueing the lifted part if necessary.

Once the leather is flat, check again to make sure that it is correctly positioned. If it is not, peel back the leather, spread a thin layer of glue over the wood, and try again.

Take a sharp scalpel and hold it at an angle, so that it slightly undercuts the leather. This prevents the bright unstained underside of the leather from appearing at the very edge.

Choose an inconspicuous area to begin, and rub a fingernail against the leather to find the edge. Plunge the scalpel through to the wood at the very edge of the border. Remember to angle the scalpel over the border, and twist the handle very slightly so that the blade tends to cut away from the centre of the leather and into the wooden border.

Cut to the nearest corner, hold the small strip of leather at right angles to the edge, and begin cutting in the opposite direction. Do not pull the waste leather; just ease it away and clear of the knife. Cut slowly and gently. Follow the edge, keeping the knife angled over and twisted, so that it tends to cut into the border.

Continue around the piece.

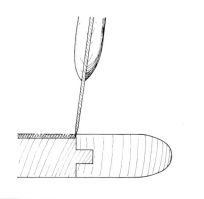

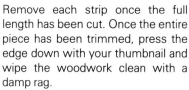

Remove each strip once the full length has been cut. Once the entire piece has been trimmed, press the edge down with your thumbnail and wipe the woodwork clean with a damp rag.

After about half an hour return to the work to check that the leather is lying properly. Press down any raised areas before leaving it to dry.

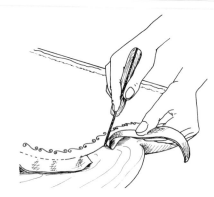

Leather tabs

These should be fitted into slots in the wooden groundwork of the leather surface. These slots must be cut before the leather is laid.

Make the tabs from surplus leather cut from the edge of the top, shaping them with a knife or scissors. Once the leather writing-surface has been glued in place,

locate the slot (by rubbing across the area with a fingernail, or by prodding a blade through from the underside).

Stab through the leather from above, and insert the tab, pulling it through on the underside. Make a wedge from a slip of veneer, glue it, and press it into the slot at the underside of the surface. Cut the leather and wedge flush with a paring chisel.

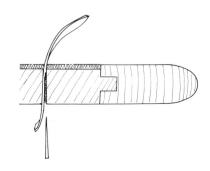

REPAIRS TO CHIPBOARD FURNITURE

Sheets of chipboard are made by compressing wood chips and bonding them with resin glue. Chipboard, and similar types of particle board, are widely used in the manufacture

of modern furniture. It is dimensionally stable, and suited to modern machining and finishing techniques.

Chipboard, however, is unable to withstand suddenly applied loads and is very brittle. Its brittleness is not equalled by resilience or

strength. When it breaks, it snaps fairly cleanly, without splitting and tearing. Using the right technique, a broken piece of chipboard can be reassembled and strengthened to the extent that the repair is stronger than the original board.

Technique

Press the broken parts of the board together, interlock the two faces as well as possible. Cover a supporting board with polythene sheet, and press it very firmly beneath the break. Shore it in place, and then tap the two parts of the break closely together. Stick some modelling clay at the ends of the break, and wipe grease or petroleum jelly over the surfaces at the edges of the crack.

Mix some unthickened epoxy resin glue, and pour a very small quantity into the crack. Allow this to seep in, and replenish when necessary. When the crack is unable to absorb any more glue, leave it to cure. Wear rubber or polythene gloves when handling epoxy resin glue.

By the time the resin has cured, most of the glue will have been absorbed into the chipboard. Clear away any remaining traces with a chisel, and regrease the surface by the crack.

Finish for Formica-topped chipboard

Mix up another small quantity of resin. Divide it into two parts. In one add some dry powder pigment to bring it to the colour of the surrounding finish. Pour a very small amount of the coloured resin into the crack and allow it to settle. Follow this with a trickle of the uncoloured resin to bring the level of the resin slightly above the surrounding surface.

When the resin has cured, scrape away the excess with a knife or chisel, and sand the surfaces. Finish with a fine grit abrasive paper, followed with burnishing cream.

Finish for wood or veneer

Where there is a wood or simulated wood finish the techniques described on pp. 171ff., 186ff. are all appropriate.

Joining chipboard

Chipboard can be dowelled or tongued with a loose tongue (see p. 61). Use machine tools fitted with tungsten carbide edges wherever possible. Joints should be joined with thickened epoxy resin glue. Most problems occur when screws pull out, or fastenings work loose. The remedy is described in the following section.

Screwing and bolting into chipboard

The problem with screwing into chipboard is that the wood fibres have insufficient holding power to allow the screw to be pulled up tight. Furniture manufacturers overcome this by bedding nuts into the chipboard, which locate onto fastening bolts and serve to spread the load over a greater area. Once the furniture is assembled, it is usually impractical or uneconomic to rebuild these joints, and a reinforced screwing technique should be used instead.

Assemble the joint and hold it firmly in position. Select an adequate number of screw fastenings, and an appropriate washer for each screw. Counterbore for the washer and screw head, and bore a hole for the shank, to the full depth of the screw.

Smear grease or petroleum jelly over the screw threads and pour some unthickened epoxy glue into each hole.

Leave the glue to soak in for about two minutes, and then add a little more as it is absorbed.

Screw each fastening into place. Do not tighten, but make sure that each screw is driven fully home. Clean around the join, and leave the glue to dry.

Tighten the fastenings when the glue has dried. This technique is also suited to restoring the grip of fastenings that have pulled free from the chipboard.

METALWORK REPAIRS

The restorer will often have to repair or replace damaged metalwork. The basic tools he will need are shown here.

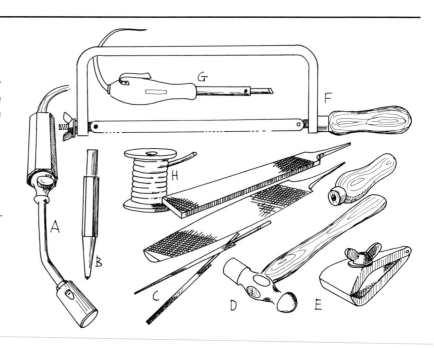

A gas torch   *B* centre punch   *C* large and rat-tailed files   *D* ball pein hammer   *E* holding clamp   *F* hack saw   *G* soldering iron   *H* solder

Sawing

Always buy good quality hacksaw blades; these are the workhorses of the metalwork shop, and much time can be wasted if cheap blades are used. When fretsawing, select the correct blade for the work. Hardware store assistants will help choose the appropriate blades.

Saw deliberately and slowly. Lubricate the blade with soapy water or oil. For cutting complicated shapes, such as escutcheons, cover the face of the metal with thin dark paint, and scribe the shape onto it. Alternatively, leave the surface of the metal as it is and draw the pattern onto it.

Drilling

Always wear safety glasses when drilling, and clamp the workpiece.

Centre-punch the point for the drill. Do not allow the drill to overheat; withdraw it frequently and cool it with oil or soapy water.

Files

Keep files clean and sharp. Never use them without their handles, otherwise the tang may injure your wrist. Hold the file in both hands and work it slowly and steadily. Draw filing gives a clean finished edge. A selection of small rat-tailed files, as well as some large flat and rounded ones, is essential.

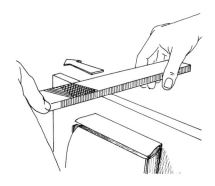

Riveting

Riveting is a simple and strong way of joining pieces of metal. The rivet should be malleable and pass through all the pieces to be joined. Countersink the rivet holes; the rivet should stand about three-quarters of its diameter clear above the surface of the metal. Support the head prior to hammering the top with ball pein hammer. Wire nails and steel woodscrews make good rivets once they have been cut to length. For more information see p. 129.

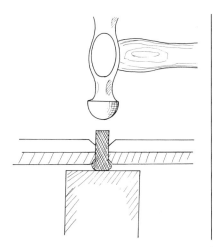

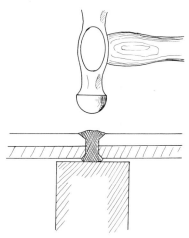

Soldering

Brass, copper, tin and iron can all be soldered, provided that sufficient heat is applied to the join. Surfaces must be clean and grease-free. It often helps to 'tin' the surfaces by applying a thin film of solder to both faces before holding them together and heating them. Too much heat causes the solder to oxidise, and this prevents the joint from running together.

In order to localise the heat, a heat sink can be used. Wrap wet rags around the part which you want to keep cool, or rest it upon a block of iron. Do not, however, place the heat sink too close to the area to be heated, or it will be impossible to raise the temperature of the solder sufficiently to cause it to fuse with the metals.

Use old files to ease away the surplus solder. Alternatively chisel it free, and clean the area with wire wool.

Hardening and annealing

Tool steel can be hardened by heating it to a glowing, bright, cherry red colour, then plunging it in oil. To make the metal springy it should then be cleaned with wire wool, and heated until it turns blue under the heat of a gas torch.

To return the metal to its malleable state, heat it to the cherry red colour and allow it to cool slowly.

Copper is annealed by heating it and then plunging it into cold water. Brass is sprung by being hit repeatedly with a hammer.

Repairing locks

This is a task that requires patience and a selection of old keys. Remove the lock from the furniture, and unscrew the backplate. In most early locks the mechanism is simple. The key is inserted into the lock, and located at a point where it can rotate. Various ridges (called wards) may be riveted to the face plate of the locks to prevent the key from turning freely. Cuts will have to be made in the key to allow it to pass across these without hindrance. Alternatively, the wards can be removed, but this renders the lock less secure. When the key rotates, it will at some point in its circuit press sideways against the locking bar. Simultaneously, this will lift a locking catch held in place by a spring, and the locking bar will move sideways.

More sophisticated locks have levers that are a variant on the locking spring. These have to be aligned by the key before they will release themselves from the notch in the top of the locking bar. The key must be carefully filed to accommodate the needs of the levers. If one lever is tackled at a time, this is not a difficult job.

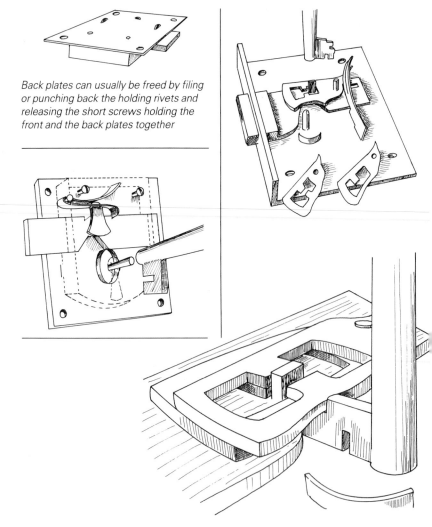

Back plates can usually be freed by filing or punching back the holding rivets and releasing the short screws holding the front and the back plates together

Specialist companies

There are a number of companies that will supply reproduction brassware for furniture repairers. John Lawrence of Granville Street, Dover, produce a particularly fine range of very convincing reproductions, and are able to copy handles and escutcheons should they be needed. Their address is listed at the back of the book.

Although there are a few specialist craftsmen who undertake metal repairs for antique restorers, most jobs can be successfully tackled in the workshop. If welding or hard soldering is required, take the work to a clock repairer, garage, or a lawnmower repairer, and ask him to help.

Ageing new metalwork

Brasswork should be fumed in ammonia until it turns green. Do not allow the brass to come into contact with the ammonia liquid, or leave it too long in the fumes, or the surface will become pitted. Clean brasswork with fine wire wool to give it the pale, aged, worn appearance.

Handle ammonia with great caution. Keep the containers well away from your face, and open them in a well ventilated place. Never inhale the fumes, or peer closely at a piece recently fumed. Wash the pieces in water immediately after fuming.

Ironwork can be aged by putting the piece in the embers of a fire and allowing it to cook overnight. Take care that the piece does not overheat and distort in the process.

9 Glueing and Fastening

Clean and dust all surfaces to be glued. Wood that is unseasoned or wet will not glue satisfactorily. Wood that has been treated with preservative should be allowed to dry.

Choose a glue that is suited to the job. Quick drying glues such as the cyanoacrylate and P.V.A. quick-grab glues have their uses in the workshop, but for many jobs a slow drying glue that will give ample time to assemble, adjust, check and clamp the joint is preferable. Always equip the workshop with a range of glues, some gap filling, some quick drying, and others that are cheap, and easy to apply.

Collect used plastic washing-up liquid bottles, cut them in half, and use the bottom half as a bowl for mixing glue. Use them in rotation, leaving used glue to harden (after which it can be slid out by compressing the sides).

GLUES

Cold water paste

This a wallpaper paste which can be bought from most suppliers of paint and wallpaper. The instructions for mixing will be written clearly on the packet. Make the glue extra strong by slightly reducing the amount of water. This is the best glue to use for holding down leather tops to writing slopes. It has an immediate adhesive quality, yet allows some adjustment in alignment of the leather. For further information see p. 117.

Scotch glue

This is the traditional woodworker's glue. It is commonly sold in pearl form. It is extremely strong, gap filling glue, which will pull surfaces together as it dries. It is ideal for use where almost invisible butt joins are required. Hardened glue can often be melted, and joints and veneers released, by the application of heat to the glue join. Dry colours can be mixed into the glue to help it merge with the surrounding wood. A few spots of linseed oil added to the glue will aid elasticity, which makes it suitable for glueing leather or canvas hinges.

Scotch glue is not weather-proof and it has a tendency to shrink as it dries; it will, for instance, pull veneers into hollows if the groundwork is not properly filled.

Mixing
Scotch glue must be applied hot. It should be heated in a double saucepan or glue pot. Joints must be together and clamped before the glue chills. It is, therefore, difficult to glue large surfaces unless (as in veneering) a heating iron is used.

Initial preparation
Place the pearls of glue in a glue pot or a double saucepan, cover them with water, and leave to soak overnight. Heat the glue in the morning and add a small amount of water. When the glue is hot enough to use, it will run from the brush like syrup. Do not allow the glue to boil.

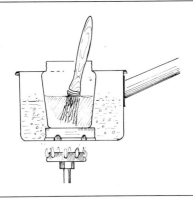

Glue which has been frequently reheated will lose its strength.

Scotch glue is ideal for all small repair jobs. It is particularly suitable for veneering, patching, and applying crossbanding. Always use Scotch glue for glue blocks where, because of its instant adhesion, tacking in place is unnecessary. Because of the problems of keeping the glue hot while the joint is positioned and checked, it is best not to use Scotch glue for large or complicated structural repairs to furniture.

P.V.A. glue (polyvinyl acetate)

This white liquid glue can be bought in 9 pt (5 l) containers from a cabinetmakers' supplier, and decanted into a cleaned washing-up liquid bottle.

P.V.A. has many uses where convenience in application is an advantage and great strength is unnecessary. It is an ideal glue to use in tight-fitting mortice and tenon joints and dovetails, and it is useful for patching and scarfing small repairs in mouldings. It should not be relied on in stressed glue joints such as scarf and V-joints to legs of tables and chairs.

P.V.A., thinned down with water and with the addition of dry colours, makes a good matt paint.

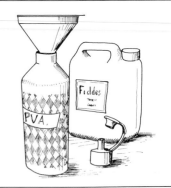

Cascamite (urea-formaldehyde glue)

This is an immensely strong waterproof glue, simple to mix and easy to apply. Small quantities of dry colours can be added to tint the glue.

Mix the glue powder into a small quantity of cold water. Once a paste is formed, it can be thinned by adding water and stirring.

Setting times depend on temperature; the mixed glue remains usable for approximately three hours at 15° C (60° F), giving ample time for making adjustments when a joint is being clamped together. It is a satisfactory gap-filling glue. Wash your hands after use, because contact with the skin can cause dermatitis.

Aerolite 306 (urea-formaldehyde glue)

This is a very powerful, waterproof (but not fully weather-proof) glue. Aerolite is applied in two parts: a resin powder/water mix and an acid hardener, to be applied to the separate pieces of the joint separately. It is a transparent, gap-filling glue, which can be coloured with dry colours. When Aerolite glue comes in contact with iron or steel fittings, nails, or clamps, particularly when it is used with woods that have a high tannin content, there is a possibility that a black staining around the joint will result. It may be possible to wipe away the stain with a cloth dampened with a 10% citric acid solution, but this may also alter the colour of the wood. To avoid such a stain, make sure that the resin and hardener are applied with brushes that do not have ferrous fittings, and that all nails, screws, etc., are punched or driven below the surface of the wood and sealed. Where a joint will be in a conspicuous position, it is best to test the wood beforehand, or use a different glue.

As this glue will dry without the action of the air, it is ideal for injecting into joints. Two syringes are needed, one for the hardener, and the other for the glue. The hardener should be injected first, and allowed to soak into the wood before the glue is pumped in (see p. 82). Wash syringes and brushes with warm water after use.

Epoxy resin glues

These are very strong, gap-filling and weather-proof glues, ideal for injecting into loose joints, and an excellent filler when very fine wood dust is added. Wear gloves when handling this glue, as contact with the glue may cause severe skin irritation.

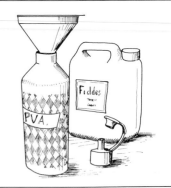

The two parts to the glue should be mixed prior to glueing, and any recommended filler should be added to the mixture. Full instructions accompany the package of glue and should be followed.

Contact adhesives (Evo-stik, etc.)

These are impact adhesives. The rubber based glue is spread on both faces, positioned, and pressed together. Thixotropic contact adhesives permit slight adjustment in the joint before the bond is secured. They are useful for holding veneers to curved groundwork, or bonding formica to work surfaces.

Cyanoacrylate glues

Some superglues are available which will bond wood. These are very useful for temporarily tacking pieces together – as in patching.

Latex-based glue (Copydex)

This is white, flexible adhesive, useful for glueing fabric repairs.

GUIDELINES WHEN GLUEING

Glueing should never be a hasty operation. Much time and effort is put at risk when glueing a piece, and it is worthwhile making absolutely certain that the operation will be straightforward and successful. Plan the glueing process carefully, and have all the necessary equipment handy.

Planning

Thought needs to be given to the order in which a piece is glued. When the piece is to be assembled, see if it is not simpler, and more certain to succeed, if the parts are glued in stages. Awful problems can occur when too many joints are being glued at each stage. Once the scope of the glueing task has been determined, make sure that all the joints fit well, are well keyed by dowels, etc., and can be satisfactorily clamped. Remember that once glue is applied it will, in some cases, act as a lubricant, causing the pieces to slip and slide about. If there is a danger of this, and locating dowels are not used, try bedding some ½ in. (10 mm) oval nails into one face of the joint, and bradawl holes to fit the pins in the other. This will ease the assembly, and reduce the amount of slippage.

Where cramps or clamps are used, protect the workpiece with soft wood blocks. If specially-shaped blocks are needed (for holding turnings, etc.) make them before the glue is applied. Where cramps are used to hold table tops together, there may be a tendency for the bar of the cramp to mar the surface of the table, particularly where joins may lift under pressure. Place some

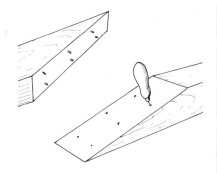

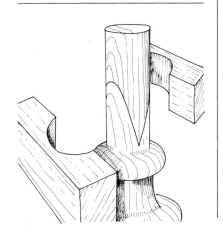

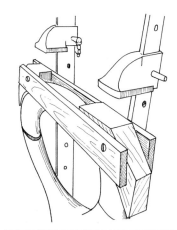

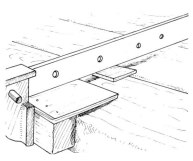

protective blocks between the table-top and the cramp.

Assemble the joints without glue to check that the order of assembly and the cramping devices are satisfactory. Before dismantling the piece make sure that each part is very clearly marked. If in doubt, tab

the joints with small pieces of masking tape, and re-mark them with the appropriate number or letter. A small amount of extra time spent checking the glueing arrangements can save hours of effort later.

Glueing

Follow the manufacturers' in-structions in mixing and applying the glue. Assemble the joints, and wipe away the surplus glue with a damp rag. Clamp together.

Check the piece for squareness, using set squares and, where necessary, diagonal battens. Cramps can be adjusted to pull a piece square if it is out of true.

Stand back and inspect the work. Make sure that all joints are together, and the piece looks right from all angles. When dealing with chairs and tables, make certain that the legs are in alignment with each other, and correctly positioned in relation to the rest of the piece.

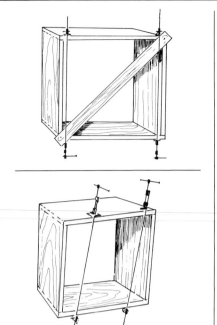

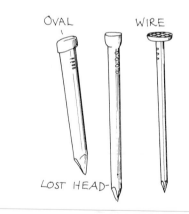

FASTENINGS

Nails

The restorer should have a good supply of nails handy in the work-shop. These should range from 6 in. (15 cm) nails down to ½ in. (13 mm) veneer pins. Ovals, lost heads, and normal wire nails should be available.

There should also be a collection of old nails rescued from old wood, sorted to size, and kept in a tray partitioned for the purpose.

Nails should only be used where the original fastenings were nails. *They should not be used to support or strengthen weak or failed joints, or to repair scarfs.* This is a fundamentally important point. Nailed joints do not stand up well to use, and often tend to weaken a piece. Where woodwork has failed, the remedy must be new wood, or repaired joints. Rebuild the structure of the joining members. Never drive nails in, hoping that this will restore the lost strength. Such a desperately bad practice merely aggravates the problem, and causes a conscientious restorer extra work.

OVAL   WIRE

LOST HEAD

Nailing

Big nails should be hit with heavy hammers, small nails and pins with light hammers. Unless the timber is very soft, it is wise to drill a pilot hole to take the nail. If the nail head is to be sunk beneath the surface of the wood (and stopped with a short peg, for example) the counterboring hole should be drilled first. The pilot hole should be less than the diameter of the nail – its exact size will be determined by the softness of the woods. Larger diameter pilot holes are needed in hard wood. Soft, easily compressed, wood can be bored with a smaller drill. The nail should always make a good drive fit, distorting the fibres of the wood around the nail without splitting the piece. Panel and veneer pins do not need to be given a pilot hole unless the wood is particularly brittle. Nails that may bend when hammering, or are difficult to start, should be held in the jaws of some long nosed pliers.

A panel or veneer pin held in the chuck of a hand drill can be used to bore pilot holes in thin mouldings, etc. before nailing

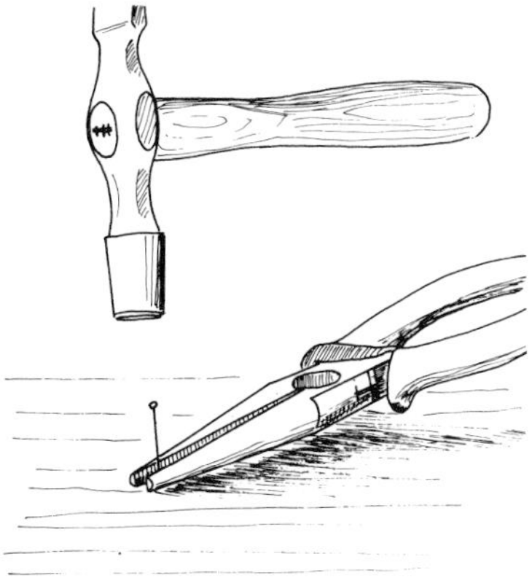

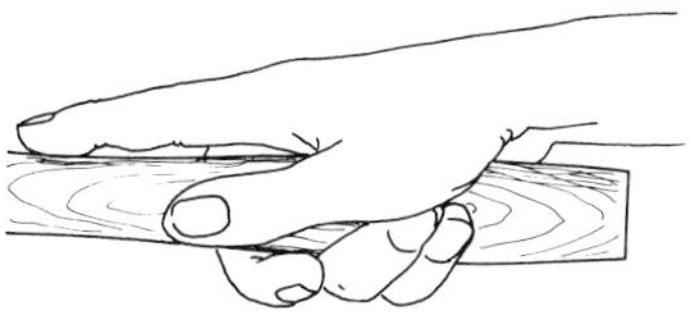

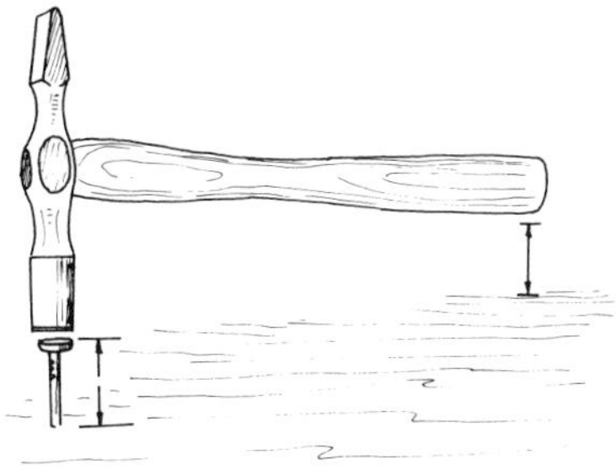

Hammers should be held in one hand, the index finger braced against its handle. The end of the handle should be held level with the nail head.

Where large nails are being driven into hard wood, the tip of the nail can be dipped in furniture wax. This will temporarily lubricate the nail and will later be absorbed by the wood, leaving the nail firmly embedded.

Screws

A full range of old and new screws will be needed. Countersunk screws are normally required in the course of restoration work; round-headed screws are not often needed.

Do not repair with screws unless it is a screw joint that has failed. Bore a pilot hole for the screw about one-third less than the diameter of the screw shank. Then drill the hole again to half its depth with a wider drill to take the top half of the shank. Cut a recess for the countersunk head with a rose countersink bit.

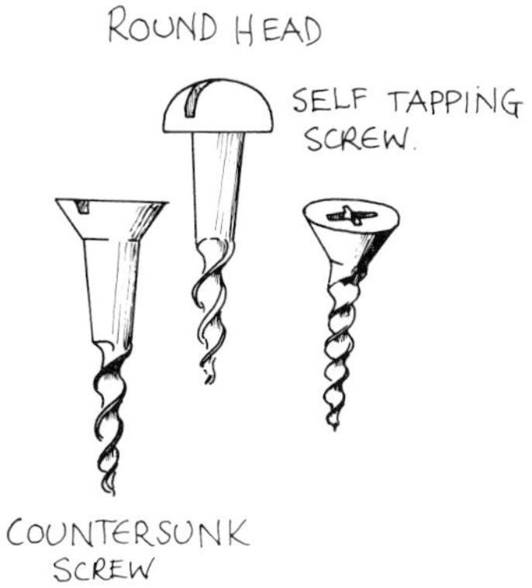

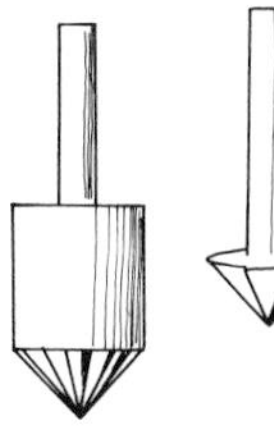

Counterboring

Drill the hole for the head of the screw with a brad point drill before drilling the holes for the shank and threads. Plug the screw with a wood pellet cut with a gouge, plug cutter, or turned on the lathe.

Various means can be adopted to provide for expansion or shrinkage. Table tops are often fastened to the base by buttons screwed to the top and located into grooves in the sides.

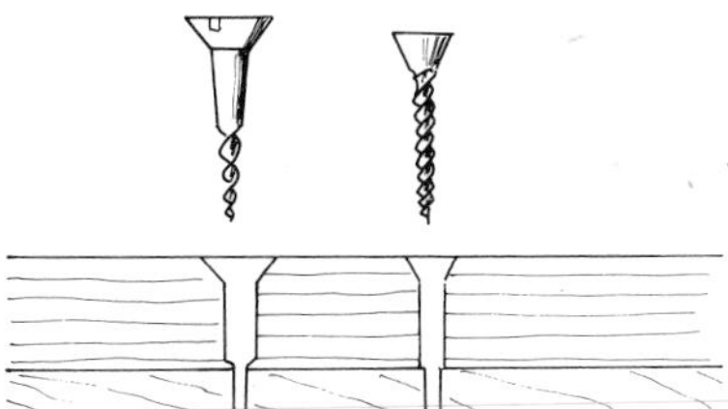

Alternatively, metal brackets can be used which permit a roundheaded screw to move in a slot when the wood moves. Where a top is to be screwed to a batten, an alternative method can be used: countersink and bore for the head of the screw and then bore out part of the shank hole from the joining face of the batten with a large diameter drill. This allows the screws to move with the wood without the ugly buttons or metal brackets.

When preparing to drive a screw into the work, select a screwdriver of the correct size. The edge of the screwdriver should exactly fit the slot of the screw. It must never be too wide (or it will tear the surrounding wood) and it should not be too narrow, otherwise it will be impossible to tighten the screw adequately, and may damage the screwdriver or screwhead. Screw slots should be aligned before being left. This looks better than a haphazard arrangement and, where the screw is to be plugged with a cross grain wood pellet or a short peg, it will make the task of a future restorer simpler when he removes the plug.

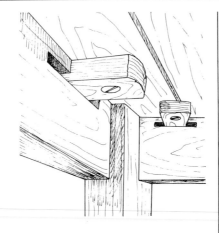

If the screw holes are correctly bored prior to screwing, difficulties in driving the screw are unlikely to be encountered. Bear in mind that brass screws and old screws will take less torsion than new steel screws.

Pegs

If wooden pegs have served to keep a piece together for a few centuries, they can probably be trusted to hold the piece for a few centuries more. Pegs should be made from good straight-grained, knot-free timber. Although, originally, many pegs were inserted unseasoned, it is better to make them from seasoned stock. Split the wood to the approximate size, and finish with flat or slightly curved gouges. Do not use the circular saw to run off lengths of timber to be converted into pegs, unless they are for decoration. By splitting, the wood is permitted to keep its strength, the grain will run parallel with the sides of the peg, and

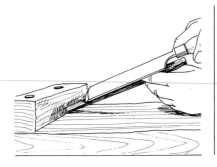
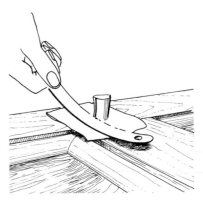

this will ease the trimming of the peg to a round section. Pegs should be cut to length prior to use, the heads sanded and stained, and then rubbed in hard stopping wax. A drop of epoxy resin glue or a fox wedge should be put in the bottom of each hole before the peg is driven home. It is not necessary to glue or wedge pegs holding mortice joints.

Where a perfectly flush-fitting peg is required, it should be driven home before it is cut to length, and then cut with a hacksaw blade resting on a piece of card. Final cleaning should be done with a paring chisel and sandpaper, if necessary.

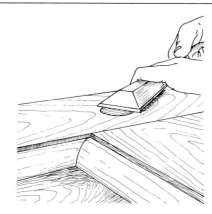

Metalwork: rivets

These can be made from nails or any other malleable metal. Pieces to be riveted should be drilled with a hole the exact size of the rivet, and the rivet inserted. A head to the rivet is not needed at this stage. Cut a nail to length, with approximately three-quarters of its diameter protruding each side of the metalwork to be joined. Use the ball of a ball pein hammer to tap the end of the rivet, supporting the other end on a piece of heavy metal. Turn the piece round, and use the ball pein to work a mushroom head on the other side. Again, invert the piece, and this time work a good round head on the first (tentative) head, and flatten it down. Turn the piece over, and give a few taps to the other side.

For an invisible rivet, the holes should be bored and then counter-sunk. The rivet should be cut in the same way, and the hammering completed as before. Final cleaning should be done with a file, followed by emery paper or wire wool.

10 Frame Furniture

It is not necessarily a disadvantage for a large piece of furniture to have slightly loose joints. Give in the framework may prevent joints from breaking when the piece is moved, and will allow it to settle when it is stood on an uneven floor. It can be a great advantage to be able to dismantle a piece for easy removal. Many large pieces of French furniture are designed with this in mind. One should not, therefore, glue the mortice and tenon joints of the framework if the pegs alone will suffice.

Where the joints are very loose, a second or third peg can be drilled and inserted, provided that this does not weaken the tenon. The joint should be dismantled. The method for drilling a pegged mortice and tenon joint is described on p. 63. If it is impractical to dismantle the piece, or if the joint cannot be easily separated, it should be tightly clamped together and drilled. The drill hole should pass right through the framework to the inside, so that the peg can be removed at a later time. The peg should be a tight fit, slightly tapered and pointed, and the head sanded, stained if necessary, and rubbed in hard stopping wax before it is driven home.

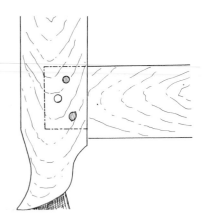

Position the third peg where it will hold the join, without weakening either the tenon or the mortice

REPAIRING WORN FEET

Often, only the feet of a piece of furniture need attention. If the rest of the framework is sound, it is unnecessary to dismantle it in order to tip the feet. The methods for splicing the new tip in place are described below, and a full description of tipping on pp. 83–7.

The problem with working on the feet of a piece without dismantling it is that joints and panels get in the way of the tools, and prevent a simple splice being made. Splices cannot be cut if tenons are seriously weakened. However, joints need not be damaged if the line of the splice is planned carefully, and the following diagrams show various ways to resolve the problem.

Back legs are even more prone to attack by worm and rot than front legs. This may be due to a cheaper

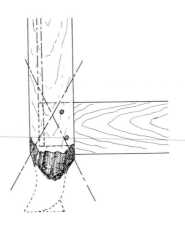

and possibly (for a woodworm) tastier wood being used, or poor ventilation between the wall and the back of the furniture. With back legs, the problem of joining new wood is less acute. The repair must be very strong, but it need not be totally invisible. A good repair can be

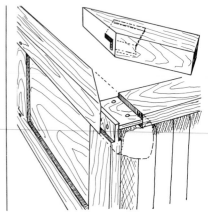

effected by building up the leg with two or more pieces of wood, glued in place. Use a router to clean the touching faces of the repairs.

A similar problem occurs with table legs that have worn down. Sometimes these will be so worn that the stretchers are touching the

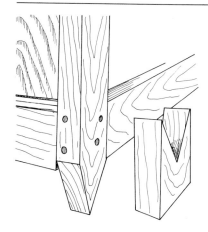

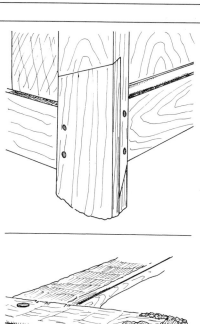

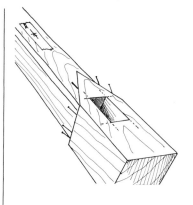

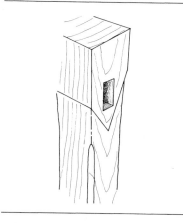

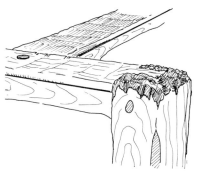

ground and the joints are open at the underside of the leg. The position of the stretcher should be marked clearly on the leg, and the stretcher removed. Cut the tip, fit it as described on pp. 86–7 and clamp it in place. The exact alignment of the leg should be checked. Small tacks driven around the joint will help to relocate the position later. Use a straight edge to mark the line of the inside leg. Mark the mortice in place.

Cut the mortice before the tip is glued and clamped in place. When it is dry, the initial levelling and smoothing, but not the chamfering, should be completed.

The stretcher can then be fitted, one end held in place by a loose tenon if necessary.

An alternative method is to mark and chop out the mortice once the tip is glued into position and shaped. This is a satisfactory method, provided that there is sufficient room to work the chisel and mallet or router.

Occasionally it is necessary to glue the tip and the stretcher in place at the same time. In this case, the tip must be planed to its finished size on the front and side faces before glueing. When the piece is glued and assembled, check the lines of the leg and stretcher very thoroughly, as misalignments can easily develop.

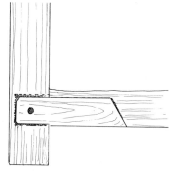

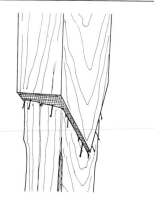

REPAIRING DAMAGED PANELS

It is difficult to repair broken, shrunken or rotten panels without removing the panel from the framework. If the piece can be removed by releasing the joints at one side of the frame and sliding out the broken panel, then the repair is simple. The panel is either patched or new parts added, coloured and replaced.

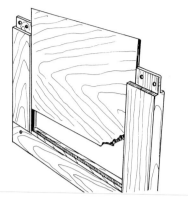

Unfortunately the task is rarely as straightforward as this, and other ways must be devised to enable the repair to be made with the panel in place.

(a)　Small areas that need repair can be patched in the manner described on pp. 92ff., 114ff. If the panel is thick, the patches need to be kept small. If there is any danger that the patch will pass right through the timber, method (b) must be used.

(b)　Where there is a hole right through the panel, a reinforced patch can be used. This is an operation in two parts. The patch itself is supported by another patch embedded on the inside of the panel. The procedure for doing this is as follows.

A patch of the appropriate size and grain pattern is selected and fitted to the panel. It should only penetrate to half the thickness of the panel, and should be a tight tapping fit. It is then removed and placed against a piece of similar wood, and used as a pattern for a second, bigger patch. This is inserted on the inside of the panel, and needs to be about ½ in. (10 mm) bigger all round.

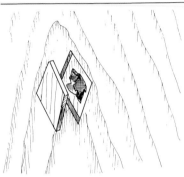

To hold it, drill through the centre of the patch, and clamp it in place with a bolt tightened on the outside with a brace across the recess of the first patch. Mark the second patch very clearly and excavate the area with a router or chisels.

The second patch can now be glued and clamped in place, using the bolt and external holding clamp

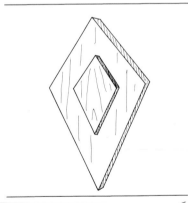

OUTSIDE
OF
PANEL

MARKING KNIFE

CLAMPING BRACE AND SCREW.

INNER PATCH

Scribe around the inside patch, which is held in place by a screw pulling against a wood brace on the outside of the panel

previously used when marking it. Any slight gaps around the edge can be filled with epoxy glue and sawdust.

When the patch is dry, the seating for the external patch should be checked and any drips of glue removed. This is now glued and tapped in place, cleaned up, stained and finished, disguised to merge with the surrounding panel.

(c)　Shrunken panels in need of a new fillet. Panels made from more than one piece of timber are usually tongue and grooved together; they are seldom glued as well. Where a panel has shrunk, the edges of the panels are often held fast by the grooves in the frame and the tongue and groove joint opens. It may be possible to close the gap by levering the parts of the panels together using an old plane iron as mentioned earlier, but this may cause a gap to open elsewhere. In this case, a small fillet of wood will have to be inserted into the panel.

Ease the tongue and groove joint right apart, and carefully remove the tongue with a small sharp chisel. Hook out any broken tongue that may remain in the groove. Cut out a replacement strip of panel, and work a tongue on one side. The length of the strip should be the length of the panel, its width equal to the gap between the pieces. The depth of the tongue should be included in the overall width of the fillet and will, in effect, determine the amount that the panel will be able to swell when it

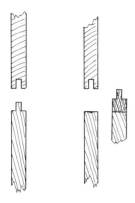

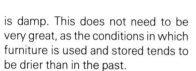

is damp. This does not need to be very great, as the conditions in which furniture is used and stored tends to be drier than in the past.

Make two small cuts at the inside of the grooved frame member to allow for the fillet to be slipped into place. Remove the waste between the cuts with a chisel.

Tuck the insert into place, colour and finish it. The colouring should be performed away from the panel, but checks for colour and age marks should be made in place. Before the panel fillet is glued, the fit between the tongue and groove should be checked, but do not force them together, as it is very difficult to separate them once they are tight together.

If the pieces fit well, the butt join can be glued and very thin wedges driven between the tongue and the groove to force the fillet back against the panel. When the glue is dry, the wedges should be removed and the tongue and groove joint pushed together. A small replacement piece should be tacked into the framework to repair the inside frame.

FITTING SHELVES

Broken shelf supports should be repaired with loose tenons screwed from the inside of the furniture.

Shelves in panelled pieces of furniture are usually made up of at least two separate pieces of timber. If this were not the case it would be very difficult to remove them.

First cut the board to fit at the back of the shelf. It need not be a tight fit. Rest it on the shelf supports and push it back against the framework and back of the furniture. Mark the line of the framework, where notches will have to be made. Use dividers to scribe the shape along the back.

If the shelf boards are tongue and grooved to the front of the shelf, the groove should be worked down the front edge of the back boards.

Tilt the back board against the rear of the furniture, cut the front boards of the shelf to length, and fit it in the

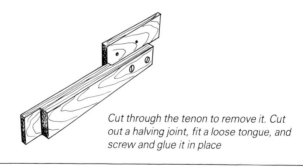

Cut through the tenon to remove it. Cut out a halving joint, fit a loose tongue, and screw and glue it in place

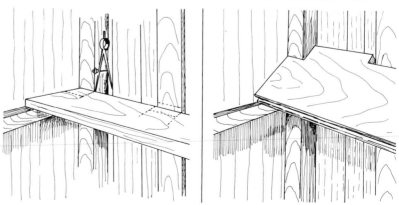

same way as the back board. Lay the back board in place above it. Scribe down the line where the two overlap. Remove the front and cut a tongue in it, using the scribed line for the shoulder of the tongue.

Insert the front board again, and lean both pieces slightly up against the front and back of the furniture, so that the join is at the base of the V. Gently slip these top edges down, and the shelf will come together.

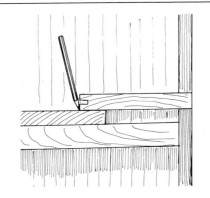
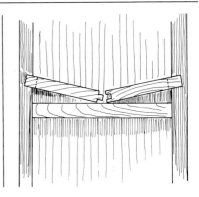

ALTERATIONS TO FRAME FURNITURE

Alterations frequently need to be made to tables to make them suitable for use. Tables should provide adequate leg room of 24 in. (610 mm) and where the legs are very worn or broken, the answer is to tip them. However, some tables, particularly heavy work tables, were not made with the dinner guest in mind, and often have deep rails that lift the top of the table well above a convenient height once the tips have raised the under rail.

In this case, it is best to consider either removing the top and cutting down the sides and legs — an operation that may seriously weaken the leg joints — or cutting away the rail at the underside of the table. This may give sufficient leg room, without raising the level of the top and without tipping. Some designs that can be used are illustrated below. These avoid having to cut away the tenon at the ends of the rail. A scribed line between the 'earpieces' and the rest of the rail may improve the appearance of the alteration.

If a drawer is set in the rail of the table, it will also need to be moved or cut down. Sometimes it is possible to lower the drawer a little without reducing the strength of the rail, but if there is a danger that a structural weakness will result, the drawer will

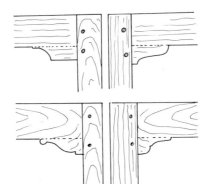

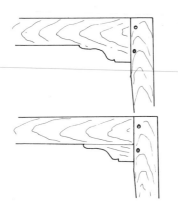

have to be cut down. It is often best to dismantle the drawer completely and rebuild it, preserving the top edges, where possible.

If the overhang of the table is inadequate (there needs to be a minimum of 2¼ in. (60 mm) at the sides, and 7 in. (180 mm) at the ends for most dining tables) the top and base will have to be separated, and the joints at each corner cut back to give the desired overhang. It is better to work on all of the joints because a longitudinal move of the top will reveal large clean areas of wood that were once hidden by the framework of the table.

When the frame is together again, position the top over it, and fasten it in place. If the original fastenings are nailed, then a temporary support should be lodged beneath the rails to support them during the hammering.

Framed furniture is very easy to alter. This is a practice that has existed for centuries, and has resulted in the preservation of a large number of interesting and beautiful pieces, albeit in a slightly different form. When considering a project, the restorer must bear two things in mind. His work should be entirely similar to the original workmanship revealed in the piece; it should be indistinguishable from it in style and finish. Secondly, the piece must not lose its strength or stability as a result of the alteration.

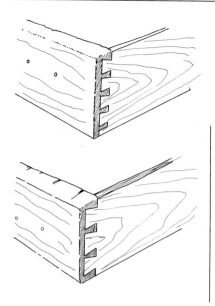

Stop drawer handle holes with wax or shellac stopping. Dismantle the drawer and cut the underside of the front and sides until it fits in the furniture. Cut new grooves, trim the back and re-assemble the drawer. Age the underside

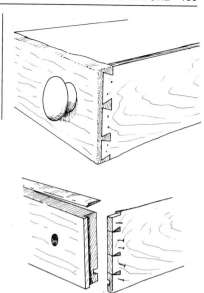

The side of the knob hole and the associated wear around the knob make it necessary to trim both the top and bottom of the drawer front. Dismantle the drawer, cut off the top and keep it for re-using when the drawer has been cut back. Trim the bottom and top of the drawer, re-use the existing dovetail pins where possible – otherwise fake pins will have to be inserted into the trimmed back drawer front, which is nailed or dowelled into the front

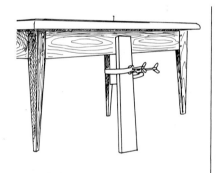

Some typical alterations to frame furniture are illustrated here

11 Carving

A selection of very sharp carving chisels and gouges will be needed (a useful selection of types is illustrated): a mallet, various slip stones and a stropping board.

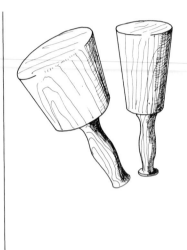

MACARONI TOOL

GROUNDING TOOL

FRONT BENT GOUGES

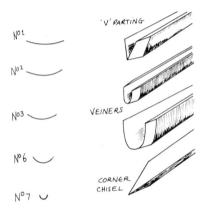

Nº1 'V' PARTING

Nº2

Nº3 VEINERS

Nº6

Nº7 CORNER CHISEL

SAFETY

Work in a good light. It is best if a low light is used, as the shadows will enhance the three-dimensional appearance of the carving and help the carver to appreciate the effect of his work.

For information and suggestions for sharpening chisels and gouges, see p. 41–3.

Hold the pieces to be carved firmly. If the wood slips or moves, the carver may damage the carving, or overbalance and hurt himself. Some suggestions for holding a workpiece are illustrated here.

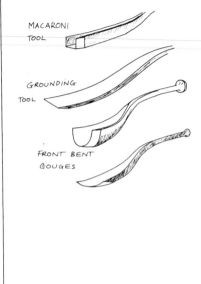

SCREWS TO HOLD CARVING

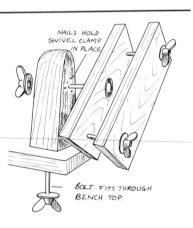

NAILS HOLD SWIVEL CLAMP IN PLACE

BOLT FITS THROUGH BENCH TOP.

The tools need to be held correctly and used gently but firmly. The handle of the chisel or gouge is held in the right hand and pushed. Often it is convenient to brace the right elbow against the body, and lean into the cutting stroke. The left hand holds the tool above the cutting edge, controlling the direction of the cut and also acting as a brake. It pulls back on the blade as the right hand pushes the tool forward. In this way a considerable amount of controlled power can be applied to the tool with the provision that the tool can always be instantly stopped or checked.

Unless a mallet is being used, never carve holding the chisel one

handed. Never have any part of the body in front of a carving tool. Work with the grain wherever possible, and be prepared to rotate the stock in order to make clean cuts.

DESIGNING A CARVING

In many cases the restorer will find that this part of the job has been done for him. Restoration work usually entails replacing damaged or broken carving by copying carvings repeated elsewhere in the piece. All the restorer needs to do is to make a rubbing of the carving, mark it on the new wood and carve it out. However, on some pieces the carving is not repeated. This is usual on some carved friezes, for instance. Where a particular part of the carving is missing, the restorer must invent a suitable design.

The technique for doing this is as follows:

(a) Study the style and patterns of carving exhibited elsewhere on the piece. Note down the typical motifs and recurring features.

(b) Study the carving to see how the spaces between the carving are arranged – does the carving take up the whole board, or does it snake

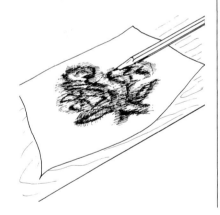

down the centre of it with, for example, leaves branching from it?

(c) Make some actual size sketches of the area to be patched. Do not mark in the detail, just the bold outlines of the patterns that may fit. Copy some of the recurring motifs and use them in the pattern.

(d) Select the most satisfying and appropriate design, and redraw it.

Clean the lines; go for boldness rather than subtle detail. Shade the areas to be cut away, with the light apparently coming from the left side of the drawing. Draw in all necessary detail, and mark a few contours across the main features.

(e) Use carbon paper to transfer the design to the wood. Do not mark in the sample contours.

SETTING IN THE WORK

This is the first stage of carving. Cut back the background (known as the groundwork) to leave the decorative parts proud. Take a small veiner gouge, and carefully cut around the outside lines of the pattern. Make the cut about 1/8 in. (2 mm) to the outside of the pencil line. Do not use a mallet, but continue to cut down, until the depth of the groundwork has been reached. Use gouges and flat chisels to remove the waste. Give flat chisels a slight sideways slicing action, to ease the smoothing strokes and to level the ground. If the original carving has been punched down, this can be copied with some improvised punches. Next, select appropriate chisels and gouges, and cut the shape to the line, making nearly vertical cuts. A mallet should be used for this work. The cuts should reach down to the level of the groundwork, but no further.

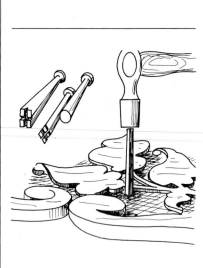

Avoid undercutting – a slight outward bevel gives strength and boldness to the carving

WORKING IN THE DETAIL

Once the groundwork is cut back, and the part to be carved stands proud, a few lines can be drawn on the wood to help in the carving of the detail. This is going to vary, depending upon the type of patterns desired. The following techniques may be wanted.

Cutting knobs

Set in the knob and remove the groundwork. Trim around the exact edge of the knob, taking care not to cut below the level of the ground-work. Several sweeping strokes, first with a number 3 and then with a number 5 gouge, will be needed to give a smooth round profile.

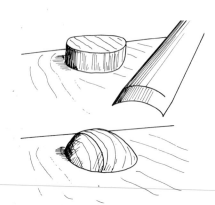

Cutting cups

Take a suitable sized gouge, hold it vertically at the circumference of the hollow and twist it to define the edge. Change the position of the gouge to carve out the centre. Cut down with a rocking motion of the gouge. Release waste wood with a second cut from the opposite side.

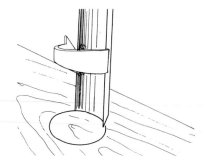

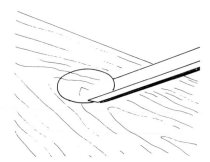

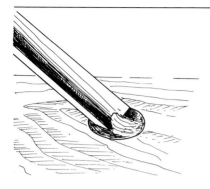

Leaves and flowers

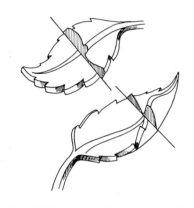

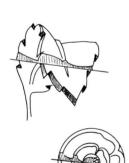

Set in, and then mould shapes boldly, only carving in the essential detail.

Tudor rose

This is cut from a basic centre boss and two concentric circles. Draw in the petals before cutting them, using a few, carefully selected gouges.

Tapered groove

Use a veiner gouge. Start with the wide end, holding the gouge slightly tilted, keep the handle down and press through the wood. Twist the veiner upright as the groove narrows.

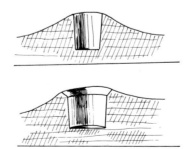

Eyes

Build these up before gouging, and then punch the eye to the level of the groundwork. Cut a slight bevel at the lip of the eye to give it an appearance of firmness.

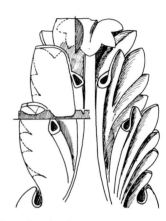

Acanthus leaf

Set in the leaf. Punch down the eyes to the full depth of the groundwork to act as points of reference when marking in the leaves. Cut in and shape the top lobe, follow with the other lobes. Finish long contour sweeps on all lobes before making final cuts around the edge.

Work methodically. Redraw the design on the work whenever tools cut away part of the line. Each gouge or chisel stroke should release its own chip. If not , plan the cuts so that a single stab will release the chips loosened in previous strokes. Do not allow rough cuts to remain; clean them as work progresses. If there are difficult areas to reach with the tools available, make new ones that suit the purpose. Do not try to make do, because the result is likely to be messy. Strop the tools frequently and regularly to keep them sharp.

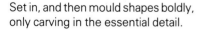

FINISHING

Carving is best left crisp and unfinished; however, when the carving is to merge with exisitng carving, the high points should be lightly sanded and rounded to give a worn and ancient effect. This can be exaggerated if a stain is applied to the piece and the high spots immediately wiped clean.

CARVING FEET

This requires a variation on the skills described above. As much as possible of the initial cutting and shaping should be completed with a bandsaw or bowsaw, and spoke-shave. When carving feet and other work in the round complete the rough shaping and check it for symmetry before beginning the detailed work. With practice, a sense of shape will develop in the carver which will enable him to refer less frequently to his patterns and contour guides.

Ball and claw feet

Mark out using the template set on two adjacent faces. Remove excess wood with bowsaw or bandsaw. Slice away two wedges from each side of the ball to give the foot more power, and a better balance.

Draw in the claws, knuckles, etc., and set in and cut the ball. Finish the ball, carve the web between the toes, and finish by carving the toes, then claws. Final shaping and smoothing is by rasp and sandpaper, but keep the claws, cuticle, and web lines clean and well-defined.

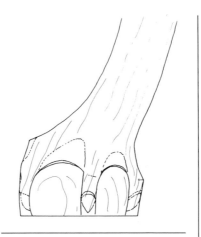

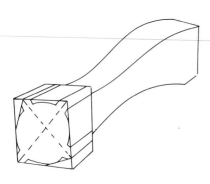

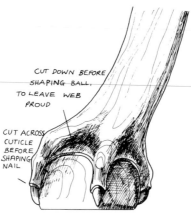

CUT DOWN BEFORE SHAPING BALL, TO LEAVE WEB PROUD

CUT ACROSS CUTICLE BEFORE SHAPING NAIL

Scroll feet

Mark using the template as for the ball and claw feet. Relieve the sides and back of the scroll foot. Locate and mark the centre-point of the scroll and draw it in on both sides. Mark major lines of scroll. Set in and trim the beading down the side, ending in the scroll. Leave the beading crisp and clean. Round and sandpaper the front of the leg.

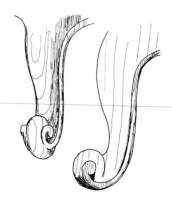

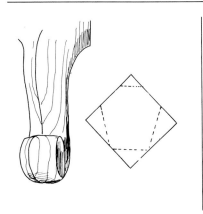

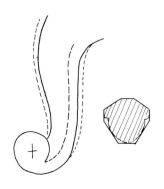

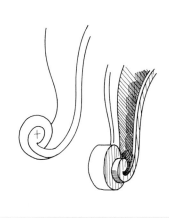

REPEATED MOULDINGS

The secret to cutting repeated mouldings is to discover the number, order and size of the chisel cuts used in its manufacture. Quite often, the mouldings are made using only two or three gouges, worked in rotation.

Stabbing strokes are usually completed before the wood chips are removed. This prevents a localised weakening of the wood, causing damage to the delicate parts of the moulding.

Once the order has been discovered, experiment on some suitable spare timber. Check the gouge size and order of cuts before making the moulding template.

This should be made from an existing part of the moulding or from the new piece if it is in any way different from the original. It is very important for the marking of a repeat moulding to be accurate, as the size and shape of the pattern is determined by the tools that are used, and it is not easy to make adjustments to the design once it is started. Cut the template in the form of a stencil, and mark through it with a pencil for small runs of moulding, and with a stencil brush for longer lengths.

12 Carcass Furniture

Carcass furniture is made from large slabs of edge-glued timber, and held together without a frame. Problems that afflict carcass furniture are usually a result of shrinkage in the wood across the grain, and are rather difficult to repair.

Shrinkage, in the sides of a chest of drawers for example, often leads to stress or damage at the front face, where the drawer runners which do not shrink significantly along their length protrude beyond the sides, or push the capping pieces away from the sides. If the results of shrinkage are not noticed at the front of the piece, they will be revealed by cracking and splitting down the sides. It is usually impossible to release the drawer runners and glue and clamp the sides, because this may distort the other mouldings, etc. that run across the grain, and may also result in the drawers becoming too deep for the chest.

Where this problem occurs, the simplest answer is often to insert wood to make up for the shrinkage.

If the sides of the carcass are veneered, it is likely that the veneer will have split around the area of shrinkage. Using a straight edge, cut back the veneer on each side of the crack. In most cases it is a good idea to make the veneer strip wider than necessary, as very narrow strips of veneer are more difficult to fade in than wider ones.

After the cutting, the veneer will be easily removed, revealing the cracked groundwork, and this can be made good. If the cracking is not too serious, a two part filler can be used instead of a wood fillet.

Flatten the patching and score the

surface to provide a key for the glue. Cut and shape the veneer, and glue it in place (see p. 146). Finish with a scraper, stain and polish.

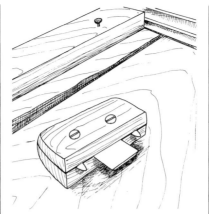

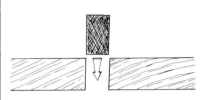

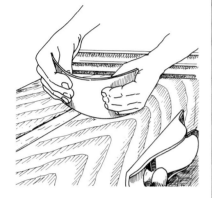

Where the carcass is made from solid wood, with no covering veneer, the crack will have to be straightened, using the tool illustrated, and a tapered strip of matching wood inserted. Glue and ram the repair in place, with glue on both sides of the strip.

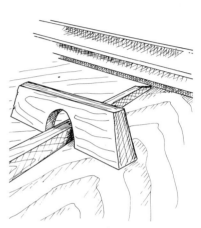

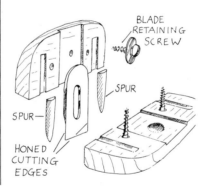

BLADE RETAINING SCREW

SPUR

SPUR

HONED CUTTING EDGES

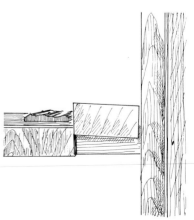

Check the levels of the split board with a bridge before planing and scraping the repair level.

EDGE MOULDINGS

Edge mouldings are very vulnerable to accidental damage, as well as damage caused by shrinkage of the sides. Repairs, however, are not difficult.

Cut away the damaged timber, angling the cut so that the replacement piece can wedge itself into its position. Repair the ground work, level it, and score it using an old hacksaw blade. Choose a piece of suitable timber, again noting and orientating its reflective qualities to match the existing capping pieces.

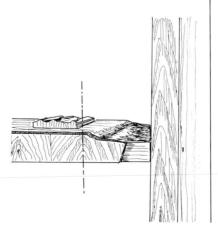

Cut the timber roughly to shape, and trim the end until it fits in place. Glue and hold it in place with masking tape. When the glue is dry, the patch can be planed level. Any moulding that is needed can be worked in using a chair scraper or scratch stock.

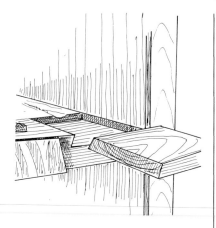

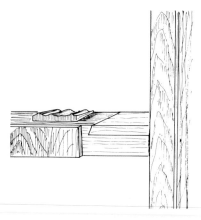

Sometimes a drawer damages the edge capping and it is always worth checking to see if this is the cause of the trouble. If the softer pine behind the capping is below the level of the capping piece and is well worn, this will almost certainly be the reason for the damage occurring. A hard filler can be used for small repairs, but any major areas of wear should be cleaned out with a chisel when the capping is off, and replaced with good wood. If the drawer is the cause of the trouble, inspect it to see if the drawer runners need building up or replacing.

If the capping piece is damaged in several places along its length, then it may be simpler to remove the old facing entirely, and replace it with new. This is always a difficult decision. Remember that this type of patch is quite a speedy operation,

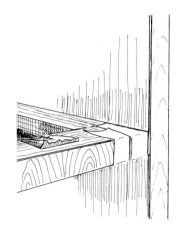

whereas ageing in new wood is often time-consuming. Consider, also, the location of the problem. If the area is conspicuous it may be best to attempt a repair. Repairs should be invisible, but often a cleverly fitted repair that falls just short of perfection can enhance a piece, while a suspect replacement may damn it. If, however, the original wood has been split or nailed, or somehow chewed up so that it has no intrinsic beauty anyway, then remove it and replace it with new wood craftily aged.

SWOLLEN SIDES

Where chests of drawers have had a considerable amount of use, one frequently finds that the sides are pulling apart from the front rails. This may be due to pressure from above, the warping of the side boards, or the vibration and stressing of the piece as the drawers are pushed into place.

This is not difficult to remedy, and the procedure is as follows.

Cramp up the piece, and check that the drawers run freely. If the drawers are tight, or difficult to open,

remember to attend to the runners and the guides before finishing with the restoration work.

Remove the drawers and the back boards. These will probably be loose in any case. Withdraw the dustboards between the drawers. Where the dustboards act as runners, adopt the following technique.

Use a paring chisel or router to work a dovetail in the bottom edge of the groove holding the dustboard to the side. Do this to all the dustboard grooves on both sides of the carcass.

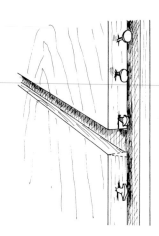

Clean the edge of the underside of each board, and glue cross grain strips to each. When the glue is dry, work a dovetail on the cross grain wood, and insert the dustboard back into the carcass. Do not glue the dustboard in place.

Once all the boards are back in place, replace the back, and nail it securely. Inject epoxy resin glue into the stopped dovetail holding the front rail in place. Allow it to dry and remove the clamps from the main structure of the carcass.

The dovetail housings on the dustboards, the tightly nailed back, and the glued front rail will hold the piece together. Do not forget to attend to the drawers if they are tight or difficult to open or close.

If the dustboards run in grooves worked on the drawer runners, or if there are no dustboards, the following technique must be adopted.

Remove the drawer runners one at a time. These are usually nailed or screwed to the side of the carcass and tenoned into the front rail. In the middle of the underside of the runner, level a slot about 4¾ in. (120 mm) wide, the full width of the runner, extending to the underside of the groove holding up the dustboard. Replace the runner using new screws, and commence work on the other runners. When all of the drawer runners have been worked on and replaced, and screwed firmly

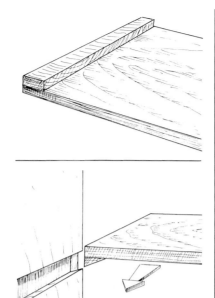

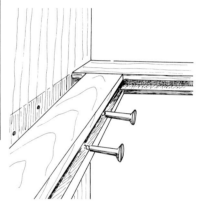
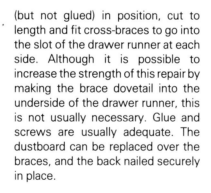
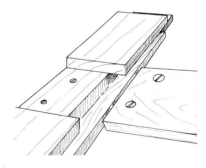

(but not glued) in position, cut to length and fit cross-braces to go into the slot of the drawer runner at each side. Although it is possible to increase the strength of this repair by making the brace dovetail into the underside of the drawer runner, this is not usually necessary. Glue and screws are usually adequate. The dustboard can be replaced over the braces, and the back nailed securely in place.

13 Veneering

Veneers should be stored flat, in a slightly damp environment. Brittle veneers are difficult to work, and tend to crack when being handled.

EQUIPMENT

A plentiful supply of scotch glue should be mixed and heated prior to veneering. The mixture should be thick, and run slowly off the brush when it is lifted above the glue pot. Glue that is too thin will have poor initial adhesion, and will not keep the pressed veneer flat.

A veneering hammer should be available. This is simple and easy to make. A copper or brass edge must be attached to the hammer and smoothed, to allow considerable pressure to be applied to the veneer without scratching or scoring the work.

A domestic clothes iron, a sharp Stanley-type knife, and an old, good quality, steel kitchen knife, with tiny saw teeth (unset) filed at its end are required, as well as a good quality, heavy steel straight edge.

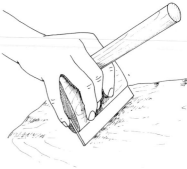

LAYING VENEER AND JOINING SHEETS OF VENEER

The surface on which the veneers are to be glued needs to be level. All hollows should be filled with a two-part resin filler. The entire surface should be levelled, and scored with a toothing blade. An unsupported panel will warp if it is veneered on only one side. To prevent this, veneer both sides, using a good quality veneer on the face side, and a

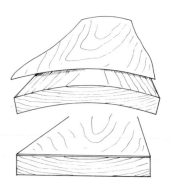

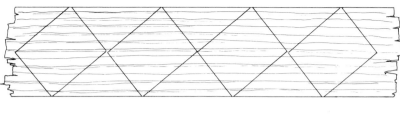

poorer quality veneer on the other. Good quality veneered pieces often have two veneers on each side: first the counter veneer at right angles to the grain of the groundwork, then the decorative veneer above.

Select the veneers (for a quartered effect see the diagram) and cut them roughly to size. They should overlap the edges of each other and the edges of the furniture by about ⅝ in. (15 mm). Mark the positions of the veneer on the groundwork.

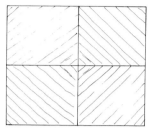

Brush the glue onto the groundwork of the piece of veneer farthest away. It doesn't matter if glue is dropped on to the groundwork in between. Apply the glue quite thickly, and overlap slightly onto the area marked for the next piece. It is important for every part of the groundwork beneath the veneer to be covered with glue.

Take the veneer, invert it and place it on the freshly applied glue. Do not press it down, let it rest there, while a similar thick coat of glue is applied to the underside of the veneer. Turn the veneer over, and position it smartly in place. When it is in position it can be pressed down.

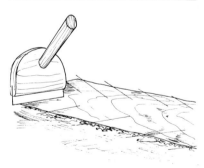

Warm the smoothing iron, and pass it over the rear half of the veneer. The iron should be hot enough to melt the glue, not hot enough to burn it or dry it out. Press the veneer flat using the veneer hammer held in both hands. Work the melted glue to the side of the veneer. Work away from the centre, moving air bubbles and accumulations of liquefied glue, until the piece lies flat. There is no hurry. If the glue chills, warm the veneer with the iron.

Use the same technique for the front half of the veneer, but do not press down the edge that is to join with the new piece.

Once the veneer is fixed down well, and lying fairly flat (it may be necessary to permit a few bumps and bubbles to remain at this stage; they can be corrected later, when the major part of the veneer job is dry),

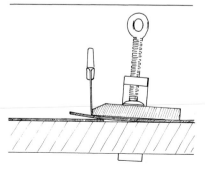

cover the adjoining groundwork with glue. Invert the second veneer over the warm glue and apply the glue to its underside.

Turn it right side up, press it in place, and begin to warm and press the glue out from beneath the veneer. This time, avoid pressing the edges down with the hammer. Make sure that the centre part of the veneer is firmly in place. Put the hammer and iron to one side while the join is made.

This is a simple operation, provided that the veneer has not been thoroughly pressed down at the join. Take a straight edge and the toothed kitchen knife. Place the straight edge along the overlap of the piece, and hold it firmly in place. Angle the knife very slightly, and, without applying great pressure, stroke it down the veneer. One or two passes will be sufficient to cut through the top veneer. Keep working the knife into the veneer at

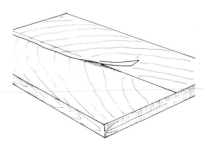

this angle until both pieces have been cut. Peel away the top piece of veneer, remove the straight edge, lift the top veneer slightly, and then peel away the second (underneath) veneer.

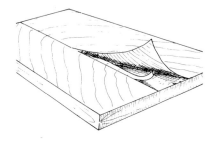

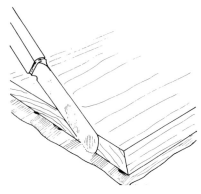

Warm the join with the iron, and press the veneers down. Work the glue out through the join, flattening one piece before attempting to flatten the second. Tape across the join.

Continue working in this way until the entire piece is veneered.

Before the glue begins to dry, cut away the surplus veneer from around the edges of the piece. Flat panels can be inverted and trimmed. Where crossbanding is to be applied, set a cutting gauge to the correct width, cut around the edges, and remove the veneer.

If difficulty is experienced in flattening some parts of the veneer (particularly difficult to hold down are veneers with confused and vigorous grain patterns), leave these until the glue has chilled and set. Return to the work next day, and heat the areas locally. The advantage of this delay is

that the heat that is used to melt the glue is less likely to lift areas that are already well glued down. Work over the high spots with the iron and hammer. If parts still refuse to lie down, try warming the glue and then placing a cold block of iron over the offending area. This may hold the veneer in place and, while it does so, serve to chill the glue.

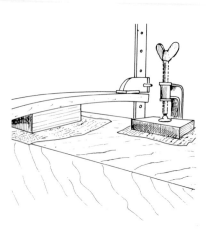

Alternatively, a wooden block can be warmed against the face of the warming iron, or placed against a radiator, and clamped over the raised area with a sheet of newspaper or brown paper between the block and the veneer to prevent the block (or caul) adhering to the veneer as it dries.

Finishing the veneer

Veneers should be scraped clean using a sharp cabinet scraper held at an acute angle to the wood, and then sanded. All surface traces of glue should be removed before staining or finishing.

ALTERNATIVE METHOD TO HAMMER VENEERING

This method uses P.V.A. glue, and is particularly suitable where inlay is to be laid down with the sheets of veneer.

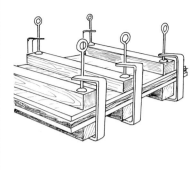

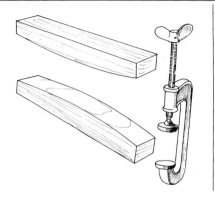

Equipment

A plentiful supply of P.V.A. glue with a roller and spreader, some veneer tape (available from suppliers of veneer), a flat board, slightly larger than the surface to be veneered, and bearers and clamps are needed. The inner bearing face of the bearers should be slightly curved so that the bearers apply even pressure over the entire face of the board when clamped at their ends.

Trim the joints between veneers with a plane worked on its side, the veneer resting on a board, and slightly overlapping its edge. Tape the joints together, and also tape the inlay in place.

Apply glue evenly and liberally to the groundwork, and press the veneer onto it. Use the wooden roller to flatten the veneer onto the ground, working from the centre of the veneer to the edges. Only gentle pressure is needed to remove the air bubbles and heavy accumulations of glue.

Cover the veneer with a layer of thin paper, and then lay the board over the veneer. Place the cramping bars in place, and clamp them firmly. Leave the piece to dry, then clean with a scraper and sandpaper.

BANDING

Small strips of veneer and crossbanding should be worked in place with the hammer veneer method. A cutting gauge can be used to cut them. Herringbone inlay must be dismantled and worked around a curve. Crossbanding must be tapered to fit around curves. Stringing that is applied between the veneer and the banding should be glued and held in place with pins, and allowed to dry before the banding is fitted against it.

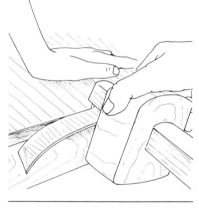

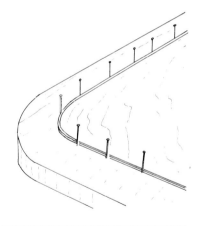

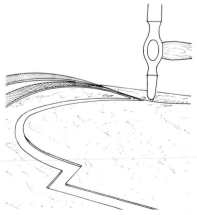

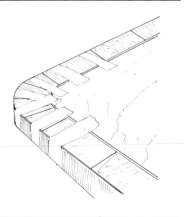

FIXING VENEER TO CURVED STOCK

Modern thixotropic glues, such as Evo-stik, can be used to hold veneers against curves and hollows. Alternatively, a negative cast of the moulding can be made from plaster or wood, and used to press the replacement veneer into place, where it can be held with scotch or P.V.A. glue.

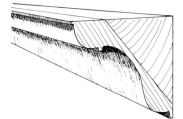

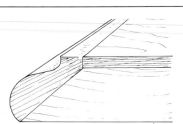

On early eighteenth-century walnut furniture thick, cross-grained veneers were applied and the moulding worked across them

To make a plaster cast of the moulding

Smear some vaseline (petroleum jelly) over an undamaged part of the moulding. Erect a simple barrier of plasticine (modelling clay) around sufficient of the moulding to make a useful pressure pad, and pour in some plaster of Paris. Release the plaster when it is dry and use it as a pad to hold the veneer in place while the glue dries.

The cross-grained mouldings on early eighteenth-century walnut furniture are made up from very thick applied walnut veneer, worked to a moulding once the glue has dried.

REPAIRING MARQUETRY

This is a time-consuming operation. First, the groundwork, and any lifted veneer, should be repaired and held down with fresh glue. Areas of missing veneer must be cleaned and the groundwork levelled.

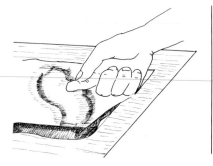

Finding the shape of the replacement parts

Lay a piece of carbon paper, face up, over the area to be filled. Cover this with a sheet of thin, clean paper. Hold the two firmly together, and rub a fingernail around the ridge left where the missing veneers were once glued.

Cut the paper around the mark left by the carbon. Choose a suitable veneer, align the grain correctly and tack the paper in place with a spot or two of glue or shellac. Cut around the very edge of the veneer using a fine fretsaw blade. The blade should just snick away at the edge of the paper as the shape is cut. Remove the paper, and place the veneer in the space.

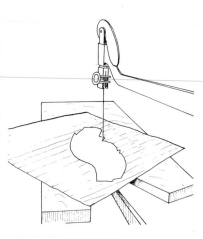

If other woods need to be inserted to restore the design of the inlay, draw on the new veneer the pattern that is required. Select the appropriate woods, and stack them together beneath the patch.

Hold them in place with small drops of superglue, just sufficient to prevent them from moving while being sawn. Saw down all of the lines, collecting any parts of the veneer that may be released by the saw cut.

Reassemble the cut veneers, selecting the woods and placing them in their correct position in the recess. Hold them together with some adhesive tape or a gummed label, then remove them and apply a thin coat of scotch glue to the underside of the replacement parts, and some thicker glue to the groundwork. Place the new pieces into the recess, heat a smooth wooden block and position it over the repair, interposing a sheet of paper between the block and the veneer. Clamp the block in place, and allow the glue to dry.

Remove the paper, and scrape and sand the new work to level it.

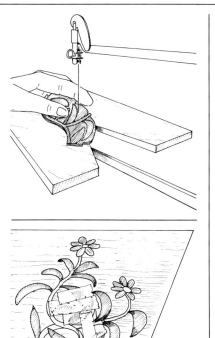

SHADING VENEER

A shading effect can be achieved by the judicious use of spirit stain, or by scorching the veneer. Heat some sand in a tin tray over the stove. When it is hot, the veneer pieces can be nestled into the hot sand. Experiment with scrap pieces before attempting to scorch the carefully cut repair pieces.

REPAIRING LIFTING VENEER

Veneers will lift for a variety of reasons. Often it will be a combination of exposure to damp, moving groundwork and decayed glue. First, stabilise the groundwork. Splits should be filled, joints secured with dowels, and the whole levelled and cleaned.

Moisten brittle veneers with a damp rag. When the veneer is slightly pliable it can be glued in place. Insert glue under the veneer using a palette knife or a slip of spare veneer, and clamp it down with a hot wood block faced with paper.

Bubbles should be treated in the same way. An incision should be made with the grain, and the glue inserted with a knife. Do not attempt to dampen the veneer, as it may swell and refuse to bed down properly. Once the glue is inserted, the wood block should be warmed and clamped over.

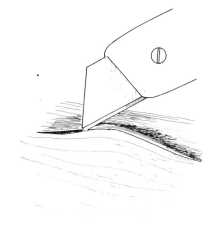

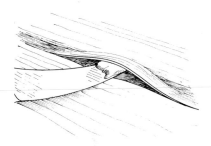

REMOVING OLD VENEER
GLUED WITH SCOTCH GLUE

Where veneers need to be removed, a procedure opposite to that of laying the veneers is used.

The electric clothes iron is heated and a tea towel or similar piece of fairly thick and absorbent material is soaked in water, wrung out and laid over the veneer. This will protect the veneer against burning, and the steam generated when the hot iron passes over the cloth may help to liquefy the glue.

Set the iron to medium heat, and work it across the cloth. The operation will take quite a long time, particularly where thick veneers have been used. When the cloth is ironed dry, soak it again, wring it out and continue working.

After a while, the veneer will begin to lift. Slide an old steel table knife

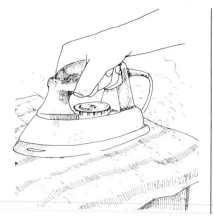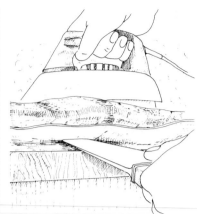

beneath the veneer, to help prise it loose. Once an edge has been raised keep warming with the iron until the veneer is lifted back.

Do not hurry this work. In time the veneer will peel away. Do not increase the heat setting of the iron,

as this will tend to burn the glue and may scorch the veneer, but it will not speed up the lifting process. If the veneer refuses to lift, it may help to strip the original finish from the veneer to facilitate the penetration of moisture from the rag.

14 Chairs

LOOSE FRAMEWORK, BROKEN AND DAMAGED PARTS

It is quite possible to repair loose joints by injecting them with epoxy or urea formaldehyde glue. The procedure for doing this is described on p. 82. In order for this to succeed, however, the condition of the joints should be basically sound. Any fracturing of the tenon or serious breaking of the mortice must be repaired, either with a loose tenon or by splicing the head of the mortice. Such repairs can sometimes be reinforced by fitting glue blocks and brackets across the corners behind the leg.

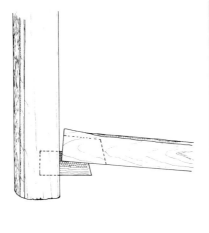

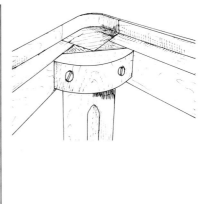

Making joints

Where the replacement piece needed is shaped and jointed, and appears to have no right angle or straight line to mark from, joints can be made in the following manner.

Make a cardboard template of the missing or broken piece. Mark out the shape on the new wood; if the length includes the tenons, these should be incorporated into the shape at this stage. If the piece is (for instance) a curved support to an arm rest, this must then be held in place with hand clamps immediately behind the mortice which will take it.

Insert a straight piece of wood the thickness of the tenon into the mortice, sight the line for the tenon on the support and mark it in. Use a pair of dividers to mark in the approximate location of the

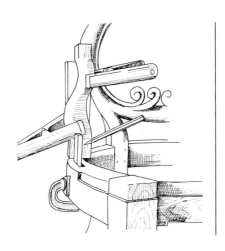

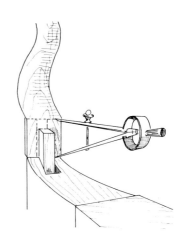

shoulders of the tenon. Cut out the tenon, leaving a little spare wood at the shoulder for later adjustment. As the tenon is lowered into position final alterations to the shoulders can

be made. Once one end of the support is in place, the procedure is repeated for the arm rest. This must be lowered towards the support, and the location of the stub tenon holding the two together should be scribed onto the top of the support. This must be considered with care, as the orientation of the arm rest may alter as it is lowered into place. Once the position of the joint is marked, the lines for the tenon can be drawn in. Check at the shoulder of the tenon that the line of the tenon will fall at the right spot on the support. This can be checked with dividers, against the edge of the mortice on the arm rest. Saw the tenon, and cut away the shoulders, leaving a small part for adjustment (as before). Where a number of such angled joins are made, a board with a mortice cut in it, with its face side rubbed with chalk, can be used to help ensure a perfectly smooth shoulder to the tenon.

When cutting angled mortice and tenon joints, always ensure that the

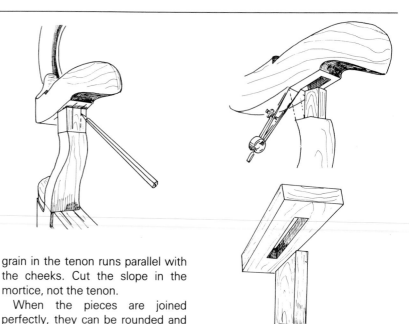

grain in the tenon runs parallel with the cheeks. Cut the slope in the mortice, not the tenon.

When the pieces are joined perfectly, they can be rounded and shaped with a spokeshave and rasp, etc.

Dowelling

Dowelling is a simpler process, in as much as the only requirement is for the joining faces to lie tightly together. Once the surfaces are close fitting, tape a pin to one of the surfaces, with its head positioned at the centre point of the proposed dowel.

Press the pieces together, and the head of the pin will make an impression on both bits of timber. A brad point drill should be used to cut the dowel hole, and its verticality can be checked by watching the cutting action of its spurs as it begins its cut. They must describe an even circle around the point of the drill.

Where new dowels need to be inserted, but old dowelling remains in the timber, flush with its surface, it is better to use morse drills, and to drill small pilot holes to lead them. Otherwise the end grain of the existing dowels will tend to deflect the bradpoint drill. Check the verticality of the pilot hole, and adjust it with a slightly larger drill before making the final hole for the dowel.

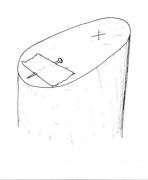

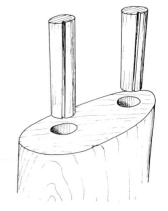

Dowels do not need to penetrate more than four times their diameter into either piece of wood. They should be a good, smooth fit, with a sawcut in the side of the dowel to allow air and excess glue to escape when the joint is driven together. Do not use P.V.A. glue for very thin dowels as it tends to bind before the dowel is in place.

If a second dowel is to be inserted, this should be marked and drilled in the same way as before, and it should be exactly parallel to the existing dowel.

Cramping

Various cramping methods are illustrated in the following diagrams. Chairs present awkward shapes to cramp, and different jigs may be needed to bring the pulling action of a sash cramp to bear on the joint. Where the pieces are shaped, or where sash cramps cannot be used, heavy string, tightened with a tourniquet, can be used instead.

Because of their light construction and absence of diagonal bracing, chairs are very prone to distortion under cramping pressure. Always bear this in mind and check the chair for true from all possible points of view.

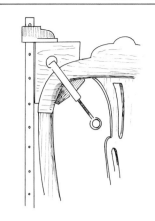
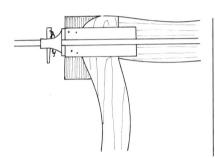
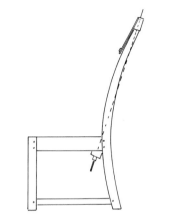

BACKS

Minor damage to the back splats of chairs should be tackled and repaired in place. The chair back should be protected and supported and the back splat securely held against a solid board. Cracks can be repaired by inserting P.V.A. or scotch glue into them and clamping with upholstery springs. When the glue joint is dry, insert a dowel across the joint, clean the end, stain, and rub it with hard stopping wax.

For major work the back will need to be removed. The method for doing this is described on p. 80. All the breaks in the back splat need to be cut and cleaned before the splat is laid on a similarly grained piece of timber and the joints scribed across.

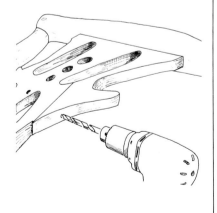
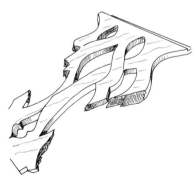

Once the joints have been made (this needs to be a slow and painstaking job) they should be, wherever possible, reinforced with dowelling. The new wood must then be levelled to the surface of the existing splat, and cut and carved to shape.

When replacing the splat into the frame of the chair, it is important for the top of the splat to be able to move freely in the groove of the chair top. Where it is considered important for the strength of the chair frame it should be glued at its centre and tacked at the edges with P.V.A. glue, which will move slightly as the splat shrinks or swells.

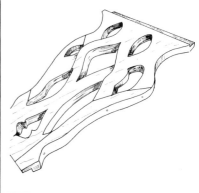

Back shrinkage

Shrinkage can often occur at the top of the back of a Hepplewhite-style chair, where the top rail is cut from a solid piece of timber. Shrinkage across the grain will cause the top rail to separate from the uprights. This can be remedied by removing the back splat, and shaving away the wood from its base.

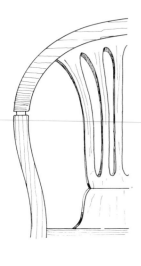

Ladder-back chairs

Where some of the rungs to the ladder back are missing, new ones will need to be made and sprung into position. These can be cut, shaped, and fitted without dismantling the chair frame, but before they are stained and finished, they should be steamed and bent over a mould. Although it is quite possible to bend and spring these in place without steaming, problems then arise when the new piece takes a different curve to the rest of the rungs. If the piece is bent to shape before being inserted, the task of springing it in place is made easier, and adjustments to its shape will not need to be made. For a description of the processes of steaming and boiling wood, see p. 167.

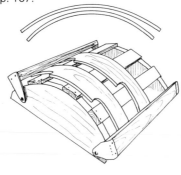

Replacing the hoop on a Windsor chair

For guidance on the bending of the hoop, see p. 167–8. The joints at the base of the hoop vary; some are tenoned into the arm rest, and others shaped to a taper and inserted into a tapered hole. For guidance on cutting and fitting the tenons see p. 153. It is very important to align the sticks correctly in the new back, and this should be done using spare dowel rods located in their seat holes, and taped or clamped against the back. Every stick should be mocked up and in position before any holes are drilled into the hoop. This prevents

unsightly irregularities from occurring in their distribution across the back of the seat. Use a brad point drill, started at right angles to the bow, then swung into the line of the stick once a start to the hole has been made.

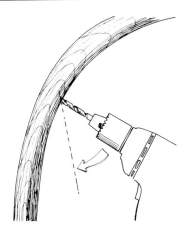

RAILS TO RUSHED SEATS

The rails that support rush seating are often badly weakened by worm, and only reveal their deterioration when they finally break. It is not possible to replace these without re-rushing the chair. I have worked on chairs where attempts have been made to extract the broken rail, and replace it by a dowel inserted through one leg, fed through the rushing, and lodged in the original rail hole in the other leg. This method results in loose rushing, a damaged leg top, and a very weak seat. The centre of the rail takes most of the stress; there is only a shearing effect at the join between the leg and the rail. The rail should therefore be stronger in the middle and thinner at the edges. Although the dowel may be no thinner than the original rail where it meets the leg, it is considerably weaker at the centre.

Rush seating can easily be

removed by slicing through the cross in the seat. Once the rushing is removed, the rails should be inspected, and any that seem weak should be replaced. These can be swiftly fashioned from ash, using an axe or drawknife, and the ends turned or shaped with a gouge.

Mark a line for a splicing cut at one end of the rail. At right angles to the

cut, bore a narrow hole to take a locating pin, and saw down the splice line. When assembling the joint, insert the pin into the hole, and clamp and tie the splice together.

When planning such a replacement operation, cut the rail slightly longer than needed, as the splicing cut tends to shorten it. For rushing see p. 216ff.

SPLIT CANE CHAIRS

The seats of these chairs are made from rattan vine, split and interlaced across the frame of the chair with the ends wedged in place. Where the framework is slightly worm-eaten, glue is used to supplement the wedges holding the cane. There is no great stress on any individual hole. When working on these chairs and preparing them for caning, it is best to repair any weak parts and replace those parts that are in doubt. Patches on the inside of the chair frame can be carried out in the normal way. Pieces should be made to fit well, and hold themselves in place by a slight dovetail effect in the edge of the join. They can be reinforced by drilling and inserting dowels through the patch into the main chair frame.

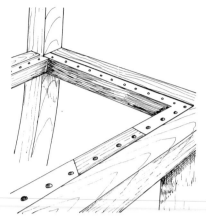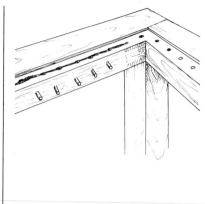

Where the row of holes has caused splits to run parallel to the holes, and there appears to be a likelihood of the edge pulling away, small dowels should be drilled and inserted between the cane holes to prevent the edge from breaking away.

UPHOLSTERED FRAMES

The same general remarks also apply to repairing the frame of an upholstered chair. These tend to be rather crude affairs, but nevertheless should be treated with the same care and attention that is spent on pieces that are on view.

15 Woodturning

This section gives an introduction to the tools and techniques that are required when replacing or repairing damaged turnings. A design for a simple woodturning lathe is included at the end of the section.

The lathe and the methods described are suited to turning spindles, legs, rails, bobbins, finials, etc. Bowls, goblets and large diameter turnings need to be fixed to a lathe face plate and turned with tools of a different design. Neither the lathe, nor the techniques described below, are suited to this.

EQUIPMENT

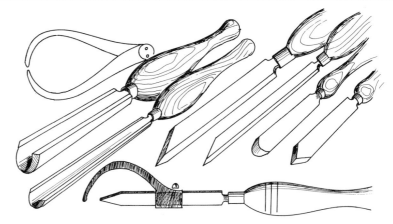

Turning tools are heavily made, and have long handles. They have heavy steel blades in order to dissipate the heat generated at the edge in the cutting process, and to prevent the tool from flexing and snapping if it should ever catch in the rotating workpiece. The long handles enable the turner to apply his body weight to the tool to prevent it from vibrating or chattering at the wood.

A selection of turning tools is necessary: two gouges, two skew chisels, a paring cutter and perhaps some scraping tools.

Skew chisels cut with a slicing action, and need to be sharpened on both sides, like a pen knife. They must be sharp, and should be stropped between cuts. Gouges and scrapers do not need to have sharp edges: these should be left with a burred and roughened edge, straight from the grindstone. In a very short period of time they can remove a lot of wood, and once their edge is dull they will tend to overheat. If there is a number of pieces to be turned, it is wise to switch off the lathe regularly and attend to the tools.

Other useful tools include calipers, thicknesser, centring jig and dowel cutter.

Safety

The only item of safety wear that a turner must use is his safety glasses. However, neckties and scarves should not be worn, and long hair should be tied back. It is prudent to wear an apron.

The tool rests must be firm and strong, and workpiece should be roughly balanced.

The tailstock centre should be firmly planted into the wood, and lubricated with oil whenever necessary.

Keep the hands away from the work, until the stock is turned to a cylinder. When roughing down, keep hands well back on the chisel, and the head slightly to one side of the cutting line.

SETTING UP

Select stock that is straight-grained and knot-free. Wood with a haphazard grain pattern is more difficult to turn than straight-grained wood. Knots may cause the chisels to bounce or chatter. Pieces to be turned should be square in section, with the corners roughly chamfered with an axe or chisel. Use a centre punch and hammer to mark the centres at each end of the wood. Place the wood against the head-stock, and tap the spindle into the endgrain with a hammer. Move the tailstock to the wood, and locate the centre in the centre punch mark. Tighten the tailstock and squirt a drop of oil to lubricate the centre.

Set the tool rest parallel to, and a short distance away from, the work-piece. Set the gear V-belt pulleys to moderate speed, and switch the motor on.

Hold the gouge very firmly in the manner illustrated.

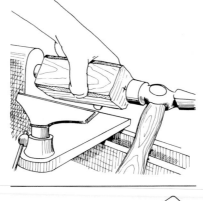

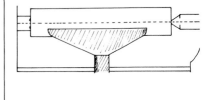

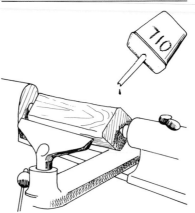

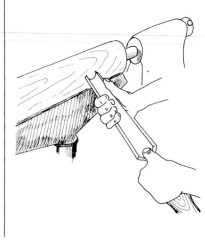

ROUGH SHAPING

Lean into the work, and make a series of slow stabbing cuts to remove the worst of the corners and unevenness. Change the hold, and run the gouge along the wood towards the headstock. Repeat this until the workpiece is reduced to a cylinder. N.B. Do not hurry this stage. Keep the motor running steadily. Do not dig the tool in, but adjust the cut until an almost continuous shaving is removed by the gouge as it is moved down the wood. Keep the hands behind the tool rest.

Stop the lathe, and inspect the work. The piece should be completely cylindrical.

Raise the tool rest so that it is just below the height of the top of the cylinder, return the gouge to its storage slot, and take up the large skew chisel. This is a cutting and not

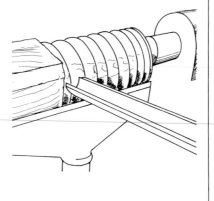

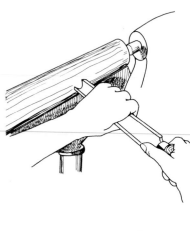

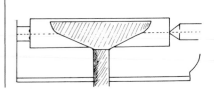

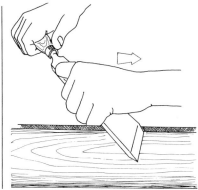

a scraping tool, and it is worthwhile practising the correct hold while the wood is stationary.

Start the lathe, and place the end of the skew chisel flat against the wood as it revolves. Rest the blade against the tool rest. Gently twist the chisel, until the bottom cutting edge touches the roughened wood, and removes a small shaving. Keep the chisel at exactly this angle, and bring it slowly along the wood. If the tool tends to chatter, lower the angle slightly, thereby reducing the bite of the chisel, and apply more pressure to the tool rest and less to the workpiece.

With a little practice the correct angle and hold will be mastered and the skew worked both away from and towards the body. Remember to press the side of the finger against the tool rest where it will act as a fence, giving the chisel a lateral stability as it moves along the turning.

Chatter occurs when the work-piece is pushed sideways out of true, or when the tool is removing too much stock too quickly. Once confidence is gained, pressure on the tool rest can be reduced. This will ease the movement of the chisel along the rest. If there is still a tendency for the chisel edge to dig into the tool rest, its edge should be slightly rounded.

A smooth and regular cylinder will result from the careful use of the skew chisel. Stop the lathe and inspect the work. This is still a roughing and sizing operation; the wood should be clean and round, with few (if any) marks of chatter.

The piece to be copied should be placed on the lathe tray, parallel and close to the work being turned. If several similar turnings are to be made, a marking stick can be made which will automatically transfer the main marks to the new wood.

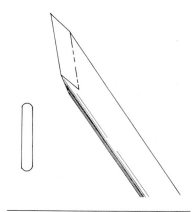
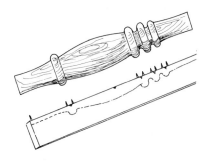

TURNING SHAPES

Gouges

Gouges are used for turning hollows or coves. They must be ground to a good rough edge, and the tool rest should be lowered to the first turning position, with the rest just below the centre line of the turning. The gouge must be held very firmly against the

rest, and its side canted up towards the shoulder of the proposed hollow. With the lathe at moderate speed, the tool is then pressed into the wood at the correct place. Its top edge makes the first cut and this effectively gives further support to the hands that are holding the gouge against the tool rest. The gouge can then be slipped into the wood, and

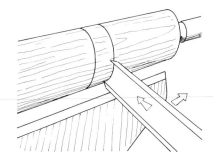

sideways into the deepest part of the hollow. It must never cut on both front edges at once. It can never be used to cut its way out of the hollow.

With the tool withdrawn, and canted the other way, a second similar, firm, jabbing and sliding cut is made, which should meet the previous cut at the bottom of the hollow.

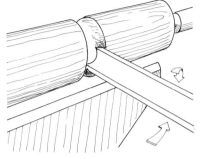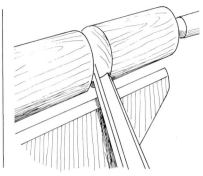

Skew chisel

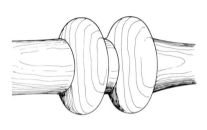

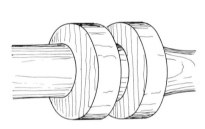

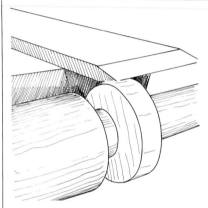

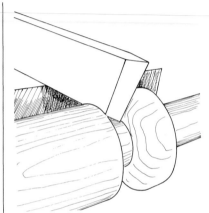

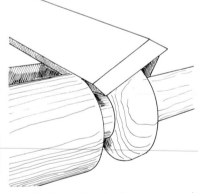

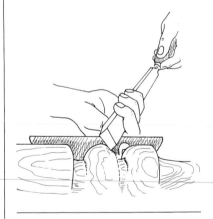

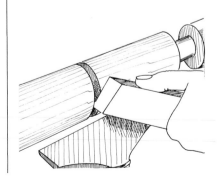

The skew chisel should be selected for cutting beads. Initial roughing for these should be done with a gouge or parting chisel. When this is done, switch off the lathe and raise the tool rest to the level of the top of the turning. Switch on the motor, and rest the small skew chisel on its side at highest point of the proposed bead. Rock the chisel sideways, and twist it. Without moving it along the rest, cut a curved shape on one side. Cuts should be made with the short point of the chisel. Return the chisel and carefully rest it at the highpoint again, and cut down the other side. Hold the chisel firmly to resist the tendency of the skew to cut back across the edge of the bead, ruining the work. More complicated cuts can be made to make balusters, etc.

simply by using both gouge and skew chisel. Neither tool, however, should ever be used to cut out of the wood. They must both be used to cut towards the centre, otherwise the workpiece will shatter.

The skew chisel can also be used inverted and resting on the tool rest. It must be introduced at right angles to the centre line of the workpiece, and is used for cutting clean sharp lines, V's, etc.

Parting chisel

The parting chisel is mainly used for removing the waste ends from the piece after the turning is completed, and for sizing the piece. Where really accurate work is required, a sizing gauge is fitted to the end of the chisel, which holds the chisel against the wood until the pre-set size is reached. This is very useful for making accurate end turnings for chair spindles, etc., but for most turning work a pair of calipers and a watchful eye are all that is required.

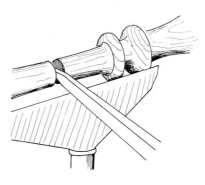

Scrapers

Scrapers should be used with the tool rest set to the centre line of the turning, and with the tool slightly canted downwards, away from the rotation of the wood. These tools are slow to use, and frequently leave a torn and rough finish. They are useful for turning tips to legs, where there is only part of a piece being turned (the original part needing no extra turning). In these conditions, it is impossible to use gouges or skew chisels, because they will be knocked out of place by the new wood.

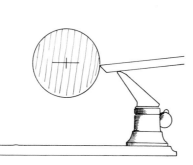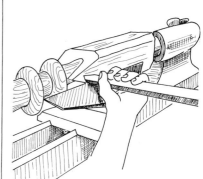

TURNING SPINDLES AND STICKS

Long, thin stock whips as it is turned, and so tends to cause chatter. Sticks should be worked by hand to an octagonal section before turning. When they are put between the centres, the gouge should be used to bring them to a cylinder. A different hold is required: the right hand holds the gouge by the blade, the handle steadied against the right forearm and the body, and presses the blade against the tool rest, while the left hand holds the gouge just behind the cutting edge and uses the palm of the hand to steady the work. No force need be directed against the

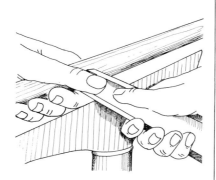

wood. Strength is used merely to hold the tool and wood together, not to plunge the gouge deep into the stick. A similar technique is employed with the skew chisel. No

fingers should be in front of the blade's edge, and the hand should brace the wood. High turning speeds should be avoided for this work, as it may cause burning to the skin.

CUTTING TAPERS

Once a cylinder has been cut, the degree of taper required can be set on the tool rest. The gouges and skew chisel are drawn along the tool rest in the normal way, except that the skew chisel will need to be tilted down as it reaches the thin end of the taper. Always work from the end with the large diameter towards the small diameter.

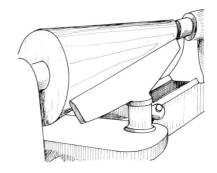

FINISHED TURNINGS

Once the turning is completed, the piece should be sanded whilst still in the lathe. Back some medium and some 220 grit paper with masking or brown plastic sticky tape. Cut a couple of strips from each about 1½ in. (4 cm) wide. Hold the medium grit in the way illustrated, and move it along the workpiece as the lathe is revolved at a moderate to high speed. Wear a face mask.

Use the 220 grit paper for the final sanding. With the parting tool cut the piece free from the waste or simply remove the work from the lathe, and brush the lathe and tray clean.

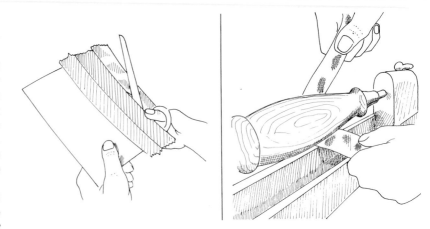

OFF-CENTRE TURNINGS

Curved chair rails are turned using four centres, instead of the normal two.

Curved chair backs

Once a template has been cut roughly to shape, the centres are marked out in the way illustrated. Mark the point where the axis of the two pairs of centres converge. This area should not be turned, but must be finished by hand.

Slower speeds are required for this slightly imbalanced turning.

A supporting stick should be tacked from the axis point to the

tailstock end while the headstock half is being turned. This will prevent the wood breaking under the end pressure of the tailstock, and the sideways pressure of the tool.

Once one end is turned, the piece is removed from the lathe, and the

supporting stick is removed and fixed to support the other end. The piece is then returned to the lathe, and the second set of centres used to turn the other end. One end should be fully turned and finished before the other is started. When

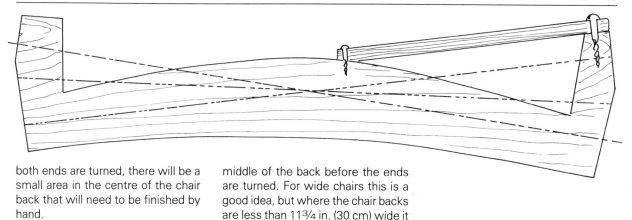

both ends are turned, there will be a small area in the centre of the chair back that will need to be finished by hand.

It may be necessary to use a third combination of centres to turn the middle of the back before the ends are turned. For wide chairs this is a good idea, but where the chair backs are less than 11¾ in. (30 cm) wide it is unnecessary.

A turned leg with a pad foot

Cut the leg to shape with a bandsaw or bowsaw and chamfer the square edges with a chisel. Mark the turning centres for the leg and for the foot with a centre punch and set the leg in the lathe using centres A A.

Shape the leg using gouges and a small skew chisel. Change the centres for A B and turn the foot. Take care that the tools do not stray onto the already finished turning on the leg.

Remove the wood from the lathe, and finish the part around the area C by hand.

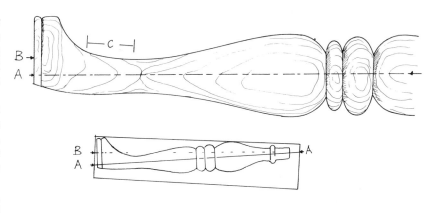

ACCESSORIES

Turning centre lathe guide

This jig enables the centre of a turned leg to be located when the original turning marks have been worn away, or obscured by a repair to the end of the leg.

The retaining screws should be sufficiently tight to hold the centre ring plate against the surface of the timber. The stock is rotated by hand in the lathe and tapped sideways until the piece is centred. Tighten the screws and remove the wood from the lathe. Tap a nail through the centre of the guide to mark the centre.

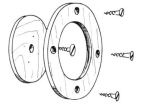

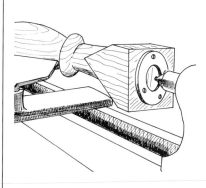

Remove the guide, punch the centre spot and return the timber to the lathe for turning.

Note: The guide only serves to help locate the centre, and should never be used to hold the piece while turning is attempted.

Calipers

Have several calipers hung on a board behind the lathe. They are used for measuring diameters of turnings. Satisfactory calipers can be fashioned from good quality ply, and pivoted around the nut, bolt and washer.

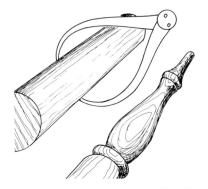

Dowelling cutter

A sharpened plane blade or gouge is clamped at the feed edge of the hole A, and arranged to make a tangential cut.

Dowelling wood should be straight-grained and knot-free, and prepared to an octagonal section. Work the cutter onto the dowel, place the dowel between the lathe centres, start the motor, hold the cutter firmly against the tool rest, and move it towards the headstock.

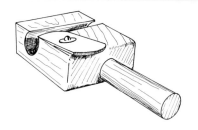

LATHE

A simple and rather limited lathe can be made in a restorer's workshop. Unlike a metal lathe, the woodworking lathe is not a precision tool. The only bearings are in the headstock. A spindle with a pulley and two bearings are all that will be needed. The tailstock, lathe headstock, bed, and tool rest can all be made of wood. The tailstock centre can be a simple pointed bar, or (even simpler) a coach screw. As long as the centres lie at equal heights to the bed of the lathe, and the whole affair is heavy and solid, this will be a perfectly serviceable tool. A washing machine or refrigerator motor will be quite adequate to drive the lathe.

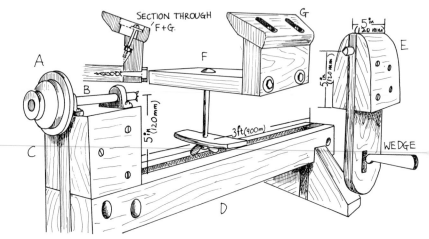

SECTION THROUGH F + G.

A V pulley drive to motor *B* spindle with two bearings *C* headstock assembly *D* lathe bed *E* tailstock *F* tool rest; coach bolt fits between timbers of lathe bed, and is tightened *G* rest can be moved up towards work by releasing bolts and sliding upwards; refasten bolts before use

16 Steaming and Laminating Timber

Prolonged boiling or steaming reduces the cellulose in the structure of the wood to a plastic state, making the wood pliable. If straight wood is then bent, held in shape, and allowed to cool, it will retain a bent shape.

For a workshop where occasional chair backs, hoops or arm supports need to be bent, a boiling tube is adequate. Where flat planks are to be bent, a steam box should be built. For very minor bending operations, a steam bag and hose can be used. A heavy polythene bag is enclosed over the piece to be bent, and a polythene tube fed into the bag. The neck of the bag is held in place by an elastic band, which also holds the end of the steam tube in place. The other end of the tube is heated and then pushed into the spout of the kettle.

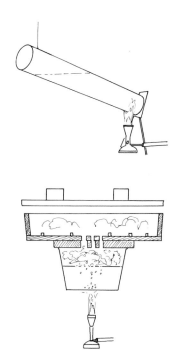

Leave a hole in the bottom of the bag to allow air and condensed water to escape.

Safety

Take sensible fire precautions. The steam box or boiling tube should be well supported. Wear heavy rubber gloves and an apron when handling hot timber. Make sure that there is easy and unobstructed access from the steaming arrangement to the mould.

WOODS

While many woods will bend after a thorough boiling, the woods normally used, because they are very easy to bend, are ash, oak and yew. The timber should be selected very carefully. It should be straight-grained, and free of knots or short-grain. It is a waste of time to try to bend second grade timber. The wood will take an irregular curve, and the result will be weak and ugly.

When choosing which side of the timber should be on the inside of the curve, arrange the wood so that it is bent as illustrated. Apart from the steam box or the boiling tube, very little equipment is required. Moulds should be made to hold the wood as

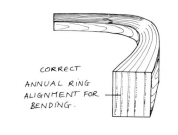

CORRECT ANNUAL RING ALIGNMENT FOR BENDING.

— SPRING BACK —

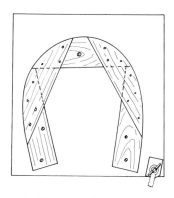

it cools. These need to be strong and designed with an extra degree of curve to compensate for the spring-back in the wood when it is released from the mould. Some suggestions for mould designs are illustrated below.

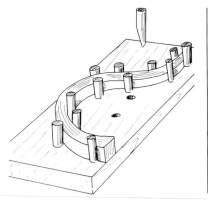

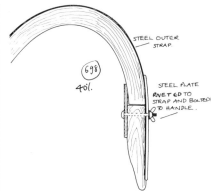

STEEL OUTER STRAP.

698
40l.

STEEL PLATE RIVETED TO STRAP AND BOLTED TO HANDLE.

Bending straps are also needed. When the wood is hot and moist (from the steam or boiling water) the fibres of the wood are amenable to compression but not to tension. The wood can be pressed around a mould but, without an outside bending strap, the outer edge of the wood will splinter. If a bending strap is used, all the force that is applied in the pulling of the timber goes into compressing the fibres of the wood. The strap with its tightly fitted end blocks prevents any stretching of the outer edge of the timber.

Bending straps are made from strips of thin gauge galvanised sheeting. End blocks should be bolted in place on the strap before the wood is boiled. If several pieces are to be bent in close succession, it is handy, but not necessary, to have several straps ready and set to size.

BENDING

Fresh-sawn or partly-seasoned wood is easier to steam than kiln-dried timber. Wood that is very dry should be planed to size with the corners lightly chamfered, and left to soak in a stream or tank for a couple of days. If the wood is to be boiled rather than steamed, this preparation is not necessary.

Place the timber in the boiling tube or steam box, and allow it to heat up. The length of time that the wood requires is dependent on the thickness of the timber, and the degree of bend desired. Chair backs made from 1¼ in. (30 mm) square ash, which have a bend or radius of about 10 in. (250 mm), should be boiled for about one hour, or steamed for the best part of a working day.

Before removing the wood from the steam-box or boiling tube, check that the moulds, bending straps, and clamps are all in place. Don the rubber gloves and apron, and remove the timber. Slip the bending strap over the wood (remember to fit it to the outside of the curve), place the wood over the mould and steadily ease it into shape. A steady pressure succeeds better than force applied jerkily. Once the wood begins to bend, it will slip into shape without a murmur. Considerable force may be needed, and if the mould, strap, or holding arrangements threaten to collapse under the stress, cease work, bend the wood straight, and place it back in the steam box or boiling tube. Reinforce the mould and start again.

Leave the wood to cool on the mould or, if more pieces are to be bent, brace across the sprung ends with string, and remove the wood to cool and set. When it is released, it will spring back slightly. You will have compensated for this by bending the wood to a greater curve than necessary. It is a good idea to overestimate the amount of spring-back in the wood, as it can always be bent straighter, but it cannot be forced cold into a tighter curve.

LAMINATING

This is a method of achieving a curved shape by bending and glueing together thin strips of wood and clamping them to dry on a shaped mould. This can be an alternative to steaming or boiling a piece of wood, the advantage being that the work is performed cold, and virtually no spring-back is experienced once the laminate is removed from the mould.

Tools

A circular saw, fitted with a tungsten-carbide-tipped blade to cut the strips of wood to size, and a good supply of G-cramps, are necessary for this operation. Use a slow drying, gap-filling glue.

Technique

Make a mould of the shape required, remembering that with laminating you only need a slight exaggeration of the final desired shape. It is useful to have a male and a female mould for compound curves. One of the two should be cut into sections and both should have facilities for clamping.

Choose clean, straight-grained timber and run it through the circular saw, cutting it into strips about ¼ in. (4 mm) thick. If a tungsten carbide tipped saw is used, the resulting saw cut should be good enough for immediate glueing; a traditional ripping blade will leave a rough cut that will have to be planed.

Apply the glue to the first stick and place it in the mould; continue until all of the pieces are in place, and the laminate is of the correct thickness.

Tighten the clamps in the middle of the mould and, working towards each end, pull the parts of the mould together, exerting as much pressure as possible to press the laminates together.

Wipe the edges with a cloth, allow it to dry, and plane and sand it to shape when the glue is fully cured.

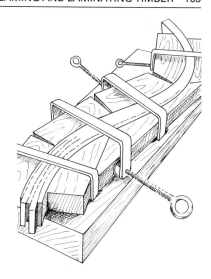

REPAIRING A BROKEN WINDSOR CHAIR HOOP

Repairing the broken hoop of a Windsor chair is rarely a straight-forward task, as the hoop is relatively flimsy, yet takes a lot of stress.

Technique

Mix an epoxy resin glue, and glue the broken ends of the hoop together. A splint arrangement will be required to hold the pieces while glueing. This splint should be held in place with a temporary fastening of whipping twine at each end. Push a two-part hard filler into the areas between the splint and hoop.

Select an appropriate repair wood: it should be clean and straight grained, and about half as thick again as the hoop. Cut into the hoop above and below the glued join, with dovetail angled cuts. If the split is on the outside of the hoop, cut a little beyond the half-way point in the hoop. The laminated build-up will be less noticeable on the inside of the hoop. Remove the waste between the cuts with a paring chisel, and insert a thin ⅛ in. (2-3 mm) slip of

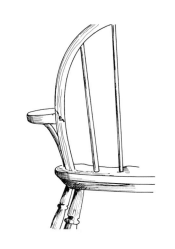

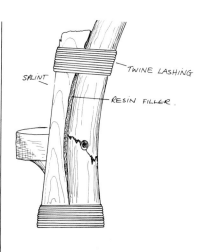

SPLINT

TWINE LASHING

RESIN FILLER.

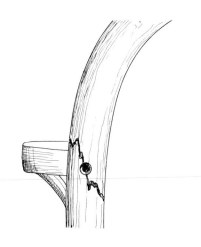

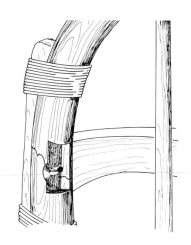

repair wood, angled to fit the dovetails at the ends. Push this in place firmly, withdraw it, glue it with epoxy resin glue, and clamp.

The next day a second piece can be inserted, longer than the first and overlapping it at each end. This should be clamped and glued. Continue this until the thickness has been rebuilt flush with the inside of the hoop.

Allow the laminates to harden. Fit a new splint on the inside of the hoop, and support it with two-part filler as before. Repeat the same process on the outside until the edge is reached.

When the glue joints are all dry, remove the splint and shape the inserts to the profile of the hoop.

This is a job requiring a lot of drying time but, provided that care is taken to align the first inserts with the grain, it is a simple task, and one which does not require much work time. Once the first insert is in place, the face of the piece can be used to steady and guide the paring chisel in its cuts for smoothing the bed of the following pieces. Disguising the work on most pieces is a simple matter, but where the chair has been bleached it is best to add a slight colouring to the glue.

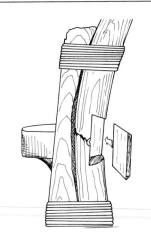
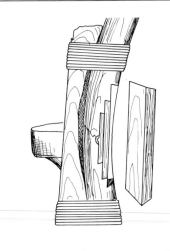
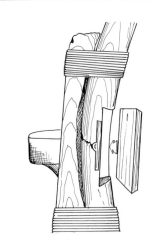
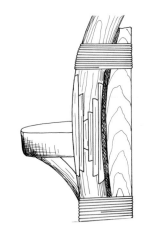

17 Finishing: Minor Work

Furniture that looks dull and in need of a clean often needs little more than a thorough application of a good quality wax. The best waxes to use for cleaning furniture are the slow-drying proprietary waxes. Apply the wax with a clean rag (buttons and zips removed!) and work the rag around and into all of the dirty areas.

A greater scouring effect can be achieved by applying the wax with a piece of fine wire wool. This should be rubbed gently over the surface. Take care not to cut away the under-lying finish. Once the wax has been applied, a very thin coating is left on the surface to dry. This should be burnished after a couple of hours.

When the piece has been cleaned, a brighter shine can be achieved by applying a thin coat of hard, quick-drying wax. This should be worked quickly and evenly over the surface, and wiped away with a lint-free rag before the residue is allowed to dry. Burnish immediately.

REVIVING A PIECE

If, after waxing, the piece still looks tired and dull, it may be possible to revive the finish. The finish on a piece of timber enhances the beauty of the wood, and provides us with a window to look into the depths of the wood. If the finish is old and crazed, or slightly decomposed, it will interpose a barrier like a dirty window between the viewer and the wood. Wax will not revive such a finish, but it should instead be rubbed all over with a reviving solution.

A simple but effective reviver is made from equal parts of methylated spirits, turpentine, and linseed oil, with a dash of vinegar added. The

solvents each have sufficient bite to penetrate the finish, but insufficient to strip it or lift it.

Reviver should be wiped over the piece and into all of the corners. Use a soft rag. If it is allowed to remain on

the surface for about half an hour, it will continue to restore the finish. Wipe the surface clean and leave it to dry. Follow with wax. Really dirty pieces of furniture can be revived with a generous application of reviver, wiped on with 0000 wire wool. Take care not to rub away the finish and leave unsightly dull spots.

Where specks of paint, glue or other marks are spattered over the surface of the piece, they can usually be lifted clear by the cautious use of a very sharp blade. This is more effective than wire wool, as the latter may tend to damage the area around the spot. Any seriously damaged areas can be restored by rubbing with shellac.

HIDING SMALL REPAIRS

The hiding of patches needs to be done very carefully and methodically. For full details of patching a piece see p. 114. The patch (if it doesn't match exactly) should appear lighter in tone and colour than the surrounding timber, and it should reflect light in the same way. If the patch is darker, it should be bleached by applying a few droplets of household bleach from a syringe onto the unfinished surface. This should be neutralised and allow to dry.

COLOURING

A fine sable-haired brush, a selection of artist's-quality watercolour paints, and a little soap and water are needed. On patches of less than ½ sq. in. (2 sq. cm) stain will not be needed. A fairly dry mixture of water-colour paints should be mixed to match the colour of the surrounding timber, but lighter in tone. This is because the wood will be darkened by the finish when it is applied over the colour. Paint brush strokes should be short and with the grain. Small areas between brush strokes should be left untouched.

If the patch is greater than about ½ sq. in (2 sq. cm) then stain can be used. For a description of the various staining and fuming techniques see p. 179ff. The rag applying the stain should be slightly damp; only the very minimum of stain should be allowed to cover the join between the patch and the main wood. If the stain is allowed to penetrate into the end fibres at the join, it will be very difficult to hide the line.

Once the initial colouring by brush or stain is completed and allowed to dry (this can be hastened by placing an inspection lamp on the surface over the patch and allowing the heat of the light bulb to warm the surface), a thin rubber or brush stroke of shellac should be applied to the patch. This will fix the colour, and bring the wood to its true colour. If the initial work is too dark, remove it by rubbing with fine wire wool dampened with a few drops of methylated spirits. Once the correct shade of groundwork colouring has been achieved, the watercolours can be used to touch in the grain and age marks. These should never be over-done; a dark patch is generally more eyecatching than a light patch, and a light patch can be darkened without stripping away the previous work.

If parts of the join between the patch and the timber remain visible, there are a number of devices that serve to confuse the eye and camouflage the join. Never be hasty in choosing the appropriate device. Any mark that is made on the patch must also be present elsewhere on the surface of the timber. Study the mark, and reproduce it exactly on the edge of the patch. Lines, blots, or subtle shading are best done with conviction.

Once the final paint marks have been made, they should be fixed with an application of shellac. The appropriate finish should then be built up in the way described on pp. 189-99. If the piece has a varnish finish, the varnish should be used for the final coats, etc.

REMEDIES FOR SURFACE BLEMISHES

Pits, scratches and holes in the surface

Conspicuous surface blemishes should be cut out and patched, or accepted and left. This is not an easy decision to make, and it is best to be aware that once a repair is finished the furniture is often so transformed by the work and care lavished upon it, that what were once regarded as blemishes become eyesores.

Small indentations (or large ones where they are not so obvious) should be remedied in one of the following ways.

Resin filler

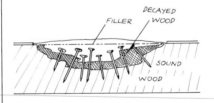

Commercial two-part fillers, or epoxy resin and fine sawdust, are suitable for covering large areas of wood, provided that they are well keyed in place. A suitable key can be provided by driving tacks into the recess to be filled, making sure that the head of the tack is well below the level of the finished surface. Stick masking tape around the perimeter of the depression. Mix and apply the filler so that the surface of the filler is above the level of the surrounding timber and can be chiselled and sanded down.

Once the filler is dried, the masking tape can be carefully peeled away. This will leave the surrounding wood clean and permit the timber to be sanded down. Two-part fillers can be smoothed with a damp knife, prior to hardening.

If the piece is to be stripped, sanding need not be quite so thorough, as the stripper will remove much of the surplus filler.

Commercial fillers are hard to colour, and have a very lifeless quality. The painting-in of the water-colour needs to be subtle and delicate to give the desired effect. Best results are achieved by building the colour and tone gradually, and fixing each coat with a fairly generous film of transparent shellac; this helps to give a translucent effect. Always start light and finish dark.

Wax and resin fillers

These can be made by the restorer and stored when not in use. Variations in hardness can be achieved by adding resin and shellac flakes to the molten wax (see p. 113). The more resin, the harder the stopping, and the more translucent it becomes. The procedure for making the filler is as follows.

Manufacture a simple saucepan from a round tobacco tin and a piece of dowel. Melt a small quantity of beeswax over a low flame, and add dry colours to give the desired colour. A pinch of crushed tree resin, and a flake or two of shellac is added to give hardness. Where woods are soft, or where movement in the timber is likely to occur, it is best to use a softer wax.

Pour the stopping into a mould

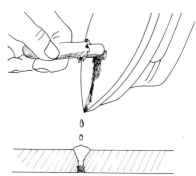

made from aluminium kitchen foil, and leave it to cool.

The stopping can be rubbed into a crack cold and the area cleaned with fine wire wool, or it can be melted with a smoothing iron and dripped into the crevice that needs filling (see p. 113). Ram a plug of cold wax or other stopping into the hole to

provide the wax with a foundation to settle on. If the wax has difficulty in adhering to the surface of the piece, the heating iron can be used to touch the timber for a moment to heat it up, and provide a ready key for the wax.

Clean the wax with a chisel or razor blade, and smooth it with wire wool when it is cool.

Shellac burning-in stick

This is an operation that requires practice. A selection of burning-in sticks is needed, a curved but flexible burning-in knife, and a spirit lamp. The knife is held in the spirit flame with its concave face to the flame, and heated until a shellac stick touching its surface will melt and run. If the knife is too hot, the shellac will sizzle and burn, too cold and it will stick to the knife.

When the knife has reached the correct temperature, the stick is pushed against the tip of the knife where a bead of shellac will form. Reheat the knife and slip its point into the scratch or depression. Agitate the knife to remove the shellac. More should be added with the knife, until the crack is filled level to the surrounding surfaces. Clean the knife by heating it and wiping it with a rag. Then reheat it, and draw it gently

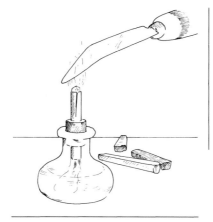

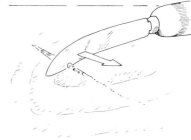

down the crack, forcing shellac into the crack, and carrying away any surplus. It is important that the knife is kept moving as it works across the shellac: any hesitation with the hot knife may damage the surrounding polish.

When the shellac is cool it can be worked down with a 400-600 grit paper backed with a wood block.

Graining effects can either be painted on or, by swapping coloured sticks as the crack is filled, a mottled grain-like appearance can be reproduced in the filler.

TREATMENT FOR SURFACE MARKS

Mark	Cause	Treatment
Black marks	Ink, paint, burns or rust. Sometimes also caused by water penetrating finish and lying beneath.	*Ink*. Remove finish. Drip small quantity of domestic bleach, allow to dry. Neutralise with water when mark is removed. Recolour and polish. *Burns/rust*. Scrape away to find depth of mark. Fill with filler or patch. *Water*. Strip affected area, allow to dry. Bleach, neutralise and colour.
White marks	Surface discoloration caused by shellac finish attacked by spirits, water, or heat.	Remove decayed polish by rubbing with fine glass paper. Colour if necessary, build up new finish. Discoloration may be reversed by rubbing area with oil/meths mix. Alternatively, rub meths onto the spoilt area, tip the surface vertical and light the meths at the *bottom* to burn up and over damaged area. Translucency is often restored in this way, but surface will need to be rubbed down and built with shellac again.
Decayed finish, crazing, flaking, cracking	Poor surface preparation.	Remove finish, and start again.
Stain bleeding into finish	Stain and finish having same solvent – no sealer applied.	Remove finish, restain. Then use sealer that has a different solvent than stain. Lightly sand and refinish.
Surface remains tacky	Solvent spilled onto it, or natural oils in wood preventing full curing of finish.	Wash finish with reviver; if this doesn't work, remove finish, wash timber with petrol (out of doors) and seal, using method described on p. 177.
	Poor quality finishing materials.	Strip off and buy new better-quality finishes.
Stain becoming faded and patchy	All stains are fugitive but tend to fade evenly and gracefully. Dramatic changes probably caused by traces of bleach or oxalic acid left in wood, attacking stain.	Strip away finish and neutralise with water or borax. Allow to dry. Refinish.

18 Finishing: Major Work

STRIPPING FURNITURE

Many pieces of furniture entering the restorer's workshop need to be stripped. There are, of course, pieces that have a good finish and a fine patina, and these should be respected. Many pieces, however, despite being of good quality, seem to have spent years in garages or farm sheds and, when the woodwork part of the restoration has been completed, will need to be stripped in order to reveal their full beauty.

There are several methods of stripping furniture available to the restorer.

Proprietary brand stripper

Always follow the manufacturer's instructions when using these dangerous chemicals. Unless otherwise stated, they can be used on all woods and will remove most finishes.

Safety
The room must be well ventilated, with a non-slip floor and a supply of clean fresh water at hand. The restorer should wear protective goggles, heavy rubber gloves (extending up the arms if possible) and a working apron. On no account should the restorer smoke while stripping furniture. Keep children, animals, and any finished items of furniture well clear of the operation. Any splashes of stripper that fall on the skin should be washed off immediately. If stripper is rubbed into the eyes, bathe them immediately in clean water. Fumes cause skin and lung irritation, so try to avoid breathing them.

Technique
If the piece of furniture is covered in thick layers of paint or varnish, it should be stripped one face at a time, moving the piece so that the face being stripped is horizontal. Remove doors and drawers and strip them separately.

Decant the stripper into a small lidded plastic bucket and apply it by brush. Where there is a lot of paint or varnish to be removed, wrap the furniture in plastic sheets, or drape damp hessian over it, to prevent the stripper from drying out. While the stripper is working, remove the sheet from time to time and agitate the surface using a short, coarse-hair brush. This is particularly necessary for cleaning awkward mouldings and carvings.

When the stripper has completed its task (this cannot be hurried) the covering sheet should be removed and washed under a tap, and the decomposed finish removed from the flat panels of the piece with a paint scraper. This should be followed with a vigorous cleaning along the grain with No. 3 wire wool.

Areas of paint that refuse to be shifted by the stripper can be carefully dislodged using a piece of pointed or chisel-ended stick.

Apply a second coating of stripper.

Clean this with No. 3 wire wool and continue as before, until all the finish has been removed from the wood.

The instructions for neutralising the stripper will be written on the container. If there is a choice between water or methylated spirits, choose the latter, as it is quick drying and does not raise the grain of the wood. Apply the neutraliser with wire wool (00 grade) and wipe it clean with a clean dry cloth.

Caution

Once the stripping and the neutralising of the furniture has been completed, leave it on one side to dry. Return to it occasionally to see if any stripper that has accumulated in a moulding or rebate is dribbling down the face of the piece. If the stripper is allowed to remain on the surface of the bare wood it will darken it. Scrub the area clean and re-neutralise with meths.

After neutralising a piece with methylated spirits a white deposit may be left on the surface. This mark is left by the rag used to wipe away the meths, after it becomes saturated with the meths and finish residue. If it is allowed to dry it may be difficult to remove later, and so should be rubbed off with wire wool. Clean, dry rags should be used when neutralising and the problem can be avoided to some extent by neutralising with refined meths, known as finishing spirit.

Caustic soda stripping

Safety

Fully protective clothing must be worn, including goggles. Have a large basin of clean water handy, for bathing caustic burns. Great care needs to be taken in handling a caustic soda solution, not only in the application of the chemical, but also in the handling of other tools, trestles, door knobs etc., to prevent the inadvertent spread of the caustic around the workshop.

Technique

Many woods will burn when cleaned with caustic, and although the darkening effect of the soda can, to some degree, be reversed by repeated washings of bleach, the life and natural colour of the wood never returns. Pine can be stripped with caustic without fear of darkening of the wood, but a prolonged soaking will bleach out the natural oils in the wood and leave it rather drab and lifeless. Test other woods before

stripping them. With some woods, such as oak (which will darken if soaked in caustic) it is possible to work very quickly and, by keeping the oak's contact with the soda to a minimum, to avoid seriously burning the surface. As caustic soda dissolves Scotch glue, carcass pieces, veneered pieces, and any that are held together by Scotch glue should not be immersed in caustic. Caustic can be used cold, or mixed with warm water. The techniques remain the same, but warm caustic works faster. Never mix caustic with hot water.

Add the caustic crystals to the cold or warm water. A concentration of about 1 lb of crystals to 1 gallon (500 g to 4 litres) of water is quite adequate for stripping. Stir the crystals until they dissolve.

Stand the piece of furniture out of doors on a waterproof plastic sheet, with logs or boards around its edge to prevent the caustic trickling away. Remove doors, drawers and

handles, then sponge or ladle the caustic onto the furniture. This will cause the paint to wrinkle and lift. Continue this operation, accelerating the action of the caustic by gently agitating the paint with a fairly soft-haired scrubbing brush. Try not to spray the caustic.

Finally, the piece should be neutralised by washing it in a weak solution of acetic acid. If small white crystals form in cracks and corners after the piece has been left to dry, wash it again with water, then re-neutralise.

Pieces of furniture that are caked in paint can be left with a porridge-like mixture of caustic and sawdust (or any other neutral binder), spread thickly over the surfaces. This will loosen the paint and prepare it for the caustic bath. Always cover these mixtures with a sheet to prevent drying, and to prevent people from accidentally brushing against the caustic and damaging their clothes.

New peel-off strippers

These are effective and can save a lot of time. When selecting a particular brand of stripper, make sure to choose one that will not discolour the wood. These strippers are rather

expensive, and still leave the restorer with a considerable amount of cleaning up to do afterwards.

Instructions for use are always printed on the packets, and should be followed.

Stripping with methylated spirits

This is only effective on shellac-based, meths-soluble finishes. Wear gloves, and extinguish all naked flames in the workshop. It is extremely dangerous to smoke when using meths or finishing spirits.

Remove doors and drawers (as for all stripping operations) and work on them separately.

Decant the methylated spirits into a plastic tub, and take a wad of 00 wire wool. Work quickly, one surface at a time. Apply the meths with the mop, scrub vigorously, then wipe clean.

It is possible to work back a surface to a cleaner underlying layer, and if it is dried quickly after the application of the meths, it can be sanded lightly and used as the basis for a new finish coat.

Take care to prevent the meths from running down the sides of the piece, as this may cause the finish to soften and necessitate a deeper cutting back in that area.

Meths need not be neutralised, but the newly cut-back finish should be left to harden. Rub the surface lightly with clean 000 wire wool or fine sandpaper, and dust with a clean dry rag. This method of stripping is only worthwhile where there is a chance that part of the original finish can be retained as a groundwork for further polishing.

CLEANING AND PREPARING FOR STAINING AND FINISHING

Once the task of stripping and neutralising the piece of furniture has been completed, it should be prepared for finishing. Despite the scrubbing action of the wire wool,

the piece may still appear to be rather dull and grubby.

On an old piece of furniture, a mottled patination caused by modest accumulations of dirt beneath a finish can look right. However, it is often better to cut through the dirt by washing the piece in a solution of oxalic acid (see p. 179).

Dealing with greasy and oily surfaces

Surfaces that have been soaked in engine or cooking oil present recurrent problems, even after they are stripped. Initially the dark discolouration under the finish will be removed by the stripper but, within days, the patch will reappear and begin to ooze oil or grease.

The problem in this case is how to remove the oil or, if that is impossible, how to stabilise it to prevent it from welling through a refinished surface.

Treatment for oily surface
The piece of furniture must be moved outside and thoroughly scrubbed with petrol and wire wool. As much of the oil and grease as possible should be leached out before beginning the finishing process. Normal safety considerations apply: wear protective apron and gloves, try to avoid breathing the fumes, and don't smoke.

Stabilising the oil
You will need a small quantity of good quality oil varnish (not polyurethane), white spirit, and some paint driers. Dissolve a tablespoon of varnish to a cupful of white spirit, and add half a teaspoon of paint driers. Wash this liquid over the surface and, after a few moments, wipe clean.

Allow this to dry and repeat this process daily. Lightly sand the piece between coats. Gradually add varnish to the mixture and reduce the amount of spirit and paint driers. A surface build up can only be begun when the amount of white spirit and paint driers in the mixture is minimal, otherwise the finish will not harden properly.

A fine and beautiful varnish finish will result from this process, which can be rubbed down and waxed, or brought to a high gloss in the normal way.

Awkward finishes

Occasionally one has to deal with pieces of furniture that have linoleum, formica, oilcloth or other impermeable materials glued to their tops. These present real problems for any restorer who needs to remove them. Unfortunately, there does not seem to be an easy way of doing this. Keep the removal processes clean. Do not attempt to dissolve the glue before a thorough and exhaustive attempt has been made to lift the material from the surface. Remove the material (by tearing away the oilcloth, levering up the formica and by pulling and chiselling the lino). Clean as much of the surface as possible with scrapers, chisels, and old plane blades, until only the glue remains on the surface, exposed and ready for stripping.

Try to remove the glue with stripper before introducing petrol or other highly toxic and inflammable solvents. If these have to be used, make sure that the work is carried out in the open where the fumes will present fewer hazards to the worker.

Sanding by hand

Where furniture is badly marked or torn by use, or if the grain has been scuffed in the cleaning processes, it will have to be sanded before being stained and finished.

Sandpaper

Sandpaper is sold in various cutting grades. The coarseness of the grit is referred to by a number printed on the back of the paper. The higher the number, the finer the grit (this does not apply to emery cloth, which uses a different system). A workshop will need a range of papers from 90 grit for rough sanding to 400 for very fine work. Do not economise by re-using worn paper for fine sanding work. Paper that has been used can be cleared by flicking the back of the sheet, but once it is worn or clogged it should be discarded.

Initial sanding passes should be at an angle to the direction of the grain, never with the grain or across it. Coarse grit sandpaper should be backed by a cork or felt-faced block, and worked gently and evenly over the surface. Follow with finer grit

papers, each worked in the same way, but altering the angle of the cut each time the paper is changed, to bring the cutting strokes of the block parallel with the grain when working the final passes. If the piece is to be stained, do not use paper finer than 120 grit, or the sanded finish will be so smooth that the stain will not penetrate the wood fibres. This does not apply if the piece is to be fumed or stained with chemical stains.

When preparing for the application of water stain, or water-based chemical stains, dampen the surface of the wood to raise the grain, then sand before applying the stain.

Electric sanders

Rotary disc sanders

Never use disc sanders for smoothing any exposed surface. They leave a very uneven finish which is difficult to remedy.

Drum sanders

These are cylinders of sponge, with a sanding belt wrapped tightly around them, rotated by an electric drill. Wear a face mask when using one of these, as they work very efficiently, and send clouds of dust into the air. These are useful tools, provided one does not want a perfectly flat finish. Unlike disc sanders, they do not leave unsightly radial scratches on the surface. They are very useful for cleaning rough and worn surfaces.

Orbital sanders

These are essentially motorised sanding blocks. They are very efficient finishing tools, producing a fine finish. Inspect the face of the sandpaper attached to the pad of the sander for any signs of tearing, foreign matter or accumulations of sawdust which might affect the

cutting action of the paper. Final finishing is best done by hand, to avoid the very small circular scratches that are imperceptible on the clean wood surface but clearly revealed when the stain is applied.

When sanding is completed, brush and then blow off the dust.

BLEACHING

Bleaching is a chemical process which lightens the tone of a piece of timber. Some woods bleach well, others may require many applications of bleach before the desired colour is achieved. There are three types of bleaches, and the techniques for using them are as follows.

Household bleach

This also has a fairly short shelf-life. For removing small stains it is most effective if it is carefully dripped onto the wood. For larger areas (table tops, etc.) it should be applied, with the grain, in long, regular sponge strokes. Wear rubber gloves and ensure plenty of ventilation because the fumes from the bleach are very irritating and unpleasant. Domestic bleaches should be neutralised with water.

Two-part bleach

This is very powerful. It is stored and applied in two separate parts. The shelf life is short – about six months – but can be slightly prolonged by storing the bleach in a cool dark place.

The instructions for using this bleach are always clearly marked on the labels of the containers, and

Oxalic acid

Rubber gloves, an apron and goggles should be worn when applying the acid. When sanding a bleached area, wear a face mask. Work should be carried out in the open, or in a well-ventilated room.

Technique

Dissolve oxalic crystals in cold or warm water to make a saturated solution. Add water and stir, then test the acid by brushing it onto a corner of the furniture to check its

should be followed. The first part of the bleach is applied to the timber and allowed to soak into the fibres. While this is still damp the second part is applied, causing the wood to turn white. It may be impossible to bleach some oily, heavy woods like ebony and rosewood, but most will succumb to the treatment. Neutralise as instructed.

cleaning effect. For bleaching, the acid should be very strong, and warm water should be used. For cleaning stripped furniture it can be weaker.

Brush the acid onto the piece of furniture and use a sponge to distribute it evenly over the surface. Once the dirt has been cut away, the surfaces can be wiped dry.

Neutralise the acid with a solution of bicarbonate of soda. When the piece is dry, it can be sanded smooth. Wear a face mask. The dust from a piece that has been washed with oxalic acid is harmful and will cause lung irritation.

FUMING

The fuming process involves the use of ammonia gas, which will darken timbers containing tannic acid when they are exposed to the fumes. Oak and chestnut are particularly easy to fume, and can be turned from their newly cut pale yellow or white to a rich dark grey, black or greeny-brown. Most other woods can also be fumed provided they are adequately primed with tannic acid. The advantage of fuming is that no colouring pigments are used to achieve a dramatic change in colour, and the grain remains clear and unmuddied.

Safety

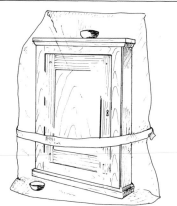

INSPECTION SLIT, CUT, THEN SEALED WITH TAPE.

TAPE TO COVER JOIN BETWEEN BAGS.

Ammonia is purchased in liquid form which evaporates to form a heavy gas, leaving a residue of water. This gas is very unpleasant, and can cause temporary blindness and severe breathing difficulties if inhaled. Handle ammonia with great care. Pieces to be fumed should be carefully contained within a pipe or some clear polythene bags from which the gas should be unable to escape; this should only be opened outside, or at night just before closing the workshop. Do not breathe in the fumes, or look into the container that holds the ammonia. Gloves should be worn when handling pieces that have been removed from the gas bag.

Technique

Some woods, such as oak and chestnut, contain a large amount of tannic acid and will readily react with the gas and turn colour. Other woods with less tannic acid, like mahogany and elm, will only change colour slightly. Those woods that do not contain significant quantities of tannic acid will not change their colour at all, unless the wood is first primed with tannic or pyrogallol acid. The strength of the solution and the length of time that the piece stays in the ammonia gas determine the final colour of the wood.

Make experiments with different strength solutions to discover what range of colours and tones are available through fuming. Mark the strength of the solutions and the woods that they should be used with on the bottles.

Remove metal fittings, and punch nails below the surface of the wood (unless one desires a blackened stain around the nail to give an aged appearance). Wash the furniture with warm water to prime the timber to take the acid, which should then be flooded onto the wood. Spread the acid with a sponge, so that all parts are covered. Once the acid has had a chance to soak in, wipe away the excess with a sponge.

Leave the wood to dry; place it in the fuming chamber, and leave it to change colour. As ammonia is a heavy gas, lengths of timber should be laid horizontally; tall pieces of furniture may need to be inverted sometime during the fuming process.

Inspect the colour of the piece at regular intervals, and change the ammonia every 12 hours or so. Most jobs will not require more than a few hours of fuming, but where the fuming needs to penetrate deep into the wood, the piece should be removed from the ammonia each day and more tannic or pyrogallol acid added to the wood. It should then be replaced in the chamber with fresh ammonia and resealed.

In this way a clean and pure colour change can be achieved, penetrating deep into the piece of wood. Newly sawn cherry, which is a pale orange or white/green colour, can be turned a rich iridescent brown/red. Yew wood, which is naturally pale pink or orange when freshly cut, can be turned a rich brown. Yew, however, is a very dense wood, and whereas cherry or oak can be fumed to a depth of ³⁄₈ in. (7 mm) or so, the colour change on yew remains superficial. When fuming, it is often worthwhile to add a few extra pieces of wood to fume. These can then be stored in the woodstore, ready for use.

Fuming can also be used to colour new wood that has been joined to old, although care should be taken to ensure that the original wood is not significantly darkened by the ammonia. Oak tips to old oak legs can be fumed simply. If the original oak legs are already a rich dark brown, then the ammonia is unlikely to affect them, yet the new part will rapidly assume the colour of the old, and adjustments in the colour of the tip can be made by adding small quantities of pyrogallol or tannic acid. A similar system can be used with yew, cherry, elm or pine. Only the

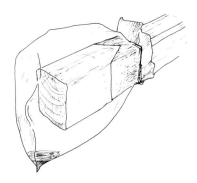

new wood, not the old, should be covered by the acid.

To provide tonal variation on the timber, or to inhibit the effect of the ammonia (on chestnut, for instance, where there is a lot of tannic acid present) the surface, or part of the surface, can be washed with borax or another alkali, which will tend to neutralise the acid present in the timber. This will produce subtle surface variations in tone that, over a large area, give the effect of weathering or bleaching by sunlight.

Once the piece has been fumed and is withdrawn from the gas bag, it should be taken outside and allowed to exhale its awful fumes. Pieces that have been thoroughly fumed may take several days to lose their smell, but most pieces that have only been fumed for an hour or so will lose their smell very quickly.

Sometimes, if it has been soaked in tannic acid, a blackish-purple deposit will discolour the surface of the wood once it is fumed. This can be removed by rubbing the purple parts with a wad of wire wool soaked in methylated spirits.

If the piece of furniture was already finished before the fuming was started (the ammonia gas will penetrate through many finishes) it should be left to air, and the surface rubbed down with reviver. This will kill the smell of ammonia.

AGEING

The appearance of age is given by a subtle balance between the colour of a piece of furniture, its wear and surface texture, and variations in colour. In order to reproduce a convincing effect of age, all of these elements need attending to. The ageing processes should, for the most part, be tackled in order.

Wear

The effect of wear can easily be reproduced with the aid of a spoke-shave, drum sander and strips of sandpaper backed by plastic sticky tape. Areas should be cut down, hollowed, and smoothed. The guiding principle should be to work the signs of wear in places where it is likely to occur. On antique chair and table stretchers, this can be carried out with freedom and style, but at no point should the marks be overdone or exaggerated.

Where knots occur in places likely to be worn, they can be used to emphasise the worn surrounding timber. Soft wood around the knot can be eased away, and the knot left

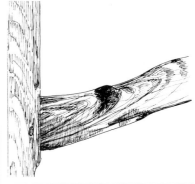

Areas of wear – front rail, front lower side rails. There will be less wear at the back and inside of the chair frame. Back rest will be worn and rounded

very slightly proud. On table stretchers, mouldings can be worn away completely, but only where it is possible and likely that shoes once rested. This is entirely a matter of observation and taste. It should be remembered that, as the piece is renewed, it will lose its derelict air and overworn parts may begin to be an embarrassment to the restorer.

Texture

Texture should be applied to the replaced parts, to break the smooth, clean surfaces that result from the sanding and shaving. Various implements can be used, and are illustrated on p. 16.

Very careful observation should reveal the extent of the variation in texture in the piece, and this must be faithfully reproduced in the new work. No new part should be smoother than any old part, nor should any be more battered than the worst part of the original work.

Remember that there has always been a relationship between texturing forces, and the smoothing effects of wear. This balance should be evinced in the new work.

Woodworm

Woodworm marks usually conform to a pattern. If they occur elsewhere in a piece, they should also be present in the new work. The patterns made by the woodworm should be studied. They seem to like the sapwood of timber (often found at the edges of pieces of wood); they infest small areas in some woods, but attack others apparently indiscriminately. Much of their activity takes place below the surface of the timber, but signs of the activity are revealed where the roofs to their tunnels collapse. Sometimes they are exposed as having been working across the grain; more frequently, they work along the soft wood between the grain markings of the timber, and cut through these at right angles to join other tunnels nearby.

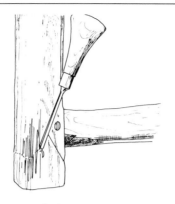

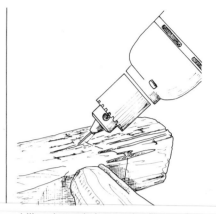

Once studied and remembered, the pattern left by the worms can be copied.

Major grain excavations should be carved using a very thin veiner gouge. These can then be followed using a panel pin held in the chuck of an electric drill, with its point snipped off. This gives a roughness to the deep cuts that adds authenticity. The

drill and panel pin can also be used to indicate the path of the sub-surface tunnels. Worm holes can be made by hitting the infected part with a stick impregnated with nails.

It is neither desirable nor necessary to cover new work in this way; a few judiciously chosen areas, convincingly executed, will suffice.

Attention to areas of grain filler

Flat areas of grain filler should always be given a surface texture that corresponds to the texture of the surrounding timber. This can be done with a variety of tools that can be scraped across the surface of the timber. Coarse sandpaper, handled carefully, can make very effective slight grain marks that are just sufficient to give a gentle texture. Nails, chisels, and broken hacksaw blades can all be used.

STAINING

The timber in most pieces of furniture over 60 years old tends to be much darker in tone and richer in colour than fresh-sawn wood available direct from a timber yard. This is an effect of age, shared by most woods, except those that stand for long periods in strong sunlight. This darkening effect is not a superficial colouring. In many cases the deepening of tone extends far below the surface of the wood, and gives the wood the lustrous and glowing quality associated with antiques. It is a mistake to attempt to achieve this effect with stain, unless the area to be stained is very small and insignificant. Heavy applications of

stain tend to darken the timber unevenly. Soft parts of the grain or end grain soak in the stain, while harder parts do not. As stain is applied, a barrier of pigment begins to build up in the surface of the timber, and this dirties and then destroys the reflective quality of the wood. The result is a caricature of the original wood, and rarely looks attractive.

Chemical stains are less offensive in this respect, and can be used very successfully. The best way to give a piece the darkness that comes with age is to fume it (as described on p. 179). This takes the colour well below the surface of most timbers without reducing its translucence.

Surfaces should be clean and free

of grease and glue marks. Sanded surfaces should not be so smooth that they resist the stain. Carefully remove any surface marks and sand the area before stain is applied. Where a water stain is to be used, the surface should be washed with water to raise the grain, allowed to dry, and then sanded with a paper no finer than 180 grit. The prepared surfaces should be blown free of sawdust. This prevents the dust from settling into and clogging the pores of the wood.

Application of stain

Stain can be applied with a wad of absorbent rag, a brush or a sponge. It should be wiped with the grain, allowed to stand for a short while, and then wiped off with the grain before it dries. When working over large flat areas, work with the grain, keeping a wet edge as the rag moves down the plank. If the entire width of a table top, for instance, is stained and worked forwards, part of the stain line will dry leave an unsightly line that is very difficult to remove. Keep the wet edge narrow, and work in strips with the grain. Areas that have been missed can be touched in with a fine brush.

Panelled furniture

The order for staining panelled furniture is as follows: stain the panel first, then the top and bottom rails, then the vertical stiles and finish

This weathered tripod table has a good solid top. Stain will bring out the colour, and finish will give it depth

with the mouldings. A board can be used to mask the cross grain at the end of the stiles if necessary.

Viewing stained work

View stained work from a distance or in subdued light. Strong light or close inspection will tend to make the work seem lighter than it will appear in normal household conditions.

Staining open grain and boards with end grain

Where the wood has an open grain, or areas of end grain on the surface, a sealer may need to be used prior to staining. Shellac sealers, either bought ready-made or made by diluting garnet or button polish with methylated spirits, will partially block the end and open-grained parts of the timber, but still permit some of the stain to enter the fibres of the wood. A very thin coat is applied, and should be sanded once it has dried.

If a stain is still difficult to control, its bite may be further inhibited by applying a second coat of sealer over the most absorbent parts of the wood. Once again, the surface should be sanded before applying the stain. Adding thinners to the stain will increase the bite, and so exacerbate the problem of uneven penetration.

Chemical stains cannot be used once a sealer has been applied to the wood. In general it is best to leave sealing the grain as a last resort, to be used when chemical stains and normal staining methods have failed.

Fixing the stain

Where an oil or naphtha stain is to be covered by an oil-based varnish, a fixing coat should be used to prevent the stain from bleeding into the varnish. A thin coat of shellac brushed onto the surface will fix the stain and provide a stable base for the varnish. Bleeding may also occur when covering a spirit stain with shellac, but this is less likely as the shellac is very quick drying. Should it occur, however, it can be remedied by running a dilute coat of varnish over the stain, and allowing it to dry. This will provide a satisfactory base for the shellac, provided that the varnish is only applied thinly. A thick varnish coat will provide an unstable foundation for shellac, causing it to craze. Lightly sand the surfaces that have been fixed.

STAINS

Chemical stains

Chemical stains react with the chemicals in the timber to change the colour of the wood. As the stains are water soluble they tend to raise the grain, so the surface should be washed, dried and sanded before applying the stains.

Handle chemical stains with care. Bottles of stain and their powders should be stored out of the reach of children. Wear gloves when handling, mixing, and applying all stains.

Always experiment with wood offcuts before staining. No woods ever stain in the same way; even separate samples from the same type of tree will stain differently. Be prepared to experiment, and the experience gained will be more use than any stain colour chart.

Potassium dichromate

This is poisonous. If it is splashed or rubbed onto the skin it may cause dermatitis, and should be washed off immediately. This is a fairly permanent stain, easy to apply, and with a good bite. It is traditionally used to stain oak and mahogany; it turns the latter a rich, dark brown. It reacts with the tannic acid present in the timber, and this effect can be reproduced in timbers like birch or deal, by priming the piece with freshly mixed tannic acid. Like most stains, this is fugitive if exposed to strong sunlight for long periods.

Ferrous sulphate

Dissolve a few ferrous sulphate crystals in water. When applied to a piece of walnut or oak and allowed to dry, it will add a grey tint to the wood, killing, for instance, any strong orange or redness in the wood. A piece of bright red mahogany will resemble walnut, and a piece of brown oak, when stained, will look weathered. The strength of the solution is critical, and should be tested before being used. When ferrous sulphate is used on sycamore the wood turns grey. This is known as harewood.

As with potassium dichromate, a priming with new tannic acid will permit the ferrous sulphate to be used on most woods.

Tannic acid

Tannic acid solution should be stored in a plastic container with a plastic lid. It should not be allowed to come into contact with ironwork. Plastic brushes, mops or sponges must be used. Nails should be stopped with wax prior to covering with the acid, metal hinges, etc. removed. If ferrous fittings are left on the surface of the wood to come into contact with the acid, a black stain will discolour the area around the nail or fitting.

When pieces that do not normally contain tannic acid in their chemical composition are primed with the acid, they can be fumed or stained with potassium dichromate or ferrous sulphate, in the same way as others that naturally contain the chemical. Old solutions of tannic acid tend to turn black, so it is best to use a new solution for staining wood, but the old solution is quite suitable for priming a piece that is to be fumed, as it can be scrubbed thoroughly with methylated spirits and wire wool after fuming is completed.

Priming followed by staining tends to be fugitive, but the colours can be very attractive. Pieces stained in this way should be kept out of direct sunlight to preserve their colour.

Potassium permanganate

This is a stain much loved by Victorian craftsmen. It, also, is fugitive when exposed to strong sunlight. Pine furniture stained with a solution of potassium permanganate takes on a clean, warm brown, and natural bleaching on such pieces as dressers or bookcases can look rather attractive.

The potassium permanganate crystals are dissolved in water to make a purple solution. This can be brushed or sponged onto the furniture, and the excess wiped clean with a rag. Those pieces of furniture that have been cleaned or bleached with oxalic acid must be thoroughly neutralised before potassium permanganate is applied, or the acid will work through and the colour will vanish. (This, of course, is the way to remove a potassium permanganate stain from a piece of wood. Remember to neutralise the acid with bicarbonate of soda after stripping away the stain.)

A darker and quicker-drying stain can be obtained by dissolving the potassium permanganate crystals in warm water, to make a saturated solution, and then adding about 30% by volume methylated spirits. This should be shaken together, very briefly, the cap of the bottle released, and the bottle taken outside to settle down, and cool.

The liquid heats itself, and then cools to leave a thick brown liquid, which can be applied with a sponge or brush, and wiped off with a cloth. *Do not breathe the fumes released by this reaction.* Wear rubber gloves for mixing and applying the stain. Brushes that have been used for applying the stain should be washed in clean water, or their bristles will be eaten by the solution.

Oil stains

These are oil soluble dyes, dissolved in naphtha or other oil. They give good strong colours, with a controllable bite. They do not raise the grain, and can be mixed and diluted to create a wide variety of colours and shades. The lighter shades give particularly fine colours but, as previously mentioned, the darker colours applied to a light wood give a muddy appearance. These stains should be fixed with a thin coat of shellac before varnish or wax is applied over them.

Water stains

These are grain raising, which is a particular nuisance where mouldings or carvings need to be stained. The surface of the piece should be dampened before staining, in order to raise the grain. Sand prior to staining. If a wax finish is to be applied over the stain, it is a good idea to protect the stain with two brush coats of transparent shellac or a thinned coat of varnish. This will prevent the stain being leached out by accidental spillages of hot water.

To increase the bite of a water stain, a dash of .880 ammonia (the same that is used for fuming) can be added to the solution. This is often used with a solution of vandyke crystals to darken oak.

Aniline spirit stains

These are non-grain raising, powerful stains with a sudden bite, and very quick drying time. It is difficult to apply a spirit stain evenly over a large area because of the speed with which the stain penetrates and dries. However, these stains come in a wide range of colours, green and blue included, and are very useful when they are applied in thin washes to make subtle changes in the tone or colour of a piece of wood. It is worth while experimenting to find the extent to which strong and crude colours can be modified by the discreet use of aniline spirit stains. They can also be used to alter the colour of furniture that has been finished with shellac.

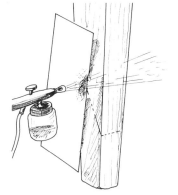

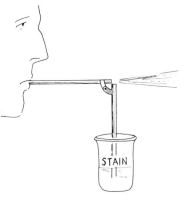

Because these stains dry very quickly, they are ideal for use with an air-brush. Chair and table tops can be rapidly coloured and then toned using a range of stains and an artist's simple air-brush. Shading and grain lines can be simulated by holding shaped and straight cardboard masks against the piece being sprayed.

For areas likely to be under closer scrutiny, a commercial artist's air-brush should be used. This will give greater control of the spray, and prevent accidental drops of moisture landing on the work.

STAINING NEW WOOD TO MATCH OLD – STAINING GUIDE

(a) Is it practical, or worthwhile, to fume the piece?

(b) Check for tonal difference. The new work should be lighter than the old. Bleach it if necessary. It is not possible to stain a piece lighter; every application of stain darkens the wood.

(c) Forget about tone and look for the colour difference between the new and the old wood. Is the new wood too red, orange, too brown? Experiment with aniline spirit washes to reach the required colour.

(d) Once the work is the desired colour, a toning stain should be mixed. This is not the same colour as the colouring stain, which is tinted to work with, or to compensate for, the colour of the new wood. Apply the toning stain, which may be aniline, oil, or water, until the correct tone is reached.

Always carry out tests prior to staining. Use wood removed from the piece during the repair operations, or experiment on a part that is hidden from view. Different types of stain can be applied one over the other, provided that the previous coats are dry. If in doubt, apply a thin coat of fixer (thin shellac) before following with stain.

Do not press ahead until the experiments have been successfully completed. Stains are very difficult to remove once they have entered the fibres of a piece of timber.

Remember that a small patch of colour will appear lighter in tone than the same colour and tone over a larger area. Err on the side of discretion, and make the toning and colouring stains a little less powerful than you think may eventually be necessary. Adjustments may be made to the colour once the finishing process has begun.

STAINING FINISHED FURNITURE

Wax, dirt and grease first need to be removed from the piece of furniture. A shellacked finish can be wiped carefully with fine wire wool dipped in white spirit, and then washed clean with soap and water. A varnish finish should be washed with soap and rubbed with wire wool. Both finishes should be allowed to dry thoroughly.

Once the pieces are dry, they should be lightly rubbed with dry 0000 wire wool, taking care to clean the mouldings and corners. This should again be wiped with a damp lint-free rag and allowed to dry.

Treatment for a shellac finish

Mix up an appropriate aniline spirit stain, and add about 20% water to the mixture. The water will inhibit the stain, reduce its bite, and prevent it from stripping the shellac from the finish. The stain should be applied with a wad of cotton wrapped in cloth, or with a neatly-bunched absorbent rag. Strokes should be with the grain, and should not hesitate or falter. Allow the stain to dry before refinishing with a coat of shellac – applied with brush (p. 190) or rubber (p. 192).

Treatment for varnish

Select an appropriate oil stain, decant enough for the work into a glass bottle, and add equal quantities of varnish and white spirit (33% each). Shake thoroughly, and apply with a rag or brush. When dry, lightly sand and finish with a coat of varnish.

REFINISHING FURNITURE

Fading in repairs

When the repairs have been thoroughly shaped and worn, they will still have a distressingly bright and clean appearance, emphasised by the obvious age of the rest of the piece. Even if old wood has been used in the repair, and so has the natural depth of colour typical of old wood, it will lack the subtle shading which a piece acquires with age.

The process of camouflaging is essentially one of shading and darkening to match the existing wood. It is important to avoid making the new wood too dark or, worse still, having to darken the old to match the new. It is easy for the new wood to become too dark because, although the shading techniques are gradual, their effect is cumulative. The more stain and paint that is put on to a piece of wood, the darker it becomes. Imperceptibly, the wood is deadened by the pigment, and loses its reflective qualities. When this happens it is time to start again, keeping a closer watch on the progress of the job.

If the new wood matches perfectly with the old, fading will not be necessary. If it is not a perfect match, it is necessary to start with the new wood lighter in tone than the old. To achieve this it may be necessary to bleach it.

The new wood should now be lighter than the rest of the piece. Matching the colours needs to be a swift and simple operation, as there

COLOURS REQUIRED

Wood colour before staining	Yellow	Green/ brown	Brown	Brown/red	Red	Grey	Black
Yellow		Brown stain (chemical if possible). Restain with weak spirit	Brown stain (chemical if possible)	Chemical stain brown. Tint with red oil or spirit stain	Red stain	Pre-treat with tannic acid (if necessary) then stain with ferrous sulphate	Black spirit stain. Follow with black shellac
Green/ brown	Bleach (two-part) thin yellow wash stain		Thin wash of orange or Bismark brown spirit stain	Orange or Bismark brown spirit stain, then wash of weak red stain	Red stain	Bleach (oxalic). Blue spirit stain wash	
Brown	Bleach (two-part) yellow wash, stain if necessary	Green wash stain – bleach with oxalic if necessary		Weak red stain	Red wash stain	Bleach (oxalic). Blue spirit wash	
Brown/ red	Bleach (two-part), yellow wash, stain if necessary	Bleach (oxalic). Green spirit stain	Thin wash of spirit. Green stain		Bleach if necessary. Red stain	Bleach (oxalic or two-part). Blue/black spirit	
Red	Bleach (two-part). Yellow finish	Green spirit stain (applied as a wash)	Weak oxalic bleach. Green/ brown stain	Blue or green wash. Bleach before if necessary		Two-part bleach, stain brown, blue wash	
Black (colour changes unlikely to succeed)	Bleach (two-part). Yellow stain	Two-part bleach. Green/brown stain	Two-part bleach. Brown stain	Two-part bleach. Brown/red stain	Two-part bleach. Red stain	Oxalic or household bleach	

are often large areas to be covered, and it is unlikely that at this stage a good faking job can be achieved. Look closely at the new wood, and identify which colours are missing, or which are too strong. Use this table to help in testing stains on a piece of spare wood.

It is possible that the new wood can be fumed to the colour of the old. This is an excellent solution if the piece is in a dismantled state, or if the repairs can be readily isolated with the ammonia (see p. 179).

If fuming is not possible, then the chart of stains above will help in achieving a satisfactory undercoat stain on the new timber. Do not be too bold in the application of stain; avoid pigment stains where possible, unless the colour change is a very minor one. Remember that once stain has been applied, it is very difficult to remove.

Once the approximate colour has been achieved, brush on a thinned coat of shellac to fix it. This also has the effect of bringing out the colour and tone (darkness) of the work that has just been done. When the shellac is dry, experiment with stains to find the appropriate toning stain that brings the new work to the general colour of the old wood finish.

When the toning stain is dry, fix it with a coat of shellac. The new work will glisten, and still have a uniform colour and tone. But the colour and tone should be about right, and the whole should merge quite well with the rest of the piece. Ideally, there should be a natural variation in the timber, so that some parts are lighter than others. This will be useful when painting in signs of age.

At this stage it is best to complete the hiding of any scarf joins or patches that you don't want seen. Take care over this work; use a sable-haired watercolour brush and good quality watercolours. Poster paints are opaque and should not be used. Use very little water. It helps to rub the brush in some household soap to improve the covering qualities of the paint. Apply the paint in small dots of colour, not as a wash. When the paint is dry the work should be sealed with a coat of shellac.

The job is now almost complete. The new wood is the same colour as the original, and the joins and patches are hidden. All that remains to be done is to darken some areas and to highlight others, to give the appearance of accumulated dirt and worn surfaces.

The dirt should be applied first. Mix a small quantity of P.V.A. glue (woodworker's white glue) to a few drops of water. Add some dry powder colours to give the colour of the furniture. Add a small amount of black and, with a rag, dab this paint mixture onto the new wood. As soon as it is applied, dab the paint off with another clean cloth. This will leave a shadow of paint behind. Repeat this process, taking care not to make areas too dark. Any mistakes can be wiped off with a damp rag.

The paint/glue mix will dry leaving a white deposit on the wood, but this will disappear when it is shellacked or waxed.

When this is dry, highlight areas by rubbing them gently with wire wool, grade 0000. Take care not to make these areas too localised and bright.

To enhance the effect of age, further marks can be applied with a paint brush; these are particularly effective on the highlighted areas. Copy marks already present on the piece, but do not overdo them: a few bold stains are much more pleasing than a host of trifling marks.

Before waxing, or finishing with shellac, the whole area that has been worked on should be allowed to dry, and smoothed with fine sandpaper or wire wool.

COPYING A DETERIORATED FINISH

This involves as much skill as any other finishing process; it also requires the touch of the artist.

Where repairs are carried out on a piece of furniture, they should be indistinguishable from the original work. The original finish, in a detriorated and worn state, will have to be manufactured, applied and textured to merge with the old wood.

There is a wonderful variety of ways of creating old finishes, and the restorer should be prepared to use any of the stains, finishes, and paints that he has at his disposal.

Paints and varnishes are essentially a gum, or pigment, mixed with a binder and solvent. The restorer should experiment with making his own. Most ancient or worn finishes can be reproduced by using one of the following recipes. Keep experimenting to increase your repertoire of faking skills, and to find ways of speeding the process.

Paints

A quick-drying opaque paint can be made by mixing dry powder colours into a mixture of P.V.A. glue and water. A thick coat needs less water. Surfaces should be grease-free. The glue must be dry before highlighting with wire wool. Do not hurry the drying, as the P.V.A. tends to dry from the surface inwards, and adhesion to the groundwork is the last consequence of the drying process.

This paint can be brushed on, or applied with a pad in dabbing motions. If a fairly wet mix is used, the pad can be used for highlighting, fading, and texturing while it is still wet.

For a subdued gloss effect, the finish can be rubbed with wire wool and brushed with shellac, then waxed.

Varnishes

Shellac is a very quick-drying gum, and can be used to copy smooth, thick varnishes or sticky and runny finishes. Take a small quantity of shellac polish (a dark polish for a dark job, etc.) and add aniline spirit stains dissolved in meths. Mix these together well, and allow to stand in the sun. The mixture will thicken as the spirits evaporate out. For texture, dust (particularly concrete dust, or pumice) can be added to the mixture. Apply this mix with a brush, allowing runs to form, and leave for a short while. The finish should look bright, glittery and uneven. Take a soft cloth, add a few drops of meths or finishing spirit to the rag, and rub the cloth over the work with increasing pressure. Knobs and bumps will become rounded, areas can be scraped clean and burnished and will appear as accidental damage marks. Opacity can be achieved by adding dry colours or pumice to the mixture.

Crinkly finish

This can be achieved by piling a quick drying finish onto an uncured groundwork (shellac over varnish, or quick drying varnish over slow drying varnish). Alternatively, heat applied to an uncured shellac surface with a blow heater will cause it to wrinkle slightly.

Ancient weathered look

Soot, mixed with water and lavishly brushed onto unfinished wood, will leave the wood looking grey and weathered. For the best effects, the wood should be left rough-sawn. The surface must be well rubbed down with a duster after the water has dried. This is a particularly swift and convenient way of toning down new backs to cupboards and chests.

Dust and age

The following is a reasonably quick and efficient means of ageing the underside of a piece of furniture where new feet or glue blocks have been fitted. Invert the piece, and use a P.V.A. semi-opaque paint to colour in the new wood. Allow it to dry.

Study the old wood in the piece, and choose a predominating colour which would look authentic as a fading stain over the entire underside. Mix up a thin stain using dry watercolours and water, and add some P.V.A. to act as a binder. Collect some concrete dust in a dish,

add some old cobwebs and perhaps a few fragments of newspaper.

Apply the P.V.A. toning stain to the underside of the piece and then, while it is still damp, carefully distribute the dust and debris in the crevices and corners. Invert the piece, and allow it to dry. Much of the dust will have fallen to the floor when it was inverted; some will have stayed and should look quite convincing. Do not make the P.V.A. mix so strong that it glues the dust in position; this will give a rough, concrete-like surface, and will sabotage the desired effect.

FINISHES

Workshop conditions

Finishing should be performed in a dust- and draught-free, warm, light workshop. If other woodworking activity will be going on at the same time as the finishing, a temporary finishing booth should be arranged with sheets of transparent polythene. This is particularly necessary when using varnish, less crucial for French polishing.

Where heating is functioning only during the day, finishing should be started early in the morning. This will allow varnishes and shellac to harden before the cold and damp of the evening creates a bloom beneath the surface.

Preparation

Pieces to be finished should be dry, and grease- and dust-free. All of the necessary woodwork should be done, all the staining completed.

Final spotting in of repairs, etc., using artist's watercolour paint, can still be undertaken prior to the last application of the finish. Doors and drawers should be removed.

Choosing the finish

There is a considerable range of finishes for the repairer to choose from. When deciding on the finish, a number of factors needs to be taken into consideration. If the piece is antique, a finish contemporary with the piece should be used. However, many old pieces that were once painted and have been stripped will need a new finish. Consider the use that the piece of furniture will be expected to endure. If it is a table, the top is likely to have hot serving dishes placed on it. Perhaps it will have spirits spilled across the surface. In this case varnish rather than shellac should be used. However, if it is a good quality table, and likely to be looked after, shellac would be entirely suitable.

Whichever finish is applied to the top, the base, which one would not expect to suffer from heat or spirits, could be finished with shellac.

Where the working surface of a piece of furniture is soft, a flexible rather than brittle finish is needed. If a simple wax finish is undesirable then a good quality yacht varnish slightly thinned with turps and linseed oil will give a resilient finish. If the top is likely to have hot things placed upon it, the finish must be worked into the wood and not left as a film, otherwise it may become tacky when in contact with heat.

There is now on the market a quick drying shellac-based finish that is resistant to heat and alcohol, and is applied in the same ways as other shellac finishes. This is called 'table top polish', and it goes some way toward bridging the gap between the beautiful but delicate shellac finish, and the slow drying, thicker varnish finish. The latter, however, is still more durable than shellac.

SHELLAC

A shellac finish gives a hard bright shine. It is vulnerable to water, heat, and spirit damage. It is easy to scratch, and bruises can cause a dis-

colouration in the shellac that is very difficult to remedy. It is, however, quick drying and beautifully translucent, and when applied with the French polishing technique, gives a brilliant and smooth finish. It makes a

good basis for a wax finish.

Shellac is normally bought from cabinetmaker's suppliers, already dissolved in industrial alcohol. It is (in this state) highly inflammable, and should be stored well away from naked flames. If a partly-used shellac bottle is stored over a long period of time, some of the alcohol will evaporate, and it should be topped up before use. If a container of shellac is allowed to stand until white precipitate is formed at the bottom of the container, it should be discarded and a better quality shellac purchased.

Shellac can be bought in several colours.

Button polish: An amber-coloured polish which imparts a warm tone to light-coloured timber.

Garnet polish: A rich brown colour. useful for finishing darker pieces of furniture.

White polish: A bleached shellac, good for applying to pale and bleached wood.

Transparent polish: An almost colourless polish, very useful when trying to match the new work into old. Using this, a finish can be built up which will not affect the final colour of the repair.

Ebony polish: A black polish, used in conjunction with a black aniline dye to ebonise a piece of timber. Small

quantities can be made up by mixing garnet polish with black aniline dye.

A full range of colours can be achieved by adding very small quantities of aniline spirit stain to the shellac. Dissolve the powdered stain in a small quantity of meths or finishing spirit, and then strain the liquid into the shellac. In this way the correct colour can be achieved without the danger of undissolved granules of stain working onto the brush or rubber, causing colour changes where they are not expected.

Storing shellac

Shellac is bought in plastic or glass bottles. For brushing it should be decanted into a plastic tub. Cut a hole in the lid of the tub to fit the handle of a good quality paintbrush or mop. Shellac can be stored this way, without the brush needing to be cleaned and without the shellac turning hard. If the shellac is allowed to stand for long, it should be topped up with a little meths or finishing spirit to thin it out.

Applying shellac by brush

A good quality paint brush should be used, about 3 in. (75 mm) wide. It is an advantage to have a brush which does not have a great thickness of bristles, as each dip of the brush is supposed to take the minimum of fresh shellac.

Dip the brush into the shellac and wipe the bristles against the inside edge of the rim. Brush with the grain, starting about 4 in. (100 mm) from the end of the piece. Work the brush both to the edge and forwards down the plank. This gives an even distribution of the shellac. The next brush of shellac is started a small distance from the place where the brush left off, and is again moved in both directions – back to meet the previous finish and forwards down the plank.

With this method it is possible to apply a minimum of finish evenly over the whole surface. Do not try to brush out ridges and brush marks

REPLENISH BRUSH BEFORE MOVING TO 3 + 4.

because shellac is very quick drying, and any extra brush marks will only add to the problem.

Once the first coat of shellac is finished it should be allowed to dry. Any final colouring can be completed at this stage. When a newly-charged brush can be worked over the surface of the drying finish without sticking or pulling, a second coat can be applied.

Three coats are usually required

with this method. A fourth coat can be applied once the finish has been allowed to dry and gently sanded, but this is not usually necessary unless the initial coats have turned ropy (into ridges).

Allow the finish to dry for at least four hours, then rub it with wire wool, 000 grade. Work the wire wool with the grain, and occasionally puff it clean to prevent the wool from clogging and losing its cutting action.

A coat of good quality furniture wax applied to this surface will result in a smooth and glowing finish.

Apply shellac by mop

This is a similar process, except that a mop is used to flood the polish onto the surface. The shellac should be allowed to dry between the coats. After the first two coats, lightly sand between applications. A considerable build-up of shellac can be achieved in this way, which is particularly suitable where open-grained, porous woods need to be finished.

Final spotting-in of repairs can be carried out between coats; final sanding should be with 400 grit paper, followed by 0000 wire wool and then wax.

Problems with shellac

Bloom

When shellac is applied in damp and draughty conditions a milky bloom will appear beneath the surface. Allow the piece to dry slowly and the bloom will probably disappear. Subsequent coats should be applied in warm and draught-free conditions.

Ropiness

Shellac dries very quickly and will not readily flood on to a piece of work. This results in small ridges building up as the shellac is applied. This is particularly a problem with brushed out shellac method. Attempts to brush out the shellac with a subsequent coat will fail and may exacerbate matters. The finish must be allowed to dry, and then flatted using fine (200-400 grit) paper backed by a cork or felt-covered block. Add a small quantity of thinners to the shellac, and be careful not to overload the brush. Spread the polish thinly and evenly; do not try to brush out ridges, or cover areas that have been missed. Rub the finish down with 000 wire wool, and wax it.

Dead or greasy areas

These appear on surfaces as areas that resist the shellac. A new application will cover the dead area, and then the shellac will creep away, leaving the patch uncovered. To remedy this, the workpiece should be left to dry, the offending patch lightly cleaned with soap and water, and wiped dry. Sand the area, and resume the finishing process.

Shellac refuses to harden

This is caused by the presence in the shellac of poor quality gums. The best solution is to strip away the finish and refinish using new, better quality shellac.

FRENCH POLISHING

This is a smooth and beautiful finish, but as vulnerable as any other shellac finish to marking by water, heat or spirits. The process requires patience and practice. Experiment on pieces of hardboard or plywood until a level of proficiency is achieved.

Equipment

A number of wide-topped bottles with screw lids will be needed for storing the polishing fads, and a range of small screw-topped bottles for storing the different colours of shellac. (Wadding uncovered by a

cloth is known as a fad. A fad covered by a soft fine cloth is known as a rubber.) The shellac bottles should each have two small holes drilled in the tops, one to allow the shellac to be poured out, and the other to permit air to replace the shellac.

These holes can be covered with a piece of polythene when the bottles are not being used.

Some polishing wadding, good quality fine linen or cotton to cover the wadding, a tub of fine-ground pumice powder, and some mineral oil or raw linseed oil will be needed.

Preparing the equipment

Fill each of the small screw-topped jars with a different colour of shellac. One should be filled with a 50% mixture of garnet polish and finishing spirit. Mark this bottle clearly: (½ and ½).

Each pad of wadding that is used to apply the shellac will be made

from a square of wadding approximately 8 in. (200 mm) each side. Make up five or six squares; this will be quite adequate for most needs. Pour a small quantity of ordinary button or garnet polish into a saucer and dip the squares of wadding into it. Squeeze out the shellac, and hang the squares to dry. When the wadding is nearly dry, fold

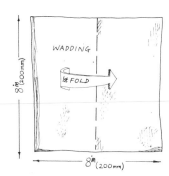

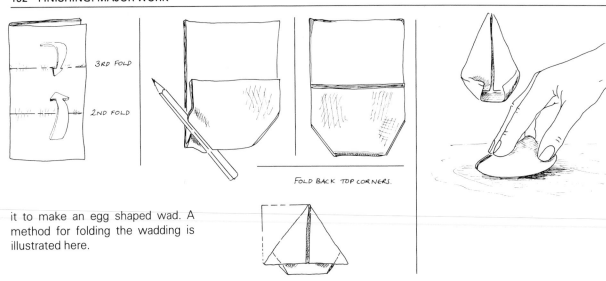

FOLD BACK TOP CORNERS.

it to make an egg shaped wad. A method for folding the wadding is illustrated here.

Technique

Pour a very small quantity of mineral oil or raw linseed oil into the cap of a bottle and place it close to the surface to be polished.

Sealing the grain
Open the top folds of the fad and fill it with a quantity of shellac; press it against a piece of paper to spread the shellac evenly over the surface of the fad.

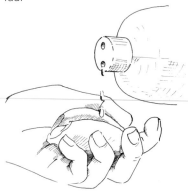

Hold the fad firmly in the right hand, and move it with the grain, across the surface to be polished. Firm pressure is needed to force the shellac into the pores of the wood. Increase the pressure as the fad dries. Cover the entire surface of the board.

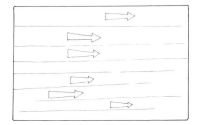

A second and third application can be made, until all of the surface is sealed by a thin layer of shellac. Leave this to dry, and then flatten it with fine sandpaper, dampened with oil. Wipe the surface dry.

Building up a finish
Recharge the fad, and spread the shellac evenly across its face by pressing it against the paper. Dip a finger into the cap of mineral oil or raw linseed oil, and flick a few drips across the surface of the workpiece. Press the fad very gently and work it in wide sweeping arcs, distributing the oil across the surface of the piece. This provides a lubricant for the fad, which eases its path over the fresh shellac, so that the arm pressure of the worker is almost entirely directed towards forcing the shellac into the pores of the wood.

Keep the fad moving, and add

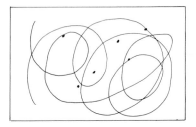

more oil until a slight steamy smear follows the path of the fad as it glides across the surface of the workpiece. If it begins to skid (this is easily felt) inspect its face. Too much oil will be the cause of the skidding, and this will be revealed by shiny patches on the face of the fad. Take a clean dry rag, and rub the surface on the workpiece. This will remove surplus oil; it may be necessary to add more to ease the path of the fad.

This process should be continued until the pores of the surface are filled and an even layer of polish has been built up. As the polish in the fad is used up, increase the pressure on the fad. When the fad is recharged with shellac, very little pressure will be required. Pressure should be increased as the fad dries out, until considerable pressure is needed to force the shellac out of the fad into the work.

If a recharged fad is pressed too soon, shellac will exude from its side and cause ridges to form that follow the path of the fad. These 'whips' should be immediately worked down with the fad or, if this is not possible, the piece should be left to stand until the ridges are dry enough to sand down using fine paper lubricated with a spot of oil.

Once the grain is filled and an even finish is achieved, charge the fad from the ½ and ½ bottle. Work lightly to avoid cutting the surface. When dry, remaining oil can be removed with a soft rag dampened by methylated spirits. Allow the work 24 hours to harden.

Building up a good body of finish (bodying)

Carefully sand the surface, using fine sandpaper backed by a pad. Any holes or dents that need filling should be stopped with wax or shellac stick.

Take a fad, charge it with shellac, and cover it with a piece of fine cotton or linen. This is now the rubber mentioned earlier.

Flick oil onto the workpiece and work the rubber in circles across the wood. Make sure all the oil drops are picked up and spread across the surface. Work the shellac into the corners and mouldings at the edge of the surface, as well as across the centre part of the panel. A series of small circles should be worked around the edge of the surface after each complete covering of the centre. Keep the rubber trim and in shape, and it will be quite easy to reach difficult corners without

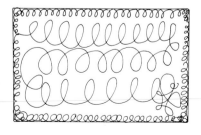

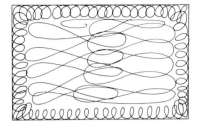

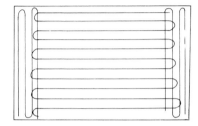

flooding the work with shellac or leaving whips on the surface.

As the finish is built up, the circles should be changed to elongated figures of eight, and then to long straight sweeps of the rubber. Always keep the work at the edge of the piece in step with the general progress of the job. Avoid recharging the rubber until absolutely necessary; it is the pressure that gives the good finish. Never allow the rubber to stop on the surface of the work; this will spoil the finish and postpone its completion. The rubber should always be glided on and off the work.

As the bodying progresses, the surface will become smooth and glossy. As before, finish with dilute shellac, wipe the surface with a rag moistened in meths to remove the oil, if necessary, and leave to dry. Sand before more bodying coats are added.

Three bodying coats are normally sufficient to provide a satisfactory finish before the final finishing process begins. This should be begun immediately after the last body has been completed. The oil should be left on the surface for the ½ and ½ coat.

Finishing

Take a special rubber reserved for this operation from its bottle, and charge it with shellac from the ½ and ½ bottle. Work the rubber quickly and lightly over the surface, first with circles, changing to figures of eight and straight lines. This should be worked very gently, until the rubber is nearly dry. As the rubber is moved across the surface, it will remove the oil smear. The rubber should be worked until dry.

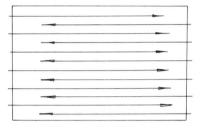

A second, special, rubber is used for the final burnishing of the finish. This is made from an old fad, completely washed clean of shellac, dried, and covered with a clean, good quality cotton or linen cloth. Drip a few drops of methylated spirits onto the face of the fad and cover it with the cloth. Test the rubber against your lips; it must not seem wet, but should feel cold and dry.

Hold the spiriting rubber very firmly, swing it onto the surface of the piece and move it rapidly around in circles. Increase pressure as the rubber dries out. This will remove any remaining oil from the surface, and soften and burnish the shellac finish. As the rubber dries, it can be recharged if necessary. Continue the burnishing until a smooth, bright and glossy finish remains.

Leave the surface to dry for at least 24 hours, before any dulling is carried out.

Dulling

If the finish is too bright it can be dulled. This can be achieved by rubbing the piece with a wad of 0000 wire wool dipped in wax, applying very gentle pressure and moving the wire wool in the direction of the grain. An alternative is to sprinkle pumice powder over the finish and brush it across the surface (with the grain) using a soft bristled brush. Areas in panelling that need masking can be covered with a postcard while the brush is worked to its edge.

Problems

The initial stages of the fadding process can be sabotaged by the fad leaving hairs on the surface of the work. If this occurs, the hairs should be removed by gently rubbing them with a finger, until they are released. If this doesn't work they should be allowed to dry and sanded out.

Filling open grain

If the wood has a particularly open grain, what is known as a grinder can be used before fadding. A fad is taken and charged with the 1/2 and 1/2 mix, and then the face of the fad is sprinkled with fine pumice powder. This is covered by a sheet of thin cloth, and the grinder (the rubber sprinkled with pumice) should be worked in circles over the surface of the wood. No oil should be used. The pumice filters through the layer of cloth and grinds the surface of the wood. A mixture of wood fibre and pumice (which will exactly match the colour of the timber) will be forced into the pores of the timber and seal it. When dry, sand lightly before commencing with the fadding process described above. Keep the grinder in a separate, clearly labelled bottle.

Bloom

Caused by work being performed in damp or draughty conditions. The piece should be taken into a warm room and allowed to dry thoroughly. If the bloom does not disappear, the piece should be stripped and refinished.

Sweating

This is caused by linseed or mineral oil breaking out from beneath the finish where it has been trapped. This is probably due to too much oil being used in the bodying of the piece, or drops of oil being buried rather than picked up by the fad or rubber.

Leave the surface to sweat for a few days and then rub a reviver over it. If this does not work, mix a warm solution of soap and water and some very fine pumice powder, and work it over the surface. Wash it off and allow it to dry. Repeat the process if the sweating continues. Repolish when all sweating has ceased.

Dullness

May be caused by using too much oil during the bodying coats. Spirit off the surface (as for finishing).

The dullness may also be the result of the spirit burning the surface. If this is the case, spirit off again, using less spirit. If this fails, sand the surface back, body, and finish afresh.

Restoring decayed areas of polish

Rub down the areas that need refinishing with fine glasspaper, lubricated with a touch of oil. Where the colour and tone of the wood has been altered by the removal of the shellac, bring it back to colour with some stain or delicate spotting-in with artist's watercolours. The area can then be bodied-in afresh, using a variety of coloured polishes to achieve the final colour match. Once this has been achieved, the final finishing processes can be completed using transparent polish. Allow the work to dry thoroughly before dulling.

POLISHING MOULDINGS

Mouldings are awkward to polish. One solution is to build up a finish with varnish and grind down the varnish with a rubber of shellac.

Seal the wood with a shellac-filled fad in the normal way for French polishing. Allow to dry. Brush a good quality varnish over the mouldings. One coat of varnish is usually sufficient. When this is dry, take a piece of used wadding, press the shellac from it, and wrap it in a rag to dry. Charge the fad with a little polish, some mineral oil and a pinch of pumice powder. Work this over a piece of paper to spread the polish and pumice evenly over the surface

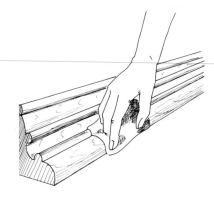

of the wadding, and then place it over the moulding, pressing it firmly into the shape of the curves. Using a finger as a fence to keep the pressed wad in its position, move it along the moulding several times. The pumice will bite back the varnish, and the polish will brighten the colour and be burnished by the movement of the lubricated rubber. Continue this until the mouldings are bright and shiny.

The rubber should ride steadily over the moulding. If it skids, too much oil has been used; too much shellac will cause it to stick; too much pumice will tear up the finish. Take a clean soft rubber and pass it a few times along the moulding to bring it to a good shine.

FINISHING TURNED WORK

There is a large proportion of end grain in turned work, making staining rather a problem. A weaker stain than would be used on flat work should be selected. If chemical or water stains are to be used, the work should be dampened with water and sanded prior to staining.

Keep the workpiece in the lathe, or arrange some temporary centres on the workbench. Apply the stain with a rag, rotating the piece at the same time. Add some more stain to the areas of flat grain. Do not allow the stain to soak into the end grain.

Allow to dry, and lightly sand the piece. This can then be sealed with a couple of brush coats of shellac, then sanded and waxed. Alternatively, a proper polished finish can be applied in the following way.

The shellac brush coats must be dry and lightly sanded. Tone in lighter areas with methylated spirit stain, mixed with a little water if necessary. Then take an old French polish fad, load it with shellac and hold it to the workpiece while rotating it in the lathe. Allow a finish to build up and then apply another brush coat of shellac.

Leave it to dry, then gently sand.

The finishing process after the body has been built up is as for French polishing, except that the final ½ and ½ coat is thicker: it should be about 75% shellac, 25% meths, and the spiriting rubber should be dipped with 25% of shellac added into the few drops of meths that are normally used. For best results, the spiriting rubber should be covered with a thin piece of chamois leather rather than cotton or linen, as it leaves a more even burnish when held against rotating stock.

VARNISH

Varnish will give a clear and durable finish, ideal for table tops or any surfaces that are likely to be subjected to hard usage.

Equipment

There is a variety of varnishes available to the restorer. The qualities and recommended uses of the varied types will be clearly outlined on the side of the can, along with the instructions for use. Follow the instructions to the letter.

Storage

Varnish should be stored and used in warm dry conditions. If a can of varnish is moved from cold to warm conditions and used immediately, a poor finish may result. Varnish should be stored with its cap tightly in place. Partly used tins can be stored upside down to prevent air seeping into the can and causing the varnish to bloom when it is applied. Never shake the varnish can before use, or small air bubbles will flow off the brush and spoil the finish.

Brushes

If varnishing is a regular workshop activity, the brushes should be stored suspended by their handles in a bottle of varnish. They should not be left to stand in white spirit or turpentine unless they are very thoroughly dried before use. Brushes that are used intermittently should be cleaned in turps or white spirit and then wrapped in brown paper held in place with a rubber band. New brushes will leave hairs and dust on the surface of the wood and should not be used for the final varnish coat.

Preparation

Surfaces should be dusted with a cloth, and corners in mouldings picked out with a pointed stick before being wiped clean. Oil stains, oil-based fillers, and naturally-oily woods, such as rosewood, should be sealed with a diluted coat of shellac. This will prevent the stains from bleeding and the natural oils from seeping, preventing the varnish from drying.

Applying the varnish

The workshop should be warm and dust- and draught-free (as far as practical) and the piece to be varnished set up level. Dip the brush and slowly twist it in the varnish.

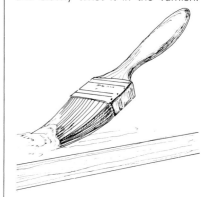

Carry the brush to the work, lay it at an acute angle to the surface of the workpiece, and draw it slowly along the grain. The varnish should flood onto the work. If the brush is moved too quickly, the varnish will creep away in areas, causing unsightly pitholes in the finish. When the brush begins to run dry, reload it and continue to cover the work. Do not overbrush the surface, but allow the varnish to assume its own level. If the varnish is applied with an even thickness over the work, the resulting finish will be satisfactory.

When the first coat is dry, it should be rubbed down with fine sandpaper, wiped and recoated. Take care when rubbing down; the varnish may be touch dry, but beneath the surface it may be quite wet. If the sandpaper penetrates through the finish, it will cause the subsurface to tear up.

Three coats are normally sufficient to seal and build up a good varnish finish. if 'dead' patches still persist in the surface (caused by areas of high porosity absorbing the varnish), these should be worked with a rubber of shellac, and allowed to dry. A subsequent coat of varnish will give a uniform finish.

Finish

Once the final coat of varnish has been applied, it should be allowed to dry for at least 48 hours. This permits the varnish to dry to its full depth, and enables the restorer to cut it down to a high-gloss rubbed finish without danger of tearing up softer varnish beneath the finish.

Worn and uneven surfaces

These can be rubbed down with 0000 grade wire wool held as a mop and worked with gentle, even pressure. Wax the surface, using a soft, slow-drying wax, followed by a harder wax.

Finishing smooth, level surfaces

Rub these down using fine sandpaper backed by a cork block. Work with the grain. Final finishing should be with a felt pad and burnishing cream. Use a soft wax to finish.

Problems

Varnish will not harden

This may be caused by an oil seeping through the sealer, preventing the finish from drying. The oil may emanate from the wood, the filler (if one has been used), or the stain. Remove the varnish, and allow the surface to dry. Brush two coats of shellac over the surface, and varnish over when dry. Where oils from the wood still prevent the varnish from drying, the surface should be washed in petrol or carbon tetrachloride. Do not smoke, or breathe the fumes; work with adequate ventilation. When dry, seal the surface with a couple of fads of shellac pressed hard into the surface, and then follow with varnish.

Runs

These are caused by uneven distribution of the varnish. If spotted quickly, they can be brushed out, otherwise leave them and sand when thoroughly dry.

Dead areas of varnish

This is the result of varnish seeping into open-grained parts of the wood. If a piece of chipboard or hardboard is varnished without sealing, this effect will be noticed over the entire surface. Dead patches are prevented by first sealing the wood with a shellac coat.

Brush hairs and dead flies sticking to the varnish

Remove these the moment they are noticed. Use a sharp pointed stick to lift them clear. It should not be necessary to brush over the area. If the marks persist, a little varnish can be run into the blemishes from a small, fine brush.

Pits

These can have a number of causes.

(a) Holes and pits in the surface of the wood, which should have been stopped before the wood was sealed. Rub these back, and stop them before continuing with the varnish.

(b) The presence of white spirit or turpentine in the brush. The piece should be allowed to dry, sanded and recovered using a brush stored in varnish (and not white spirit or turpentine).

(c) Moving the brush too quickly over the surface of the wood. These pits may be painted in using a small pointed brush, charged with varnish. When dry, the finish should be sanded smooth and, if necessary, another coat of varnish applied.

(d) Grease spots resisting the varnish. These areas should be rubbed back, then washed in soapy water. Dry and refinish.

Bloom

This is caused by moisture settling on the surface of the varnish before it has time to dry, and can be avoided by working in a warm and constant temperature. If this is impossible, the piece should be varnished in the morning so that it has the whole day to cure before the night chill causes harm to the surface. Washing the surface with reviver may remedy the problem, otherwise it will have to be stripped and refinished.

Flaking

This results where the varnish is inadequately fixed to groundwork. This may be because an inappropriate sealer has been used or because the varnish was applied to a greasy surface.

The only solution is to remove the finish and attend to the groundwork, which should be dry, and free from grease. A thorough washing with soap and warm water, followed by gentle rubbing with 000 wire wool, will generally remedy the problem.

LINSEED OIL AND VARNISH FINISH

This is a very durable, but time-consuming, finish. It is heat and spirit resistant, and because the finish is entirely in the timber, it is resistant to scratches and surface abrasions which would tear up a polished finish.

Varnish preparation

A quantity of raw linseed oil, turpentine and a supply of good quality varnish are needed. The linseed oil and varnish should be mixed together with turps in the proportions: 20% varnish, 50% oil, 30% turpentine. Carefully warm this extremely inflammable mixture in a double boiler over a stove. Apply the mixture when it is hot, with a paintbrush or mop.

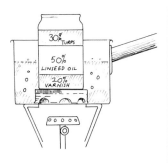

Surface preparation

This is a finish that penetrates the surface of the wood and hardens in the pores of the timber. No sealing coat should be used, as this would prevent the oil from penetrating. Fuming, or chemical water or spirit stains, can be used to stain the piece prior to finishing. Oil stains cannot be used.

Application

Swab or brush the hot mixture onto the surface of the wood. Leave it for a short while to soak in, and remove the excess with a clean cloth. Put the varnish and oil mix to one side to cool. It will not be required for a day or two.

A second soft cloth is taken, formed into a pad, and rubbed vigorously over the surface. If a large table top is being finished, a weight can be wrapped inside a layer of rags, and pushed across the surface. Rub the surface until no trace of the mixture remains on the surface. Leave the surface for a couple of days to dry.

Subsequent coats are applied in the same way. As the number of applications increases, the proportion of varnish can also be increased. The finish, however, must never be allowed to remain on the surface of the wood.

A very delightful finish can be achieved in this way, at the cost of much time spent rubbing the

surface. The finish will be durable, water resistant and have a subtle glow.

Problems

One of the major problems for the restorer is in knowing how long the process of finishing will take. This is dependent upon the porosity of the wood, the temperature of the mixture, and the rate at which the proportion of the varnish is increased. Drying times between the initial coats should be about two days; as the proportion of varnish is increased, this can be reduced by a day. By introducing a large proportion of varnish early on in the process, the amount of time can be dramatically reduced, but the finish will not be so beautiful – it will have less depth and more glitter.

Matching old wood with new

This must be completed before any oil and varnish is added to the surface. Oil stains cannot be used: any paint or stain that lies on the surface of the wood is likely to be rubbed off in the finishing process. Use chemical stain or fume where possible. Remember, when selecting the appropriate wood for a patch, that this finish above all others emphasises the iridescent qualities of the timber, and so a similarity in its reflective qualities is at least as important as similarities in grain pattern.

WAXING
Wax finish

This is a beautiful finish, which improves with age and handling. Wax can be applied and rubbed into a piece for many years, and each application will revive the existing finish and add more lustre to the piece.

A wax finish is simple to apply, simple to maintain and easy to revive. It is, however, prone to collect dirt, and is easily damaged by heat and water.

Because of these latter two factors it may be unwise to give a purely waxed finish to pieces that will be handled regularly. (See the later section on Sealed wax finish.)

Preparation
Pieces to be waxed should be well sanded, with woodwork repairs and faking completed before the wax is applied. Oil stains should be allowed a couple of days to dry before being covered with wax.

When using quick-drying waxes, ensure that there is adequate ventilation. Do not smoke.

First apply a slow-drying wax to the unfinished wood. A tinted wax can be used to give a general darkening effect. Avoid using a black or dark-brown wax early in the process, or the grain may take on a muddy appearance. The wax should be applied evenly and freely. Remove the surplus wax with a coarse rag, and allow it to dry for an hour. Repeat this process a couple of times. As the wax is applied, the colour of the piece will tend to darken, but as the wax dries it will probably resort to a pale dull finish.

Each application of coloured wax will tend to darken the piece slightly. Once an acceptable depth of colour has been achieved, a quick-drying wax can be used to build a bright shine.

Quick-drying waxes need to be applied with care. The wax should be applied in small areas at a time, and wiped clean with a lint-free rag. Work in a regular pattern over the surface of the piece. Apply the wax using the wad of cloth, and immediately wipe off all the surface wax.

Do not try to build a shine at this stage, but concentrate on removing surplus wax from the surface before it dries into smears. For an antique effect, allow the wax to remain in corners and parts of the moulding.

Burnishing

Tuck the ties into the mop before burnishing wax

An electric drill with a polishing mop attachment makes an excellent burnisher. Set the drill to high speed,

remove from the face of the mop any grit or wood shavings and work the mop over the surface, firstly in light, rapid sweeps across the grain of the wood, finishing with sweeps along the grain. The movement of the mop will be reflected in the burnish of the wax; these marks can be removed by wiping a soft duster down the grain of the wood.

Mouldings
The edge of the polishing mop can be used for working into the mouldings. Alternatively, a soft-haired shoe brush could be used.

Carving
Apply a thin coat of slow-drying wax to carvings, using a stiff-haired shoe brush. Work the inaccessible areas clean with an old toothbrush. Do not allow wax to accumulate in the details of the carving. Once the wax is hardened, burnish the carving with a soft-haired shoe brush.

Turnings

A slow-drying wax should be used for polishing turnings. Apply the wax in the normal way (with a wad) or rub it on the piece using a strip of cloth loaded with wax. Once the wax has hardened, it can be burnished by passing a strip of soft cloth around the turning, and working the cloth strip backwards and forwards and up and down the turning.

Sealed wax finish

For light woods, and where the piece is likely to be frequently handled, it might be a good idea to apply a sealant onto the wood before waxing. Where the wood is very pale it should be brushed with a couple of thin coats of white polish, dried and then rubbed down with 000 wire wool. Use a darker shellac on darker woods. Bring to a high gloss with a quick-drying wax. The disadvantage of this finish is that the wax serves only to fill and shine the surface, and it will never quite acquire the beautiful patination of waxed pieces that have been handled, rubbed and waxed for years.

Waxing antique and finished furniture

As with all of the above finishes, do not use waxes that clean and wax with a dual action. Avoid using quick-drying waxes where a piece already has a built-up wax finish, because these waxes contain strong solvents which will tend to strip the existing wax from the finish.

Select a slow-drying wax and a few soft rags. Remove from the rags zips, buttons, and hooks that might score the surface. Apply wax very thinly over the piece, rubbing it carefully into the corners and around the edges of the drawers, doors and doorframes. Wipe all parts clean of excess wax.

Allow the wax to harden for a short

while, and then burnish. Work gently at first and, as the shine begins to appear, work with greater speed and apply more pressure.

Problems

Most problems with wax finishes are caused by the wax decaying. Heat marks, water marks and areas where the wax has been dried and bleached by the sunlight can all be revived by rubbing the affected area with turps and then wax. Just sufficient solvent is required to reconstitute the wax finish. The wax and turpentine should be given a while to work.

A localised darkening of the wood will appear at the area where the turps has been applied. This will slowly disappear. Refinish using a slow drying wax.

Patching into wax finish

Patches need to be carefully selected and very tidily inserted into the wood. Chemical and water stains can be used to help match the colour; oil stains should be avoided.

Once the patch is in place, the problem is to build on the patch a surface which matches the surrounding wax finish.

There are two methods that can be used.

(a) If a cosmetic job is required, stain and colour it, and seal it with a built up body of shellac. Allow this to dry, and rub it down with wire wool and wax to finish. This is only a superficial repair but it will be quite satisfactory in places where the surface is not subjected to much wear or rough usage.

(b) A more thorough repair can be achieved with the following process. Warm the area with a hair dryer or fan heater, and rub in a mixture of slow-drying wax and a little turpentine. Rub this well into the surface, and allow it to cool and harden. Repeat the same process, with an undiluted quick-drying wax, and allow it to cool. Finish with a few application of slow-drying wax. Burnish the area until an even shine is achieved.

IDENTIFYING A FINISH

Shellac (including French polish)

A new shellac finish is bright, translucent, and thin. French polish is glass-like and without any signs of brushmarks, sandpaper, etc.

Neither finish stays unmarked for very long; shellac is a vulnerable finish. It decomposes with heat to form white opaque marks. Water left to lie on the surface will leave areas of white semi-transparent polish. Bruises and scratches are emphasised by the broken and flaked finish at the edge of the scratch and rim of the bruises. These appear a yellow-white colour. If a piece is old it is likely to have a shellac finish. Pour a drop of meths in a back corner; shellac will soften, and lose its shine.

Varnish

This is a more durable finish. Sometimes runs and puddles of varnish collect in areas difficult to work with a brush. A slightly flexible quality prevents the finish from being so easily damaged by bruising or scratching. A piece that has had a lot of use without showing the marks mentioned for shellac, may have a varnish finish.

Check by dropping a very small quantity of meths in a back corner. Varnish will be unaffected by the meths; white spirit or turpentine, however, will tend to soften it.

Wax

A faded wax finish will immediately revive if rubbed with a slow-drying wax or a cloth dampened with a drop of turpentine. A wax finish can be scraped and marked with a fingernail. Wax that has been sujected to heat will decompose to a crumbly, white, opaque appearance.

Cellulose

A cellulose finish is hard, and difficult to mark. It is applied to modern furniture, where it forms a brittle, glass-like film. A cellulose finish will be untouched by turps or meths, but will be softened with cellulose paint thinners.

Varnish and linseed oil

This gives a beautiful finish. Faded and dirty pieces can be restored by rubbing with turps and linseed oil. Much of the polish is below the surface of the timber. The polish looks thin and yet (unlike cellulose) appears to penetrate deep into the fibres of the wood. Scrub an inconspicuous corner with a damp brillo pad, remove all trace of the finish, and then wipe boiled linseed oil over the area. The finish will be restored (temporarily) and no sign of the damage will be evident.

19 Upholstery

Upholstery requires only a limited range of tools, most of them inexpensive. The webbing strainer can be made at home, using the designs on pp. 201-2.

Upholstery supplies are best bought from an upholstery supply specialist, where advice on suitable materials will be available.

TOOLS – AND THEIR USES

The tools generally required for upholstery work are illustrated below. If a number of chairs is going to be upholstered, it is handy to make up some boards to bolt to the top of the workshop trestles. These will restrain the chair legs once the chair is perched on the trestles.

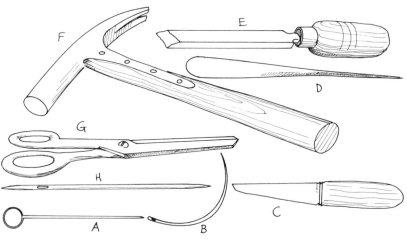

A skewer *B* spring needle *C* sharp knife *D* regulator *E* ripping chisel *F* upholstery hammer *G* sharp scissors *H* straight needle

Ripping chisels

These are used for removing old and worn upholstery. An old screwdriver or chisel will be ideal for this purpose. The chisel is lodged against, and angled down beneath the head of the tack, and struck sharply with a wooden mallet. A couple of sharp blows with the mallet will be enough to loosen the tack which, because it is tapered, will lift out easily. The ripping chisel should always be used with the direction of the grain, otherwise the hard sideways strokes

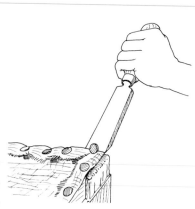

of the mallet may split the framework of the chair. At corners, the blow should be struck against the outside of the tack, forcing it into the centre of the rail; this will prevent the tack from splitting the vulnerable end grain at the corners of the chair.

Hammer

This can be a normal pin hammer, standard equipment in a restoration workshop, or a purpose-built upholstery tack hammer. The latter has a claw at one end of the head, and a specially-strengthened handle to permit tacks and nails to be levered out. A cabriole hammer should be used where tacking is needed close to a finished wood frame. It has a finer head, which reduces the danger of accidentally striking and damaging the finish of the chair.

Tacks

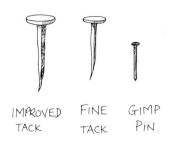

IMPROVED TACK   FINE TACK   GIMP PIN.

Upholstery tacks should be purchased loose. Pre-packed tacks tend to be blunt, and once nailed into place are very difficult to remove. Blued cut tacks are ideal and can be bought in two kinds, the fine and the improved. Fine tacks are thinner than the improved.

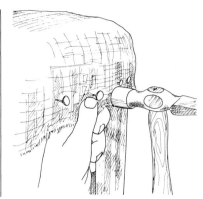

Cut upholstery tacks have a sharp point and can be pressed into position, through the material and into the framework, with the thumb. The left hand should hold the material while the thumb acts as a guide for the hammer as it strikes the tack home.

Scissors

These should be of good quality and comfortable to hold. Their sharp cutting edges can be maintained by occasional honing with an oilstone.

Needles

Needles should be kept clean and free of rust. Semi-circular spring needles for sewing down springs, bridle ties, etc. will be needed, also one or two straight needles. These are double-ended, with the eye close to one end. Those with a triangular section (bayonet needles) are used for stitching; buttoning is done with the smooth, round needles.

Regulator and skewers

The regulator is a simple steel tool used to manipulate the stuffing to a regular and even distribution. The pointed end can be worked beneath the scrim covering to manoeuvre the hair filling. The flat end is used to press a crease into the corners and tucks. Skewers are used to provide temporary fastening for the materials, freeing the hands for other work.

Webbing strainers

These are used to pull the webbing tight across the framework of the chair. They are easily made, and simple to use. Great care must be taken, however, to avoid over-straining the webbing and distorting the framework. Web tension can be checked by bouncing the tack hammer on the webbing. If the hammer bounces back smartly, it is tight enough. If the hammer fails to bounce, the webbing is too loose.

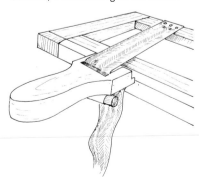

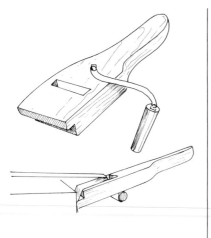
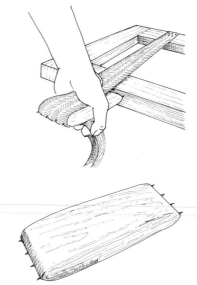
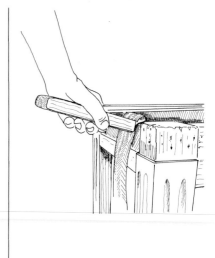

MATERIALS

Webbing

The black and white, herringbone-pattern webbing lasts well and stretches very little. It can normally be bought by the metre (39 inches), or by the roll (approximately 18 metres, 19½ yards).

Hessian

This is coarse, brown, open-weave cloth, made from jute, and sold in 1 m (39 in.) widths. Always use best quality hessian for upholstery work.

Scrim

This has a more open weave than hessian. It is used for the first covering over the initial fibre stuffing.

Calico

An unbleached cotton cloth, used as a final cover over the wadding, prior to finishing with the decorative cover.

Wadding

Cotton wadding can be bought by the roll in varying thicknesses. Some wadding has a skin to one side; this should be used over the fibre filling, skin down, soft side uppermost. Thicker wadding can be bought without a skin. This needs to be separated and laid to the correct thickness. Wadding serves both to fill irregularities in the surface of the stuffing, and to prevent the fibre or hair fillings of the secondary stuffing from working through the finished cover.

Upholstery hair and fibres

All kinds of materials are found as stuffing in upholstered furniture. Straw, woodshavings, shoddy (shredded rags) and any other dirty and compressed fillings should be discarded. Where the filling is hair, coconut fibre (coir) or black Algerian palm grass fibre, it may be possible to tease the fillings by shredding them in the hands, removing the lumps and compressed parts, and washing and drying the fibres. This is a messy operation which should be done out-of-doors.

It is often possible to buy bags of horsehair (which is usually a mixture of horses' tails and manes, hair from cows' tails and short hog hair) from junk shops where the proprietor has had the opportunity to rip apart old mattresses. This may be excellent filling material, but should always be teased and washed before being reused. Any extra filling material can be bought from an upholsterer's suppliers.

REPAIRS TO DAMAGED CHAIR COVERINGS

Tears and cuts

These should be repaired immediately, before the material distorts and stretches around the rent. Cut a patch of calico that is about 7/8 in. (29 mm) wider than the damaged area, and cover it with a thin layer of latex adhesive. Insert this through the tear, work it carefully beneath the material, holds its edges by skewers worked into the stuffing and gently press the cloth upon it. Only gentle pressure is required, otherwise the cloth will become distorted and rucked. Match and align the torn fibres and allow the repair to dry.

Replacing broken spring webbing

This is a temporary solution, which only postpones a full re-upholstering. If the webbing supporting the springs has failed, then it is very likely that the hessian over the springs has also worn through and that, before long, the stuffing will begin to fall through the seat. However, the technique is to invert the chair over the table or workbench, and remove the old webbing with a ripping chisel and mallet. Misalign the springs, so that the new front-to-back webbing can be tacked and tensioned in place. Weave the first crossing web, tack and tension it. Replace the first row of springs, move to the next strip of webbing and repeat the process. It may not be possible to use this technique on the third or last row of springs, as the framework of the chair may make the displacing of the springs impossible. In this case, weave the webbing across the framework, tack one end in place and

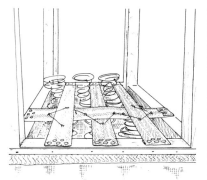

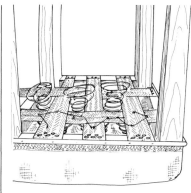

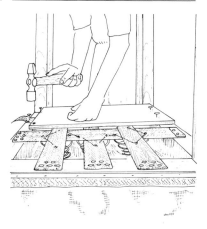

position the springs. Before tensioning the webbing, tack a flat board across the underside of the chair to compress the springs, ensuring that the board does not hinder the fastening of the web. Tension and tack the web in place and remove the board. Stitch the springs in place from below.

STRIPPING AWAY OLD UPHOLSTERY

Much can be learnt from the old upholstery, so it should be removed with care. In general, it is best to work in the reverse order to the way in which it was upholstered. Be careful to avoid damaging the showing surfaces of the woodwork, and remember to use the ripping chisel with the direction of the grain; working inwards at the corners. Preserve the outer covering as a rough template for the new material. If the chair has upholstered armrests and back, as well as the seat, the old cloth can be used to arrange a repeated pattern on the new material.

It will be noticed that the original

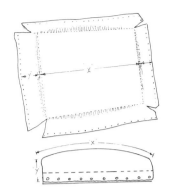

will show, by the wear and the fading of the cloth, as well as by the creases in the fabric, the exact contours of the chair. With an overstuffed piece of furniture, this information may be very useful when restuffing.

All tacks, webbing, and hessian should be discarded. Springs should be tested; those that are rusty or compressed out of shape should be thrown away. If the filling is still resilient it may be possible to reuse it.

CHECKING THE FRAMEWORK OF THE CHAIR

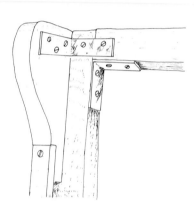

Before re-upholstering is commenced the chair must be thoroughly checked for broken parts and loose joints. Any breakage should be repaired, and any surface abrasions, bruising, or other damage cleaned up.

Test the chair for loose joints by grasping the arms and feeling for indications of weakness or looseness. Press against the back to test the joints between the back legs, the seat, and the front legs. Any sideways wobble will be revealed by holding the seat of the chair and pushing it firmly sideways.

Techniques for repairing broken or loose joints are described on p. 82. Often these will be inappropriate, as the framework of upholstered chairs is fairly complicated, and does not permit single pieces to be removed without dismantling the entire piece. If this is the case, metal brackets and wooden supporting pieces can be glued and nailed in place. This,

however, can only be done if the repairs are to be covered later with material.

It is extremely difficult to assess the strength of a piece of furniture. Err on the side of caution, and reinforce any weak parts before the upholstery makes a later repair impossible.

Worm holes should be injected with woodworm killer and the surrounding wood treated and left to dry before the upholstery process is begun.

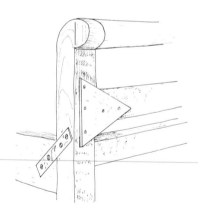

MAKING A LOOSE SEAT FRAME

This is often necessary when upholstering the loose seat of a dining chair. Many old and worn chairs can be bought in a derelict state, and may not have any loose seat frame at all.

Others may be so badly made that they require replacement. The state of the loose seat, or the quality of its construction, rarely reflects the quality or age of the chair.

Loose seat frames can be made from pine or hardwood. Hardwood is preferable, as tacks held in pine tend

to work loose. A length of planed wood is needed, equivalent to the perimeter of the chair seat (with a little spare for cutting), approximately 1 x 3 in. (25 x 75 mm). This should be cut to lengths that fit into the rebate of the chair seat, with about ⅛ in. (2-3 mm) space at one end.

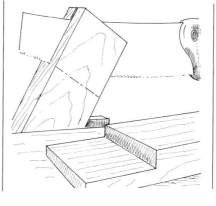

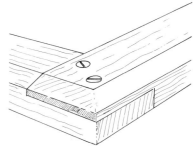

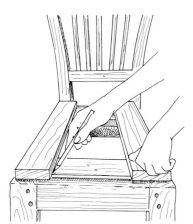

Once each piece is cut to length and fitted, remove the side pieces from the chair rebate. Place the front and back pieces in the rebate, and place the side pieces across these. Align them with the edge of the rebate and, in each corner, draw a pencil line where they overlap. Without moving the boards, mark the same for the underside. Number the boards and cut each corner with cross-halving joints. Re-assemble the framework in position in the rebate, and check it for size. Glue and screw the frame together, and leave it in the rebate for the glue to dry.

Once the glue is dry, remove the frame and mark a bevel on the top outside edge. Hold the frame in the vice and cut this bevel with a plane or chisel.

When the bevel is in place, the final fitting can take place. Take two scraps of the finishing upholstery material and place them together in the front rebate. Put the frame in place. It should be an easy fit. If it is tight, remove a shaving from the front until it fits easily into the rebate. Repeat this operation at the side. The double thickness of material should be about the equivalent of the final thickness of cover when the job is finished. If the frame is a sloppy fit in the rebate, tack some card to the sides to pack them out.

UPHOLSTERING A LOOSE SEAT

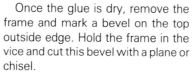

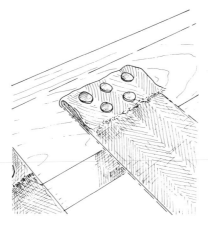

Place the loose frame on the work surface, with its front edge facing away. Take some webbing, fold the end back about ⅝ in. (15 mm), place the fold about ⅞ in. (20 mm) in from the edge of the frame, and tack it to the centre of the front frame, using five ⅝ in. (15 mm) tacks. Tension the webbing and tack it to the centre of the back frame, holding it with three ⅝ in. (15 mm) tacks. Cut off the webbing, leaving about 1 in. (25 mm) overhanging the edge of the frame. Repeat the procedure on each side of the centre web. Turn the frame to one side, weave the webbing through the front to back webbing, and tack it. Loose seats usually have two transverse webs.

The front webbing and the webbing on one side of the frame will be held by five tacks per web, driven through the folded material. The other ends of the webbing will be held by three tacks with the ends left unfolded and flapping at the side of the loose seat.

Cut some hessian to cover the framework. Allow about ⅝ in. (15 mm) overhang of hessian all round for a fold.

With the frame again positioned with its front edge away from the worker, fold back the edge and tack the centre front of the hessian cover. Align the hessian so that its weave is centred with the centre of the frame, and place a temporary tack in the middle of the back rail to hold the hessian in place.

Fold back the hessian and tack it to the front rail, working from the centre of the frame using ⅜ in. (9 mm) tacks at about 1½ in. (40 mm) centres. Remove the temporary tack in the back frame and, pulling the hessian towards you to achieve a slight tension, tack the centre. Continue as before, but without folding the hessian. Work to the sides from the centre, spacing the tacks at about 2¼ in. (60 mm) intervals. Repeat the operation at each side. Only very slight sideways tension should be put on the first side to be tacked, otherwise the weave of the cloth will be distorted. Tack both sides as described for the rear frame member. Do not fold the

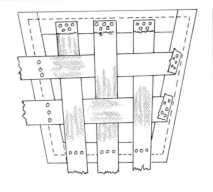

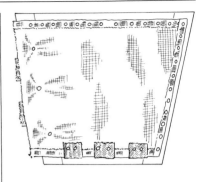

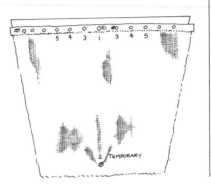

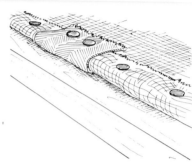

hessian. Drive the tacks at about 2¼ in. (60 mm) centres.

When the hessian has been tacked all round, work round the frame, folding the edges back and

tacking them down. When the loose ends of the webbing are encountered, they should be folded over the hessian fold and held with two ⅝ in. (15 mm) tacks.

Tying bridle ties

Take a spring needle and about a yard (metre) of twine. Start off with a slip knot at one corner of the frame, 3¼ in. (80 mm) in from both outside edges. Sew long loops of twine parallel with the side, until they reach a point about 3¼ in. (80 mm) from the front edge. Work round the framework until there are loops about 3¼ in. (80 mm) from each edge. The loops should be large enough to hold a handful of hair or fibre stuffing. If the loops are too large they will be ineffective at holding the stuffing in place. A

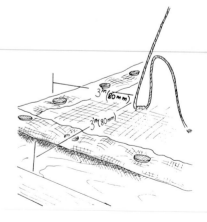

simple guide is to make the loop so that your hand can just be slipped beneath it. No knots are required when tying bridle ties, except at the ends of the twine; a simple running stitch is all that is required.

Stuffing the seat

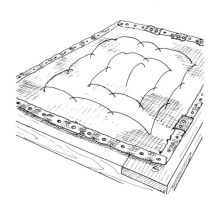

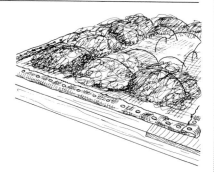

Most upholstered seats look best if they have a gentle curve, rather than a mole-hill profile. When stuffing the seat, bear in mind the final appearance of the chair. Good-quality fibre or hair fillings will not compress more than the natural spring in the fibres will allow. The calico and final coverings will look strained and lumpy if an attempt is made to change the profile of the chair once the stuffing is in place and completed.

Once the outer row of ties has been completed, work in a second row, closer to the centre, keeping the ties the same size and the same distance from the first row: 3¼ in. (80 mm).

Take a handful of stuffing and push it beneath an outside bridle tie at one corner. Continue around the edge of the chair until all of the outside row is filled. Next fill the centre ties. Use a similar amount of stuffing for each tie. When all of the ties have been filled, work around the seat, pushing stuffing between the ties, between the rows of stuffing and between the stuffing and the edge of the frame. Do not overstuff the edge; allow for a gentle graduation in thickness, from the first row of bridle ties to the bevel at the edge.

Calico covering

Once the stuffing is in place, moderately domed and even, take a tape measure or a flexible rule and measure the dimensions for the calico cover. Mark out and cut the calico cover, and lay it over the seat. Fasten the calico to the centre of the front row, and then to the centre of the back. Do not stretch the calico. It should be sufficiently tight to hold the stuffing down, but not so loose that it folds up and rucks the chair cover. Tack the centre of the sides, as for the front and back, driving the tacks partly home in the edge of the chair, just below the bevel. Drive in one or two more tacks each side (only partly in) to hold the calico in position.

Lift the framework and hold it, upholstered side inwards. Pull the calico around the edge, remove the front temporary tacks, start from the centre, and nail the calico in place. Work around the underside of the frame, tacking the calico in place. Test the undercovering for tension. Place your hands on the seat, one at

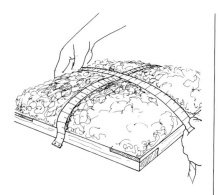

each side and, without pressing them into the upholstery, move them over the calico towards each other. If this movement pulls up a fold of cloth at the centre of the seat, the fastenings on one side will need to be removed and the calico tensioned slightly. Leave fixing the corners until the tension of the calico and the fit of the loose seat into the frame have been checked. The

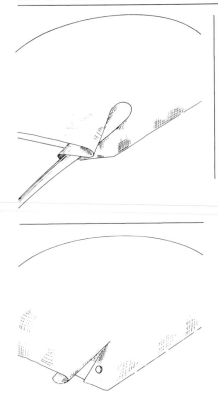

corners can then be tacked and cut as illustrated in the diagrams.

Trim the calico around the underside of the frame with a sharp knife. Lay the seat, face-up, on the work surface and cover it with a layer of wadding. This should not extend below the point of the bevel on the seat frame, otherwise the loose seat will not fit into the rebate in its chair.

Take the covering material, centre the pattern, and mark and cut the cloth to shape. Some upholstery materials need to be laid with the pile oriented in a certain direction. If a set of chairs is being covered, the pattern or the direction of the pile should match on each chair. Seek advice on the particular requirements of the cloth when it is purchased.

Cover the seat in exactly the same way as before. Make sure that the weave of the cloth is centred on the centreline of the frame. Tack it temporarily, check, and then tack it to the underside of the frame with ⅜ in. (9 mm) tacks, neatly spaced at ⅞ in. (20 mm) centres.

Throughout this operation great care should be taken that the upholstered seat fits neatly into the rebate of the chair. If there is difficulty in fitting it in place, on no account force it. Considerable damage can be caused to the joint and to the rebate of the chair, more difficult and more expensive to repair than the relatively simple task of removing a row or two of tacks and planing down the wooden edge of the frame.

RE-UPHOLSTERING A SPRUNG DINING CHAIR

Remove the old covering and stuffing, invert the chair over two trestles, and remove the webbing holding the springs. Discard any rusty or distorted springs. Take an example of the springs you need to the upholsterer's suppliers, to help in replacing them.

Check the framework of the chair for loose joints and woodworm. Remedy all faults before commencing with the re-upholstery.

Webbing

Invert the chair and tack the webbing to the underside of the chair rails. Tension and secure each end with five tacks. Turn the chair right side up for the rest of the work.

Springs

Place the springs at the intersection of the webbing. Provided that the new webbing is put back in approximately the position of the previous webbing the springs will be placed correctly. The illustration here shows the normal webbing and spring positions for a dining chair.

Place the springs on the webbing, and use a spring needle and twine to sew them into position. The top of the springs will emerge well above the level of the seat rails. If a firm, high, front edge to the seat is required, then it is usually a help to screw a batten on top of the front rail to avoid building up an excessively deep and firm edge of stuffing.

Take a length of laid cord, or some good quality string, and hammer a 5/8 in. (15 mm) improved tack at the middle front of the seat, and one at the centre rear of the seat. Hold the string over the springs, add about 12 in. (300 mm) to the length, and cut it.

Start at the back of the seat, with a slip knot around the back tack, and work towards you, knotting the centre row of springs as you go. Do not attempt to depress the springs; they simply need to be restrained from moving in a lateral direction. Tie the end of the string to the tack in the front rail. Repeat this procedure for the other lines of springing, and then from side to side as well. Front and

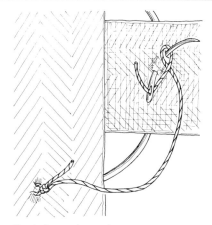

Knots for sewing springs

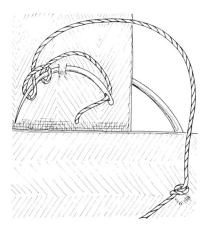

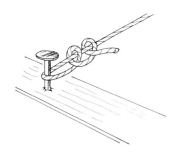

The double hitch will prevent the springs working loose should the sewing twine break

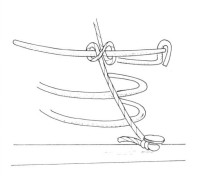

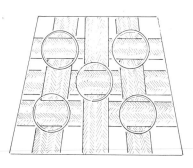

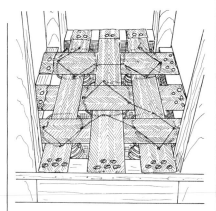

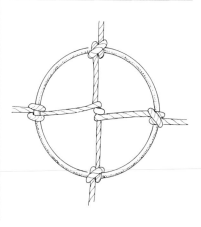

Underside of chair, showing the springs sewn into position

side springs can be given a slight lean towards the edge rail as they are tied.

Measure, fit, and nail a heavy quality hessian over the springs, and down to the top of the chair frame. Use the spring needle again to sew each spring to the hessian cover, using the same sewing technique used in the bottom webbing.

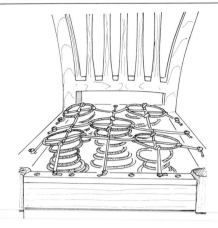

Bridle ties

Sew these in position as for the loose seat, knot the end and run the bridle ties around the seat, keeping about 3¼ in. (80 mm) away from the edge. Sew in a second line, closer to the centre of the chair.

Filling

Fill the bridle ties as for the loose seat, and pack any hollows between the ties and around the edge with a little extra filling to give the edge firmness. Cover the stuffing with a piece of scrim or hessian, cut and tacked temporarily in place.

Sewing the first stuffing

With the first stuffing beneath the bridle ties, and the scrim cover temporarily tacked in place, prepare to stitch the stuffing in place. Take a long needle and twine, and mark the position of the stitches on the top of the scrim. These should be spaced regularly, starting about 34 in. (90 mm) from the edge of the chair, and working around the seat, towards the centre of the chair.

Work the needle from the top. Push it down through the scrim, and out between the springs. Reinsert it a short distance, about ¼-½ in. (5-10 mm) away, in the line of the running stitch, and push it back, emerging close to the original entry point. Tie a slip knot, pull the loop quite tight and continue working around the edge of the chair. Avoid pulling the needle clear of the springs and webbing. As soon as the point of

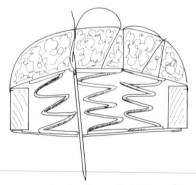

the needle is clear of the hessian, twist it sideways and push it back up. This will prevent the twine from becoming entangled in the springs. Make a running stitch, pausing to tension the twine as it works around the chair. Finish in the centre of the seat, fastening the end of the twine with a knot.

Check the stuffing of the seat. It should be firm and even. Badly filled parts should be supplemented before the scrim is permanently tacked in place.

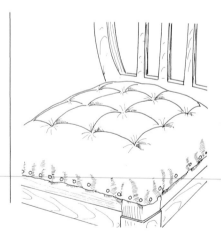

Fold under the frayed ends of the scrim, before tacking it onto the bevel on the outside top edge of the seat rail, or to the very top of the rebate. Make sure that no wisps of stuffing are left straggling after the scrim is tacked. Tuck them into the seat with the regulator as the fold is made and tacked.

Blind stitching

Rows of blind stitching, parallel to the framework of the seat, serve to stiffen the edges of the upholstery. The first row of stitching should be started close to the framework. The same needle is threaded with about a yard (metre) of twine and held with the eye of the needle closest to the hand. Knot the twine to the scrim and push the long pointed end of the needle up through the scrim and stuffing at an angle of about 40°. The needle should emerge from the scrim about 2¼-3¼ in. (60-80 mm) from the edge. Pull the needle through until the eye reaches the scrim. Then make a sideways movement with the needle, and push it back through the stuffing, swinging the needle sideways and back out, close to where it entered the scrim. The object of the swinging action is to scoop as much fibre as possible into the loop as it is worked

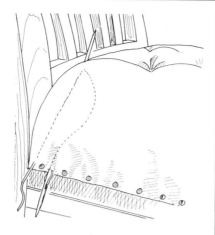

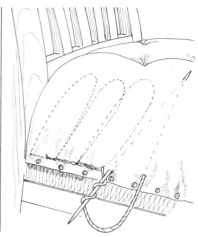

back to the edge. Before pulling the needle from the scrim, take the loop of twine and make three or four turns around the needle with it. As the needle is pulled clear, these loops will form an overhand knot on the side of the scrim, which will prevent the loop from loosening as the next blind stitch is made.

This stitching is carried on around the edge of the chair. For most seats a second row, a little higher up, and perhaps a third, may be stitched into the edge. However, one or two rows are usually sufficient to build up a firmness to the edge with should then be finished with a rolling stitch.

Rolling stitch

This gives a vertical hard edge to the chair front. As the evenness of the edging roll will, to some extent, depend upon the line of the stitching, it is a good idea to pencil in a line around the top of the chair seat about 1½ in. (40 mm) from the edge, both around the top and around the side of the seat. Hold the needle as for the blind stitch, and push it into the scrim at the line in the side and about 1 in. (25 mm) from the back leg. Push the needle right through the scrim and stuffing until it emerges on the top line about 1 in. (25 mm) from the back leg. Move the needle back towards the rear leg, and push it back through the scrim down to the line on the side, as close to the leg as possible. Tie a slip knot around the thread close to the needle, and pull the twine tight. The start of the roll will begin to form. Move the needle

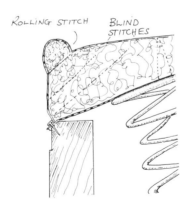

ROLLING STITCH   BLIND STITCHES

forwards about 1 in. (25 mm) from the first stitch and repeat the operation. As the needle is returned down next to the first stitch, make three turns of twine around it as it is pulled clear (as for blind stitch). The rolling stitch is continued right around the sides and front of the seat. For stools, it is carried round the entire perimeter of the seat.

Second stuffing

Once the edge roll is complete, the seat will appear to have changed shape. From the originally domed seat, the edge stitching has lowered the centre and raised and hardened the edge. In-filling will be required to build upon this firm base the desired final shape for the seat. Bridle ties are again worked into the top surface of the scrim, and more stuffing is tucked beneath them. A softer, springier stuffing is generally used for this layer, but whatever is used it should be laid carefully to avoid lumpiness and, where necessary, to even out depressions in the first stuffing.

Calico covering

Once the second stuffing is completed, the calico cover should be tacked in place. This will need to be fitted at the front corners as for the loose seat, and around the rear legs and arm supports. Use this calico layer to perfect the cuts that will be necessary when the final covering is made. Some suggestions for cuts are illustrated here. Be cautious, and undercut rather than make too great an incision. Use the regulator to make folds lie flat.

Tack the calico in place, and finish the edge with a sharp knife. Cover the calico with a layer of wadding, and then with the final covering cloth. Fold the pleats in the front, and cut around the back legs and arm supports. Where necessary, sew any gaps using the ladder stitch with a small semi-circular needle.

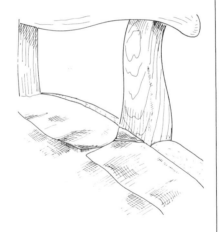
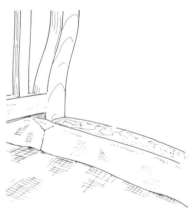
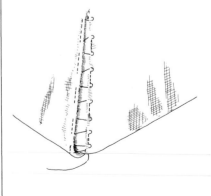

Gimp

The raw edge of the final cover will need to be hidden, and a specially-made, decorative tape called gimp should be purchased for this. Choose the tape carefully. The colour of the gimp can either be used to complement the seat covering, or to emphasise it. Experiment with a scrap of the covering material before buying.

Fasten the first piece of gimp to the back of the chair. Back tack the end to the chairleg, using two gimp pins. Cut the gimp to length, allowing about ⅝ in. (15 mm) for a fold at the end. Cover the inside of the tape with a thin coating of latex-based adhesive. Press the gimp in place, fold the end under, apply a little more adhesive to the face of the fold, and hold it in position with two gimp pins, nailed one above the other.

Repeat around the side and front edges of the chair. Pull the gimp tight before pressing it into position and

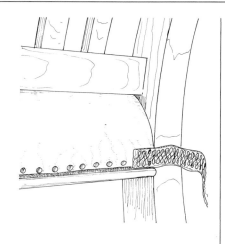

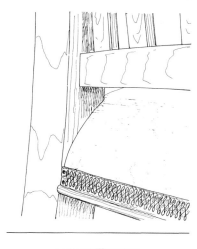

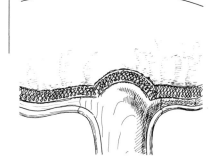

ensure that only a thin layer of adhesive is pasted to the back of the gimp. At awkward corners sometimes found over chair legs, the gimp can be glued and sewn into place.

FOAM UPHOLSTERY

The use of foam eliminates many of the skilful and time-consuming procedures necessary in traditional upholstery. Care should be taken to choose a foam that is non-inflammable, or that at least does not produce toxic gases when it burns. It is also worthwhile to remember to cover latex foam with calico, or another closely woven cloth lining, to prevent the foam from deteriorating if it is left for long periods in direct sunlight.

It is not necessary to use traditional coil springs when re-upholstering a sprung dining chair; an extra layer of foam, or the use of rubber webbing, is a satisfactory alternative.

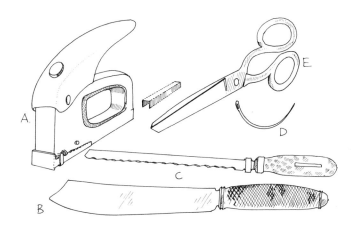

Tools for working with foam upholstery.
***A** staple gun **B** carving knife **C** electric carving knife **D** small semi-circular needle **E** scissors*

Materials

Two slightly different methods can be used. The first includes the use of rubber webbing, to give spring to the seat; the foam in the second method is rested upon a wooden or traditionally-tensioned webbed base.

Some rubber webbing, a supply of 2 in. (50 mm) medium density foam, and some 1 in. (25 mm) medium density foam, a suitable foam adhesive (ask advice from the supplier), some calico, a selection of upholstery tacks, and gimp pins will be needed.

Upholstery using rubber webbing

Rubber upholstery webbing comprises two layers of rayon reinforcing tape cut on the bias, to allow the web to stretch. These are impregnated with rubber, and sandwiched between layers of rubber. This permits the webbing to be nailed without the fastenings tearing through, and also gives a graduated spring to the web – the rayon layers put an increasing restraint upon the stretch of the rubber as the load upon it is increased. In this respect the webbing is very much like a traditional steel coil spring and it is ideally suited to replace worn springs

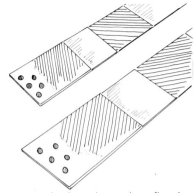

or stretched tension springs fitted to a wooden framework.

Laminated rubber webbing is obtainable in 2 and 1½ in. (50 and 36 mm) widths. For small chair seats the 1½ in. (36 mm) webbing is the most suitable.

Procedure

Remove existing upholstery using the techniques described on p. 200. The webbing fastened to support the coil springs was originally tacked to the underside of the seat frame. Tack the new webbing to the topside of the frame. Space the webbing its own width apart, and tension it before fastening.

Work with the chair front farthest away, and tack the end of the rubber webbing to the centre of the front rail. Use five ⅝ in. (15 mm) improved tacks per end, making sure that the tacks are driven perpendicular to the supporting frame. This is important because tack heads nailed at a slant have a tendency to damage the rubber webbing.

Pull the webbing straight and mark with felt tip pen the point where it crosses the back frame. The amount of pre-tension applied to the webbing determines the degree of punchiness of the seat. For a front to back measurement of 17¾ in. (450 mm) the webbing should be stretched about 2 in. (50 mm). This should give a firm seat. It is very important for each webbing strap to

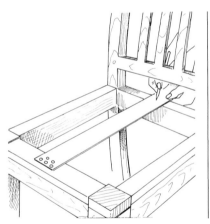

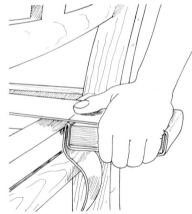

have the same tension. The simplest technique is to hold the webbing over the back of the chair frame, and mark the rubber web where it crosses the edge. Measure in (for instance) the 2 in. (50 mm) tensioning measurement, and mark it on the web. Pull the webbing until the tensioning mark reaches the back-rail edge. Fasten the tape with five ⅝ in. (15 mm) improved tacks.

Use the same procedure for each line of webbing. If the chair seat is tapered or curved, a degree of variation in the amount of tension will

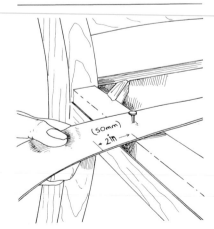

have to be made. Longer spans of webbing should be tighter. Keep to the marks, however, and assess the slight variations in relation to the tensioning marks.

Once the front-to-back webs are fixed, tack the transverse webs in place. These should also be tensioned before fixing, and should pass either above or below the front-to-back webs. If they are woven between the webs the friction between the rubber surfaces will inhibit the stretching of the webbing.

Covering the webbing

A very loose covering of hessian should be tacked around the edge of the seat. At no point should the hessian support the weight of the occupant of the chair. Make sure that the hessian is not too tight.

Fitting and cutting the foam

Before cutting the foam to shape, make a cardboard template of the seat. The edges of the foam seat padding should be clean, straight and vertical. Once the initial cut is made, subsequent adjustments are very difficult. For a simple slab effect the template can be laid upon the 2 in. (50 mm) medium density foam and the foam cut to shape.

If a slightly domed appearance to the seat is required (more accurately simulating a traditionally upholstered seat) a packing piece of foam will be needed to place beneath the upper foam, and the top foam must be cut larger (see below).

Cutting the foam

When using a carving knife, lubricate the blade with a wet rag prior to slicing through the foam in long, clean cutting strokes. Support the foam on a table, with the cutting line overhanging the edge by about ½ in. (10 mm). If the foam distorts under the pressure of the hand holding it to the table, place a board over the foam before pressing down. Where an electric carving knife is used, move it steadily through the foam, using the side of the table as a straight edge.

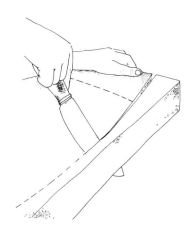

Making the domed effect

Where a slight doming in the seat is desired, the top 2 in. (50 mm) medium density foam should be cut to shape using a modified template which allows for the loss in width caused by the extra height in the centre. Take a second piece of medium density foam 1 in. (25 mm) thick, and cut it to size about 2¼ in. (60 mm) smaller all round. Cut a bevel on the upper side of the foam as illustrated. Glue this piece to the underside of the thicker top foam. This forces the top foam up, causing the domed appearance in the chair seat.

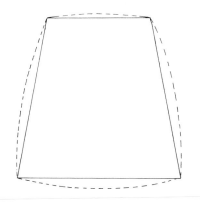

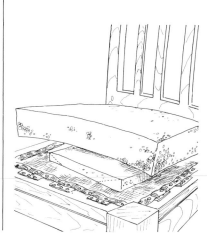

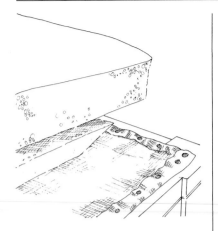

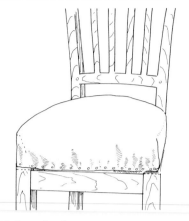

Fixing the foam

Cut some strips of calico, the thickness of the top foam plus the depth of the nailing rebate on the seat frame. Glue these around the side with the extra width hanging below the lower edge of the foam. Position the foam on the seat frame and, starting from the centre of each side, tack the calico strips to the frame. Where the domed effect is desired, the foam will need to be pushed down against the framework.

Take care not to form irregular bulges in the surface of the foam. No further stuffing will be used, so the foam must be the desired height, profile and smoothness.

Once the foam is tacked in place it should be covered by a layer of calico. This prevents the foam from rotting in the sunlight and also provides a barrier between the covering material and the foam, permitting them to move and avoiding the build-up of wrinkles in the cover. The procedures for covering the seat and applying the gimp are described on pp. 207, 212.

RUSH WEAVING

It is difficult to rush-weave chairs or stools unless the seat framework has raised corners. This is because the twisted rushes brace against the corners of the chair and are prevented from working loose. The rails for a rush-woven seat should be smooth, with all sharp edges rounded before commencing the weaving.

Rushes

Rushes are bought in bundles — bolts. A bolt is about 3 yd. (3 m) long, with a circumference at the base of approximately 1 yd. (1 m). In each bolt the dry rushes are packed with their tapered ends together. This gives the bolt a conical shape.

Bolts can be stacked on end, but loose rushes should be kept level, well-ventilated and dry. A roof space where they can rest between rafters or across sticks makes a good storage area. In such conditions rushes can be stored for a number of years, although it is best, if large quantities of rush weaving is undertaken, to arrange a rotation of stock to prevent an accumulation of old and probably damaged rushes at the bottom of the pile.

Preparation of the rushes

Select sufficient rushes for the work in hand. If in doubt, prepare less than is needed. It is a simple and quick matter to prepare them, but a nuisance to dry those that have been wetted unnecessarily. Wet rushes should never be stored with dry rushes.

Select about equal numbers of thick and thin rushes (the bolts contain a variety of sizes), and place them in a bath of cold water. Rushes will be fractured and weakened if they are folded dry, so gently bend the tapered ends to fit into the water. Weight the rushes with an old wet towel, and leave them to soak in the water for about two minutes.

Remove the rushes and fold them in half. Wrap them tightly in a towel and leave them overnight.

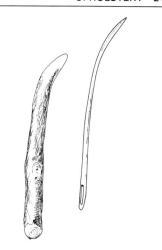

Equipment

Some thin, good quality string, a rushing needle and a padding stick are necessary, but it also handy to have a couple of old towels to wipe the rushes, and an assortment of dry rush tips and butts (thick ends) for the padding.

Technique

The basic rushing technique only works on seats with a rectangular frame. Where a seat has tapered sides and perhaps a curved front rail a special starting technique is used which reduces the shape to a rectangle. This is described in a later section.

Select two rushes, one thin and one thick. Give the tip of each rush a gentle tug to break away any weak parts, and wipe them clean. Wipe from the tip to the butt to avoid splitting the rush.

Hold the two rushes together tip to butt, and tie one end of the pair to the inside edge of the seat with a short length of string. Keep the ends and the knot on the inside so that the top and edge of the seat are not distorted by their extra thickness.

Twist the two rushes together, working each round each, to give a regular and even rope of rush. As only a small part of the rush will eventually show in the finished seat, only twist the part that will be visible. Work the rushes in the pattern illustrated, twisting only where the rushes will show on the top and sides. As the end of the rushes is reached, tie a new rush to each with a reef knot or a simple half hitch, and continue weaving. Keep the twist of rushes as even and as thick as possible.

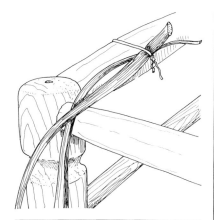

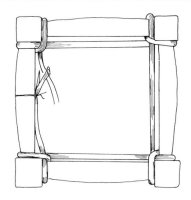

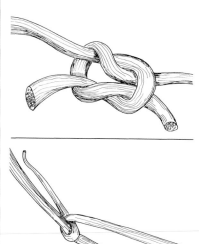

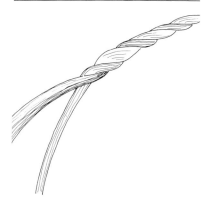

If a third rush is needed to increase the width of a pair of thin rushes, it can be introduced into the twisted part of the weaving where the turns are being made at the corners of the chair. Leave the thin end about 2-2¼ in. (50-60 mm) free of the twisting, to be tucked into the padding space in the seat. The new addition will be firmly bonded into the lay of the twist, and will require no additional fastening.

As the seat takes form, insert

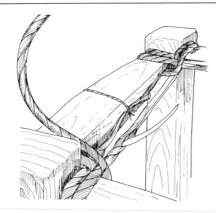

packing into the spaces left between the top and bottom layer of weaving. Invert the seat, and work into the spaces wads of folded dry rush. Do not use damp rushes for padding, as they will not only shrink, but may cause mould to grow in the interior of the seat.

Continue with the weaving until about 2¼ in. (60 mm) of seat has been woven all round. Put the chair aside so that the rushes can dry.

Finishing

Once the work has dried (24 hours is usually sufficient) press the strands of the weaving together to tighten up the previous work and continue weaving as before. Unless the chair frame makes a perfect square, the final turns of rushing will have to be in a figure of eight form.

As the distances between the turns of rushing become less, it will be more difficult to pad the spaces between the top and bottom layer of rushes. Where the space is too confined, bridge the padding across the gap and weave over and under it.

As the centre of the seat is

approached, mark the centre point of the front and back rail. When the figure of eight weaving reaches this point, reverse the twist of the rushes so that, although the actual end of the weaving may be well to one side of the centre, the opposing twist makes it appear to meet in the middle.

The final twist of weave must be worked in place with the rush needle. To finish, tie the end of the rush to the strand opposite, underneath the centre of the seat. Tuck the ends of all the knots and stray wisps of padding into the seat to leave the bottom looking clean and tidy.

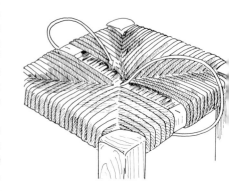

Rushing irregular seats

The techniques described below are used to square-up an irregular frame so that the bulk of the weaving can be completed in the straightforward method described above. In each case, it is worthwhile to square across from the back to the front, and mark a point about 1 in. (25 mm) in from each back leg, onto the front rail. These marks will help in bringing the shape to a square.

(a) Measure the difference in length between the front and rear seat rail. Divide the difference in two and estimate how many twisted

turns of rush will be needed to make up the distance. If each twisted pair of rushes takes up approximately ¼ in. (5 mm) of rail, and there is, for example, an extra 1 in. (25 mm) of seat rail to cover at each side (of the front rail), five pairs of rushes used once each side will be needed to make up that space.

Select five pairs of rushes, clean them, and place them in pairs, tip to butt. Tie all five pairs tightly to the centre of the left side rail. Twist and weave the first pair around the front left corner, take it across to the front right, and finish it with a temporary tie close beside the front right leg. Continue with the other rushes, temporarily tying each pair to the right seat rail. The fifth pair of rushes should complete the rectangle and so, before weaving this, gather the ends on the right-hand rail, and tie them securely to the centre of the side rail opposite to the ends on the left hand side.

Continue weaving with the fifth pair of rushes, around the front right leg, and then to the back right, etc.

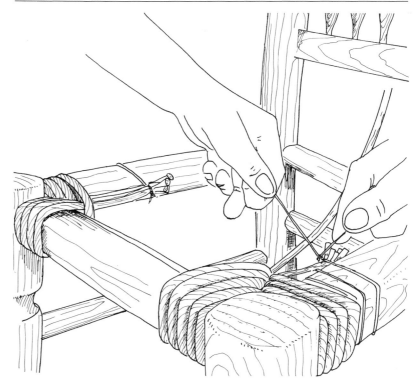

(b) This method is simpler than the previous, but requires more attention to the changing proportions of the seat while weaving is in progress.

Start weaving as for a normal rectangular seat, but after the first complete circuit of the frame is finished take two turns around each front leg every other complete time round. Take great care to keep the lay of the rush perpendicular and parallel to the front and back rail. It is easy to neglect to do this, and the resulting shape is very difficult to finish neatly.

SPLIT CANE WORK

Repairs to split cane work

It is possible to repair split cane seats and backs by pre-staining the new cane (with a water or oil stain) to a matching colour, and then weaving it in place using the techniques described here. Alternatively, the new cane can be stained with a brush once the repair work is complete. Old cane is dry and brittle and, where the damage is extensive, it is easier to remove and replace it all than to repair the fault. Cut the canework from around the framework using a sharp knife, and keep it to use as a guide when recaning.

Clear away the remaining cane, slice through the loops in the underside of the chair frame and

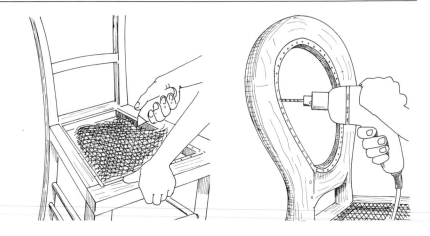

remove the pegs holding the ends of the cane, by pushing them out with a clearer. Where caning is blind (that is, where it does not pass right through the frame of the chair) the pegs will have to be drilled out.

Tools

A sharp penknife or Stanley knife will be needed for cutting through the chair seat and removing the old cane work; a punch and a light hammer for clearing blocked holes. One or two doublers will be needed; these are slightly tapered steel rods each set in a wooden handle. The ends should be rounded to prevent them from damaging the cane as they are thrust into the holes to anchor the cane and maintain the tension in the weave. The doubler should not be so narrow that the rod passes right through the hole, as it will not hold the cane, and may even snag the cane as it is passed under the frame, leaving the weave loose. A clearer will also be needed. This is like a doubler, except that the steel rod is of a smaller diameter. This is used to clear a way through the hole to allow more cane to be inserted. Both the clearer and the doublers can be made from wire nails, with their ends slightly tapered and smoothed.

A worn and very blunt kitchen knife, without its handle, will be

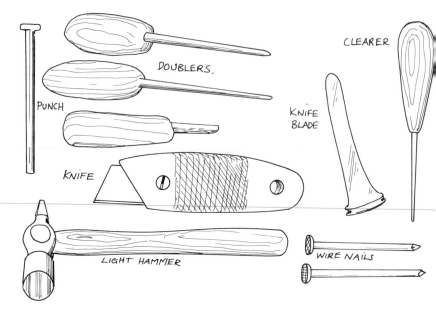

needed to help pass the cane through the weave of the seat. The blade should be ground to a thin, rounded end, and the edges burnished and smoothed to avoid damaging the cane or injuring the hands.

Split cane work

Cane

Split cane is obtained from the rattan vine, which grows in South East Asia. It can be bought in graded thicknesses. No. 1 is the narrowest, about 1/16 in. (1.5 mm) wide. No. 6 is the widest, about 1/4 in. (6 mm) wide. Two thicknesses of cane are used in the weaving of the cane seat, and a wider third cane for the perimeter beading. The cane comes in lengths of approximately 3 yards (metres), and is sold in hanks. Each hank will be sufficient to reseat about four bedroom chairs.

Cane splits very easily. If an end is split, cut it off before the split runs the full length of the cane. Cut cane with its shiny side against the blade. If the cane is too brittle to work, wipe it with a damp cloth.

Preparation

Once the old cane work, pegs and odd tails of cane have been removed, the chair should be checked for soundness. All joints must be strong and any damage or weak parts in the framework repaired. Stain and repolish the repairs before caning.

The first stages of caning exert a fair degree of stress on the framework. Thin or weak structures may distort under the tension of the cane and should be supported with temporary battens, to be removed when the caning is completed.

Count the caning holes in the side of the chair. There should be an equal number on each side. If there is not, glue and plug some holes on one side and redrill to give the correct number. If there is a large discrepancy between the sides it may be necessary to plug and redrill parts on each side.

Most chair seats have 3/16 in. (4.5 mm) holes set about 5/8 in. (16 mm) apart, and should be caned with number two and number four cane. If the holes are larger and spaced further apart, a wider cane should be used. No. 1 and 2 cane may be needed when the holes are smaller, and spaced closer together.

The central medallion must be firmly braced in position before the old cane is removed. Caning starts with the radial canes pulled and fastened very tightly

Using a doubler

Technique

Doubling

Doublings are the first canes woven into the framework. In all but curved chair backs they run from front to back on the seat, and top to bottom on the back.

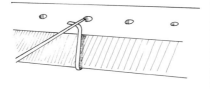

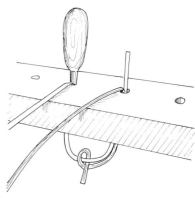

Work with the chair front closest to you. Find the centre hole in the back row and mark it with chalk. Do the same for the front row. Choose a long No. 2 cane, fasten it at the back and feed it down through the front centre hole. Pull it tight.

Making sure that the cane is still shiny side up, pass it to the right and poke it up through the adjacent hole. Take it to the back rail (it will run parallel with the first) and push it down the hole to the right of the centre hole. Pull it tight and wedge it with a doubler. Bring the cane up the next hole in the back row, and pull it to the front and down the hole next to the previous two. Use the doubler taken from the back row to wedge it tight. Add new cane if necessary, and continue working across the chair seat, tensioning and wedging as you go.

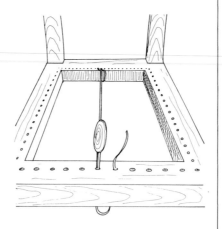

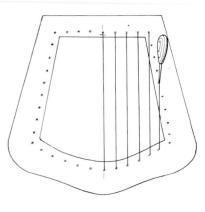

As the side of the chair is approached, it will be evident that, in order to keep the spacing of the cane regular, only a few of the side holes will be used to take the doublings.

When half of the chair has been covered with a single row of doublings, work back again, passing down the same holes as before, doubling up on the first ones.

Continue across the chair, past the first centre cane and on, across the left hand side. Use identical holes in the left side to those used on the right side. This will help maintain the symmetry of the canework. Double back to the centre and finish off. Each cane should be paired and each hole in the front and back row should have two canes passing through.

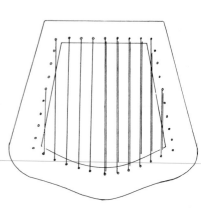

Setting

The setting pieces are the cross pieces of cane which complete the basic grid pattern on the chair seat.

Start at the front of the chair. Locate the corner holes and place a straight edge across them to assess the probable position for the foremost settings and weave them across.

Start from the right, and weave over, then under at each pair of doublings. Pull the cane tight, but do not fasten the ends. (This allows for adjustment later).

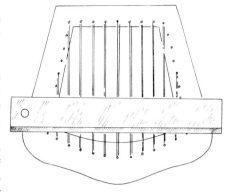

Take a second long piece of cane, and start at the left hand side and, against the back edge of the first setting, weave a second cane. This must pass over then under at each pair of doublings.

Pulling this tight, press the two settings as close together as possible and straighten them up. Take the long end of the second setting (which will be at the right hand side of the chair frame) and poke it down its hole in the side, and up through the next hole back, or perhaps two or three holes back,

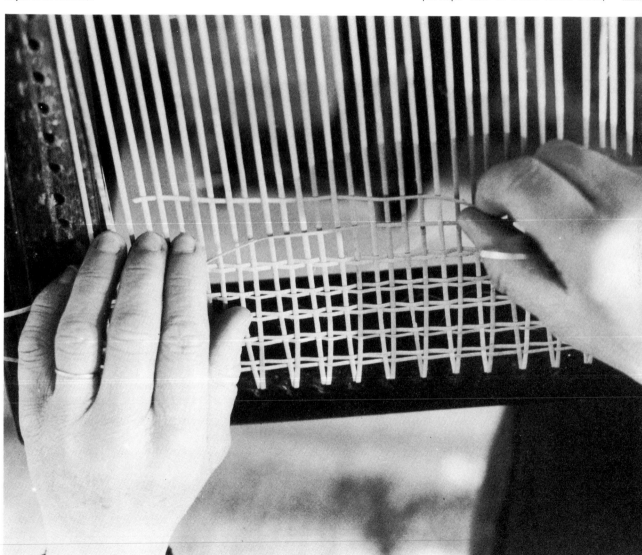

Setting

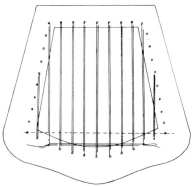
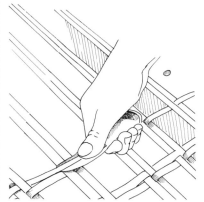
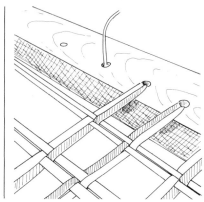

depending upon the shape of the chair. Weave it across the doublings, going over and then under as each pair is reached.

Do the same on the other side. Notice that each setting will alternate between the front and the back of the pair as the weaving progresses. Keep the settings tight and straight.

Once the centre of the seat is reached start again at the back and work towards the front. This enables

the final weaving to be carried out in the centre of the chair, where there is more room to work, and more give in the cane. Ensure that the weaving sequence is maintained, so that the pattern merges at the centre.

When the setting operation is completed, take a damp sponge, and lightly wipe the seat. While the cane is still damp, straighten and adjust the doublings and settings to leave them square and true.

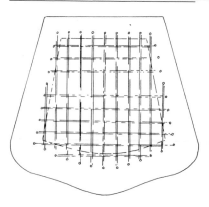

Crossings

The diagonal canes are known as crossings. Select a length of wider cane (No. 3 or 4). Start close to the front left corner of the chair seat, fasten one end, and pull the other diagonally across the seat. Weave it across under settings and over the doubling, take it to the corner, and poke it down a convenient hole. Continue this operation, each time inserting the end down a hole when the side is reached. Crossings from the right hand side of the chair go over the setting and under the doubling. It is not necessary or helpful to do all the left to right crossings first. Some of the others can be worked in too, and their ends tucked in as the work progresses. Keep the canes tight and straight. All the weaving should look flat: if there

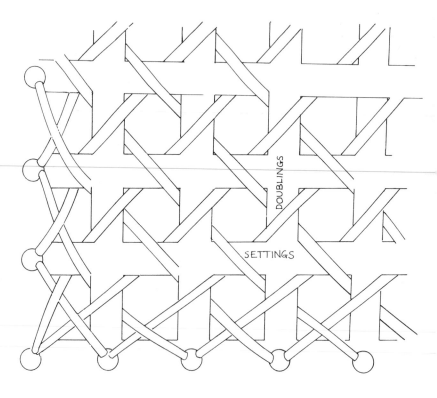

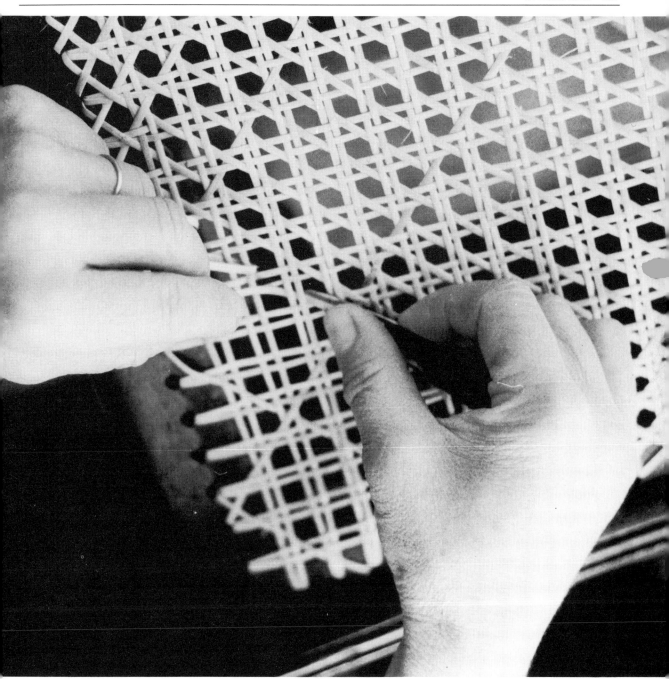

are rucked up areas at the edge, loosen and rearrange them to look flat.

When the crossings have been woven in, study the edges, look at the pattern of the crossings, and rearrange them to follow the pattern of the weave. Each hole should have two crossings. Rearrange canes so that the long passes are covered by shorter ones, thus breaking up the irregularities. If there are two or more holes to choose from, tuck the crossing into the one that will tend to pull the pattern of the weave together.

Working the crossings in no particular order

Pegging and beading

When the caning looks straight and flat, and all of the edges are trim and neat, the holes can be pegged. Take a piece of straight-grained seasoned pine and split it to a sliver, about the size of the holes to be pegged. Roughen the end down to a tapered point.

Do not peg the left hand back corner hole, or the holes immediately adjacent to it. The end of the beading is inserted into the corner holes and the first tying loop to hold the beading in place passes through the second hole.

Also leave unpegged holes where there are sharp turns in the shape of the seat, which will entail bending the cane sideways around the curve and keeping it flat. Extra loops of cane will be needed to hold the beading at these places.

Take a very light wooden mallet, or a spare offcut of timber about as heavy as a tack hammer. Tap the pine into the hole. Too much force may damage the cane or split the seat frame. Snap the stick by jerking it sideways and then, without removing the freed part of the stick, give the peg an extra tap or two to lower it beneath the level of the canework.

Peg every other hole (except at curves and corners). Tap, snap, and tap again, move on to the next, occasionally trimming the end when the pine refuses to be pushed into the hole.

When holes need pegging (and occasionally a chair will be simply pegged and not beaded at all, in which case every hole, including the corners should be pegged) take a doubler or clearer and use it to lower any splinters of peg that may still protrude beyond the surface level of the canework.

Select a thick beading cane, and put it to soak for a few minutes in a tub of cold water. While the beading is soaking, take a thin No. 2 cane, and pass it up through the hole nearest to the back corner hole. Pass it down

the same hole again and leave a loop at the top. If there is any difficulty in passing the cane through the hole, a clearer should be used to clear the way. Use it gently, twisting it as it is forced into place.

Wipe the beading with a rag to remove excess water, pass one end through the loop of No. 2 cane and, after checking that the shiny side is uppermost, insert the end into the corner hole and bend and press it in place. Knot the loop on the underside of the rail and pull it tight. Continue working the beading around the edge of the chair, lacing the No. 2 cane under the rail, then up through the unpegged holes, over the beading and back down the holes again. Use a clearer where necessary. Take care to keep the beading cane flat where it turns the corners, dampening it again if it is necessary to keep it lying flat.

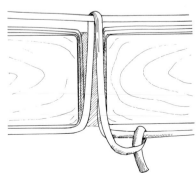

Finishing a corner

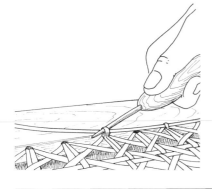

When pulling the looping tight over the beading, it may be found that the tension of the loop tends to pull the beading sideways, or to cause it to lie awkwardly over the edging of the canework. In order to avoid this, the clearer should be held over the beading and the loop pulled across it. When it is tight, slip out the clearer and pull the cane home.

End off the beading in the same way that it was started. Tuck the spare end down the corner hole, work it flat with the side of the knife, tighten the loop over the cane and secure it beneath the framework.

Once the beading is completed, invert the chair, and clean up the underside. Tuck in or cut off any spare ends.

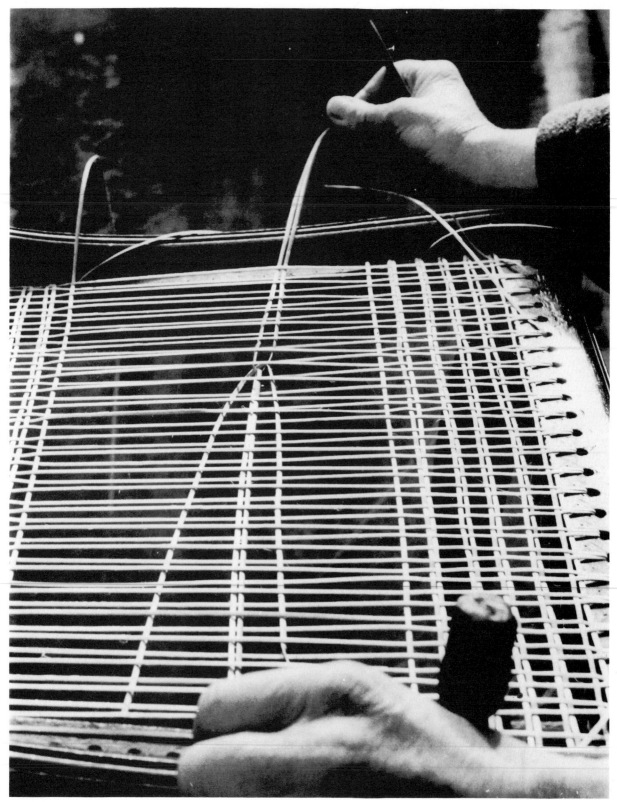

A steamer in use

Staining or finishing

Once the cane is dry, it can be stained using oil or water stains, and then sealed with a brush coat of clear shellac. Experiment on some spare cane before applying the stain. Remember that the stain will appear to be darker on the chair than it does on a separate strand of cane because of the density of the strands and the number of exposed edges of the cane (which absorb more stain than the shiny outer surface). Do not brush on the shellac until the cane and the stain are completely dry.

The use of a steamer

A steamer is a very simple device which enables the caner to weave one half of the settings extremely quickly. Once the doublings are in place, the steamer, which is merely a loop of cane, is passed between each pair of doublings. A second loop, made from a separate piece of cane, is linked to the first loop (this enables the steamer to be pulled back through the doublings like a shuttle), and whenever a setting is needed the cane can be tucked into the loop and swiftly drawn through the doublings. The steamer is then returned to the other side of the chair seat to await the next setting from that side.

It is only possible to use one steamer for each job, and it is best to arrange to use the steamer for inserting the setting which you find most difficult to weave. The setting that comes from the left side of the chair to the right hand side (as you face it) is inserted through the cane with the left hand and collected and pulled through with the right hand holding the blunted knife. The opposite is the case for the setting that comes from the right to left. If the worker finds difficulty in collecting and pulling the cane through using his left hand, the steamer should pull the right-to-left settings. It is unwise to use a steamer unless some experience has been gained in putting in the settings without one.

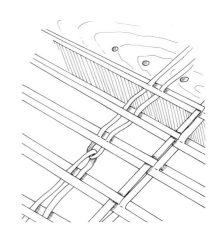

Curved backs

Where the back or seat of the chair is curved as, for instance, in a bergère chair, the doublings should work with the curve and not try to cross it. Any attempt to work the doublings across a curved back would result in a loose and uneven weave.

A corner prior to beading

Dummy caning

The procedure for caning blind holes (holes which do not pass completely through the framework of the seat) is the same as for the normal caned holes except that each piece of cane has to be cut to length and glued into the holes before any further caning is started. All of the doublings can be worked in place, and should be held by injecting a small squirt of P.V.A. glue into each hole and then wedging the cane with a suitably sized wire nail. Leave the glue to dry and remove the nails next morning. The setting can then be worked into place and glued and wedged. Peg every other hole as normal, prior to beading.

When beading blind holes, the same procedure is adopted, except that, instead of pulling the loop tight from below the framework, each loop holding the beading is cut to length and looped like a staple over the beading. Insert glue into the hole and ram the loop into place over the beading.

Finishing Supplies

Small quantities of:

Transparent shellac polish
Coloured wax stopping
Liquid driers
Polishing oil
Methylated spirit soluble stain in
   following colours:
   green, blue, black, oak, mahogany,
   walnut, Bismark brown
Water soluble chemicals and stains:
   potassium bichromate
   potassium permanganate
   ferrous sulphate
   tannic acid
   borax
   mineral black, Venetian red, brown,
     umber, flake white, yellow ochre
Wire wool 0000 grade

Large quantities of:

Button polish
Garnet polish
Brown and black beeswax polish
Stripper – spirit washable
Urethane varnish
Pure turpentine, or turpentine
   substitute
Raw linseed oil
Methylated spirit, or finishing spirit
Oxalic acid crystals
Ammonia
Naptha base stains:
   light oak, dark oak, brown
     mahogany
P.V.A. glue
Pearl glue
Cascamite, and Aerolite 306 urea-
   formaldehyde glues
Epoxy resin glue
Wire wool:
   grades 3 (coarse), 00 and 000
   (fine)
Abrasive paper:
   400 silicon carbide, 180, 120, 60
     garnet paper
Barrier cream
Hand cleansing cream
Plastic gloves
Wadding
Masking tape, 1½ in. (38 mm)
   wide

Mail Order Suppliers

U.K.

Tools
Sarjents Tool Stores Ltd
44-52 Oxford Road
Reading
Berks.
RG1 7LH

Tel: Reading 586522

Bahco Record Tools Ltd
Parkway Works
Sheffield
Yorkshire
39 3BL

Tel: Sheffield 449066

Woodcarving tools
Henry Taylor (Tools) Ltd
The Forge
Lowther Road
Sheffield

Tel: Sheffield 340282/340321

Saw blades, supplies, sharpening, grinding
Tewkesbury Saw Co. Ltd
Trading Estate
Newtown
Tewkesbury
Glos.
GL20 8JG

Tel: Tewkesbury 293092

Finishing supplies
Fiddes and Son Ltd
Florence Works
Brindley Road
Cardiff
CF1 7IX

Tel: Cardiff 40323

Reproduction brassware
John Lawrence and Co. (Dover) Ltd
Granville Street
Dover
Kent

Tel: Dover 201425

Cane, rush and upholstery supplies
Touchwood Craft Centre
15 Warminster Road
Westbury
Wilts.

Tel: Westbury 823381

Leather – ready tooled
S. Doctors
5a Lansdown Mews
Farm Road
Hove
Sussex

Tel: Brighton 774630

U.S.A.

Tools
Garrett Wade Company
161 Avenue of the Americas
New York
New York 10013

Woodcraft
41 Atlantic Avenue
Box 4000
Woburn
Massachusetts 01888

Frog Tool Co. Ltd
700 W. Jackson Blvd
Chicago
Illinois 60606

Saw blades
Woodcraft
(address as above)

Frog Tool Co. Ltd
(address as above)

Finishing supplies
Garrett Wade Company
(address as above)

Mohawk Finishing Products Inc.
Amsterdam
New York 12010

Reproduction brassware
Ball and Ball
463 W. Lincoln Highway
Exton
Pennsylvania 19341

Cane and rush
The Woodworkers Store
21801 Industrial Blvd
Rogers
Minnesota 55374

Upholstery supplies and cane
Jim Dandy Sales
Box 30377
Cincinnati
Ohio 45230

Leather
Roberts Leather Studios Inc.
214 West 29th Street
Unit 403
New York
N.Y. 10001

Berman Leathercraft Inc.
145 South Street
Boston
M.A. 0211

Bibliography

Furniture repair

Brown, Margery, *Cane and Rush Seating*, Batsford, London, 1976

Frank, George, *Adventures in Wood Finishing*, Taunton Press, Newtown, Connecticut, 1981

Hayward, Charles, *Antique or Fake*, Evans, 1970

Hayward, Charles, *Furniture Repairs*, Evans, 1967

Hayward, Charles, *Staining and Polishing*, Evans, 1959

Jack, George, *Wood Carving*, Pitman, London, 1903

Macdonald, Robert, *Modern Upholstering Techniques*, Batsford, London, 1981

Macdonald, Robert, *Basic Upholstery Repair and Restoration*, Batsford, London, 1977

Wood

Edlin, Herbert, *What Wood is That?*, Thames & Hudson, London, 1969

International Book of Wood, Mitchell Beazley, London, 1976

Johnston, David, *The Wood Handbook for Craftsmen*, Batsford, London, 1983

Index